Recent Title in
Contemporary Language Education
Terry A. Osborn, Series Adviser

Foreign Language Program Articulation: Current Practice and Future Prospects
Carolyn Gascoigne Lally, editor

The Future of
Foreign Language Education
in the United States

The Future of
Foreign Language Education
in the United States

Edited by
TERRY A. OSBORN

Contemporary Language Education
Terry A. Osborn, Series Adviser

Bergin & Garvey
Westport, Connecticut • London

Library of Congress Cataloging-in-Publication Data

The future of foreign language education in the United States / edited by Terry A. Osborn.
    p. cm.—(Contemporary language education, ISSN 1531–1449)
    Includes bibliographical references and index.
    ISBN 0–89789–719–6 (alk. paper)
    1. Languages, Modern—Study and teaching—United States. I. Osborn, Terry A.,
    1966– II. Series.
    LB1580.U6F88   2002
    418′.0071′073—dc21   2001043012

British Library Cataloguing in Publication Data is available.

Library of Congress Catalog Card Number: 2001043012
ISBN: 0–89789–719–6
ISSN: 1531–1449

First published in 2002

Bergin & Garvey, 88 Post Road West, Westport, CT 06881
An imprint of Greenwood Publishing Group, Inc.
www.greenwood.com

Printed in the United States of America

∞™

The paper used in this book complies with the
Permanent Paper Standard issued by the National
Information Standards Organization (Z39.48–1984).

10 9 8 7 6 5 4 3 2 1

Copyright Acknowledgment

The author and publisher gratefully acknowledge permission for use of the following material:

Material from J. L. Watzke, 2000, The History of Foreign Language and Secondary Education Reform: Prospects for Achieving Standards-Based Goals. Ph.D. diss., The University of Iowa.

An earlier version of Chapter 3 was published by ACTFL as T. Reagan, 1999, "Constructivist Epistemology and Second/Foreign Language Pedagogy," *Foreign Language Annals* 32(4): 413–425.

In memory of
Mario Ciotola and Terry Jean Smith
Their departure has made this Earth a much poorer place.

Contents

Tables and Figures

Tables

Figures

Acknowledgments

An edited text, unlike almost any other endeavor, involves a broad range of people working in cooperation with one another. It has been my pleasure in assembling this volume to work with a most professional group of scholars, meticulous about deadlines, and amenable to the rigors of text preparation. Beyond the contributors themselves, I would like to thank Nancy Lauckner for guidance and suggestions. Additionally, Jane Garry and the staff at Bergin and Garvey were, as always, quite helpful and appreciation is extended to them. My colleagues in the Department of Curriculum and Instruction, Neag School of Education, are a most supportive and knowledgeable community of scholars with whom it is an honor to work. Finally, Dina, Joshua, and Juliana are incomparable blessings.

Introduction

TERRY A. OSBORN

If you do not think about the future, you cannot have one.

John Galsworthy

The future is made of the same stuff as the present.

Simone Weil

Being involved in language education is an exciting, yet trying adventure. For the past century in the United States, language education has been the center of many controversies, many hopes, and possibly many a wasted moment. The firestorms surrounding the use of German during the early part of the twentieth century, the exalted goals of the Sputnik era, and even the scathing indictment of the President's Commission have all faded into history now. During the last half decade, the profession has been looking toward the future under the auspices of the *Standards for Foreign Language Learning: Preparing for the 21st Century*. At the same time, the country's story of diversity has continued to evolve. Unquestionably, we have historically been a diverse group of people. Only recently, however, has that diversity been seen as a strength, rather than a blemish to be obliterated in the crucible of assimilation. And in the picture that shall eventually take focus as the status quo of language education, *The Future of Foreign Language Education in the United States* finds its impetus.

We are in another time of change for the profession. We may not be in a state of siege nor urgency, but we press on toward attainment of the grand potential we recognize in our undertaking. As we begin to assume our place as part of the core curriculum in a diverse America, the worlds of difference within and surrounding the classroom provide us the opportunity to actuate a fundamental reexamination of the work we do. It is, then, with this question that I invited the contributors to concern themselves: How does the changing social and academic context of language education in the United States impact the future of our discipline?

Deborah M. Herman chose to focus on the past as prologue. Chapter 1 analyzes the internal debates among foreign language education professionals during a preeminent historical period in the field's development, roughly from 1890–1920. This period coincides with the development of the K–12 public school system in the United States, during which time political, religious, and intellectual battles over the content of curriculum raged. Her analysis points out that the interpretations foreign language educators make and responses to key events are vital to understanding the place of foreign language education in the American school system, both past and present.

Chapter 2 presents the work of several scientists from outside of traditional language education that should encourage speculation of how radical the future changes in language education may be. Two of the authors, Kercel and Brown-VanHoozer, are researchers for the U.S. Department of Energy in Oak Ridge, Tennessee, while the third author, VanHoozer, is in private practice and has worked as a psychotherapist, a learning specialist, and a freelance contract researcher in learning and behavior. In addition to the blind review that I employ, their work is peer reviewed by their own colleagues. In this chapter they argue that traditional science is based on the assumption that *all* effective processes can be represented by a list of numbers, including much of current positivistic research on language acquisition and learning. This reductionist assumption requires that the readily observable self-referential mental processes of neurophysiology be dismissed. However, the scope of scientific inquiry need not be limited by the assumption of reductionism. Most relevant to this discussion, irreducible processes of life and mind are observed to abound in nature, as pointed out in the work of Bateson and others. The human mental processes of learning and language are neither algorithmic nor irrational, but they are tractable (albeit incompletely) with self-referential mathematical models. Thus, the successful language learning strategies of the future may well not be found in contemporary research camps. Instead, the authors argue that the most effective future inquiry will be based on rational models of learning and language similar to those known in engineering as endogenous, or bizarre systems.

In Chapter 3, Timothy Reagan highlights a series of philosophical questions related to constructivism that will greatly impact the future of curriculum development and instructional delivery in the field. As the population grows increasingly diverse and that diversity is recognized, the epistemological questions related to "knowing" and "learning" a foreign language will involve much more than a simple, clear-cut learning and acquisition distinction. He sheds light on the impact of changes to the deepest levels of language educational theory and practice.

In Chapter 4, I join Philip Anderson to explore the uses of literature in a future foreign language classroom. This pedagogical resource has enjoyed a status in foreign language classrooms since the days of grammar-translation methodology, though its popularity has waxed and waned over the years. Anderson's work in aesthetic response in the English/Language Arts context over the past decade has substantial implications for how literature can be viewed in our setting over the coming years. As a component of fluency, attention to the aesthetic dimensions of language use will likely ensure the continued place of literature in curricula.

David Gerwin and I, in Chapter 5, begin the task of conceptualizing connections in the form of an interdisciplinary unit which will balance the tensions inherent in both cultural representation and academic disciplinary divisions. Utilizing the history-as-mystery approach he has been investigating along with my own theoretical work in regard to unit development involving the foreign language class, we strive to combine the discussion of these theoretical frameworks to achieve overarching objectives. These connections among disciplines, not only prescribed in the newest standards, represent good educational practice. Knowledge is not as neatly divided as we seem to want to keep it in the academic world, and foreign language education has long suffered from this lack of recognition, in that we continue to have to justify our existence in various forms.

A. J. Vogely turns to the individual in a teacher preparation program in Chapter 6, as she describes how personality typing can be utilized to educate preservice and in-service foreign language teachers. Focusing on the development of nonjudgmental language related to teaching practice and learning, she explores how an enhanced understanding of ourselves can lead to improved service to students in our classrooms. She seeks to nurture the pluralistic persona, and in doing so celebrates diversity in teachers who open up new worlds to their students.

For Chapter 7, I am joined by Jacqueline Davis in describing the program we built at Queens College, City University of New York. This setting makes the program, in effect, a de facto vanguard of the future in the profession. As a gateway to the United States, institutions of higher education in New York often reflect the diversity that is to change the context of foreign language education in the United States. We believe that our experiences will provide a thought-provoking glimpse into the future of us all.

Timothy Reagan points out in Chapter 8 that in the context of public schooling in the United States, only three languages—French, German, and Spanish—are, together with Latin, commonly offered as foreign languages. He examines the "less commonly taught languages" in terms of the social, political, economic, cultural, and ideological elements that affect these languages in contemporary American society. Beyond merely containing lessons for language education, though, the teaching and learning of the less commonly taught languages also impact in a number of other areas, among which are multicultural education programs, global education programs, and critical language and language awareness programs. As a result, one can see that foreign language education's future is significantly linked with its social context.

Chapter 9 reports on an innovative program to reverse native language loss in migrant students. Claire Sylvan and Migdalia Romero demonstrate the power that language educational activities can have for heritage language learners, even those who speak the less commonly taught languages. This account of a bold initiative in one New York school should have broad implications for educational language policy and planning, in addition to the curricular reforms currently undertaken to address the needs of heritage language learners in the foreign language classroom.

Finally, Xaé Reyes reflects on her own experiences in Chapter 10. As both a speaker and instructor of Spanish, Reyes' insights into the cultural mediation that takes place in language classrooms and departments across the country support her suggestion of "authentic migratory" experiences as a form of macrocontextualization for students. The significance of her suggestions should not be underestimated in the diverse classrooms we now have. Foreign language classes in the future must become sites of social activism geared toward recognizing the strength of linguistic and cultural diversity, not marginalizing those who speak the very languages we love.

To be sure, as many writing in the field today have also done, for this text I struggled with the appropriate label to give our discipline. Though as scholars most of us have utterly rejected the "foreignness" of non-English languages, sadly the broadest strokes of our professional picture still reek with its abhorrent rhetoric. It is for this reason alone that I have chosen to keep the phrase "foreign language" as the marker, to serve as a reminder of the profound responsibility before us. Tennessee Williams, in *Orpheus Descending* penned, "The future is called 'perhaps,' which is the only possible thing to call the future. And the only important thing is not to allow that to scare you." The work presented here hopefully sets the stage for a future in which the discipline and the profession of foreign language education take on a greater social consciousness and a role in the center of the educational experience for all students in the United States. It is a future we should embrace with courage and determination, with an eye toward making a difference in the lives of our students. And that vision is one that we can indubitably realize. Perhaps.

1

"Our Patriotic Duty": Insights from Professional History, 1890–1920

Deborah M. Herman

"Must we always be in crisis?" Herbert Lindenberger's answer to the question posed in his *ADFL Bulletin* article in 1998 was "no." But over the past ten years the profession's major journals, and *The ADFL Bulletin* in particular, have been filled with discussions of the most recent crises afflicting foreign language education in the United States: precipitously falling enrollments in French, enrollments in Spanish burgeoning to the point of straining the quality of instruction, a number of articles frankly asking if German is not already a "less commonly taught" language, and reports of the constant struggles of Slavic, Chinese, Russian, Japanese, and other language programs for survival. While there is much condemnation of (or advice on successful adjustment to) the newly corporatized version of American higher education which attacks the traditional humanities education, such enrollment patterns also bring to the fore an ongoing internecine argument over the nature and purpose of foreign language education. Most authors fall on one side or the other of the traditional "humanities vs. utilitarianism" divide, or seek somehow to blend these apparently opposing aims under the rubric of proficiency—which does not resolve the dilemma: proficient at what?[1]

Are such enrollment crises or arguments over the inherent value of foreign language new? Clearly not. Within the context of the modern U.S. educational system, they are rooted in the very origins of the modern language teaching profession at the turn of the twentieth century. If we are to address a patterned and repeated cycle of crises which is embedded in group culture and the nature of our discipline, a response must be fashioned within a meta-framework for analysis that is sociological, political, and historical. To date, however, there has been little sociohistorical analysis; sociopolitical factors such as race, nation-state politics, and language prestige have also been largely absent from American curriculum design. In fact, it is the lack of interest itself and concomitant failure to incorporate the realities of sociological, political, and historical forces into design which has had a significant impact on foreign language curriculum. This absence complicates attempts to reinvent curriculum for the twenty-first century. Emerging changes in the socioeconomic and ethnic/racial demographics of children in the United States mean that we must begin to consider the sociopolitical history of our profession and the subsequent issues generated in revisioning curriculum design. The reason is clear: the student populations we have served at both the high school and postsecondary level since the 1910s, predominantly middle- or upper-class Anglos, will simply no longer be the majority populations in U.S. public institutions within a few short decades (Educational Research Service 1995).

FOREIGNNESS AND THE STUDENTS WE SERVE

In the United States the very term *foreign* language education carries a history of sociocultural implications rooted in nationalist ideology which defines those who are inside and those who are outside the sociocultural body of the political nation. Those who are "alien" or "foreign" are outside the body.[2] We have not in the United States used the term *second* language education despite the fact that the United States' linguistic history is characterized by constantly renewing multilingualism. Instead, we use *foreign language education* to refer to the teaching of languages other than English to students who are implicitly assumed to be Anglo or White (labels which have shifted in meaning over the decades), who speak English as their first or primary language, and who are middle- or upper-class students with the resources to travel outside the United States. Most often these assumptions are implicit; sometimes they are openly stated: "As opportunities for travel have spread from the upper to the middle classes, the notion that language study might allow students to interact face-to-face with members of a foreign culture . . . has become commonplace" (Joseph 1988, 31; see also James 1996 for a rare and blunt discussion of class prejudice in foreign language education). Comments like these make transparent two working assumptions of the foreign language profession: foreign language study is essentially for the well-to-do, and its pedagogical aim is preparation for interaction with "culture abroad." Despite a growing interest in attracting African Americans and Spanish–heritage speakers to our classrooms, such students continue to be a tiny minority in our classrooms (see Dahl 1999; Finn 1998; Harris-Schenz 1990; Moore 1998; Valdés 1991; Wilberschied and Dassier 1995).

The question we face is: What relevance will *foreign* language education have in a future where, according to estimates by the Educational Research

Service (1995), by the year 2030 only 49 percent of school-age children will be Anglos, while Hispanic children will constitute 23 percent and Black children 18 percent of the school-age population?[3] What relevance will a foreign language curriculum that is traditionally designed for college-bound, middle- or upper-class students have for the increasing number of children raised in poverty?[4] What relevance for Hispanic and Black children whose participation rates in higher education may or may not increase in proportion to their population?[5]

Even if we were to presume that significant changes in economic structure and political policy will ease the poverty rates of children, or that large-scale federal intervention to aid Hispanic and Black youth will considerably increase their college participation rates—a new G.I. bill for a new generation—we cannot escape the fact that foreign language curriculum is rooted in presumptions about the likely racial and socioeconomic characteristics of the foreign language student population. How did these roots develop and what implications do they now hold for the future of foreign language education in the United States?

These are questions that require an analysis of our disciplinary culture. A crucial historical period with which to begin is 1890–1920, the period when battles over the developing high school curriculum were being fought. By considering the roots of the profession's current definition, we find fruitful avenues for discussion of a future which must, perforce, involve a redefinition of who we are and whom we serve.

PURGING POLITICS FROM AMERICAN CURRICULUM DESIGN

As poetically phrased by one historian (Chambers 1980), the first two decades of the twentieth century were governed by "the tyranny of change." Industrialization, large-scale immigration, urbanization, and the rise of the United States as a world power were among the changes weaving a genuine societal upheaval. During this period, too, the number of children aged fourteen to eighteen attending public high school increased dramatically from 8.5 percent in 1899 to 28.8 percent in 1921 (Watzke 2000). That increase came about from a combination of factors: compulsory attendance laws passed in most states (although often to little effect), pressure from labor groups and child welfare groups to eliminate or curtail child employment, and the growing view of the school as a site of "Americanization" for the cities' large immigrant population. These factors increased the pool of children who had completed elementary school and were thus eligible to attend high school. In addition, high school attendance was fueled by parents' increasing perception of the diploma as a requirement for the emerging white-collar job market, and continued concerns, especially in urban areas, about the need to keep unemployed youth "off the streets." Increasing participation in public high schools led to what Kliebard termed "the struggle for the American curriculum" (1995). What would the ultimate aim of the high school education in particular be? How should that aim be fashioned if the high school would serve a large—even a majority—of the country's adolescent population, rather than an elite minority?

Some historians of education contend that one consequence of these struggles was that all curriculum design, regardless of discipline, avoids overt sociopolitical discussion. Such avoidance is seen as the result of: (1) an element of the progressive movement which aimed to "keep politics out of the schools" (Tyack 1974); (2) hegemonic forces, including the schooling system itself as tied to nation-state structures (see, for example, Apple 1979; Karabel and Halsey 1977); (3) pressure groups, such as industry, parents, and political activists; and, (4) the interplay of textbook markets, producers, and practitioners in maintaining the status quo (see Apple 1986; Apple and Christian-Smith 1991; Heilenman 1993). Apple (1979) asserts that the content and goals of curriculum came to be viewed as apolitical as part of a larger movement between 1880 and 1920 to create the illusion of schools as politically neutral institutions. Tyack makes a similar observation, "Talk about 'keeping the schools out of politics' has often served to obscure actual alignments of power and patterns of privilege" (1974, 11). The creation of this image of schools as neutral sites was part of the credo of some of the most prominent curriculum design specialists, such as the highly influential "social efficiency experts" John Franklin Bobbitt and Frederick W. Taylor. Social efficiency experts sought to tie curriculum design to the needs of an industrializing society: curriculum should prepare students with the practical skills needed for their intended careers. Social efficiency, with its skills training curriculum, was offered as a substitute for the traditional literary school curriculum, portrayed as outdated and inappropriate for the majority of the country's youth. It was also offered as an alternative to local curriculum control, portrayed as unscientific and inevitably entangled with ethnic and class politics.

The concept of social efficiency did not go uncontested, however. Many of Bobbitt's and Taylor's contemporaries, including John Dewey, G. Stanley Hall, and William Torrey Harris, fought for a school and curriculum not tied to perceived market requirements, or that channeled students into vocationalized tracks appropriate to their purported abilities or interests. Instead, they proposed their own (often competing) visions of a modified humanities curriculum, focused on literature and languages, as appropriate for the human development of all children. (For a detailed description of groups vying for control of the curriculum during this period, see Kliebard 1995.)

While the result has been an ongoing battle between those proposing a "well-rounded" education for all children and those demanding an education that is "useful" and "accountable," Apple contends that the efficiency experts were largely successful in at least one respect: purging sociopolitical analysis from the field of curriculum design. Once the content matter of curriculum becomes viewed as "rationalized"—that is, based on the perceived economic and/or cultural needs of society—curriculum design becomes merely a technical search for the best method of achieving preset goals. The goals may change, but the focus on methodology as the delivery system for curriculum design, and the search for the "best" methodology, will still dominate curriculum design.[6]

It is possible, then, to see the "method obsession" often complained of in the discipline of foreign language as merely part of a larger bias in American education. But the implications and historical roots of these tendencies in foreign language education are more complex. The politics of language was especially salient during the period 1890–1920: this was a time when the language one spoke was considered to form the very essence of a person's intellectual thought patterns. Wilhelm von Humboldt's views on the relationship between language and culture were representative of this line of thought in the nineteenth century, and were influential on early twentieth-century anthropologists and linguists such as Franz Boas and Edward Sapir, and subsequently Benjamin Lee Whorf (Schlesinger 1991). Humboldt felt that "Differences between languages correspond to differences in *Weltansichten*, or world perspectives" (Schlesinger 1991, 14). The respected nineteenth-century philologist W. D. Whitney likewise wrote in 1875: "Every single language has thus its own peculiar framework of established distinctions, its shapes and forms of thought into which . . . is cast the content and product of [the learner's] mind" (ibid).

These historical roots of a strong version of the Sapir-Whorf theory were well established by the turn of the century; thus, the study of another culture's great literature, even the study of the grammatical forms of its language, were seen as molding the logic and philosophical bent of the young student's mind and inculcating the values of the culture embedded in the language. This intimate language-culture-thought connection was expressed by Richard Kron, author of the textbook *German Daily Life: A Reader* in 1901:

There is a radical difference between the history of a people which asks "Qu'est-ce que c'est que cela?" and that of one which asks "Was ist das?" The point of view of a man who says "J'ai quelque chose" is entirely different from that of one who says "Es fehlt mir etwas." (v)

The content matter of foreign language study was, then, explicitly cultural and political, and therefore in opposition to the notion of the politically neutral school. In addition, its content made it more vulnerable than other disciplines to several of the most powerful sociopolitical forces of the period: nationalism, nativism, and the Americanization movement.

The foreign language profession made two responses to the changes and trends in American education and society which helped establish its place in the K–12 curriculum. First, modern foreign language advocates battled with advocates of Latin and Greek for legitimacy and space in the developing high school system, an internal struggle that dominated the profession's attention

5

from the 1890s to the opening of World War I. Proponents of modern languages (that is, spoken languages of powerful western European nations) argued that their content matter was just as demanding, rigorous, and prestigious as that of Latin and Greek. Some modern language teachers also asserted that these languages were of "practical value" to all students. In either case, the goal was securing a place for modern language study alongside (or in place of) Latin and Greek in the high school curriculum. Second, upon the collapse of German language study in 1917, numerous modern language professionals aligned themselves with the patriotic mission of the Americanization movement, disavowing German *Kulturkunde*, "the study of the language, literature and civilization of a nation" (Langenscheidt 1974, 964), and claiming a place for modern language study in service to the nation's economic expansionism. The goal initially for many may have been to court students and parents who abandoned study of German after the United States entered World War I, but it quickly became a struggle to secure the survival of a profession under pressure from those who wanted all foreign language study banned.

MODERN LANGUAGES AND THE BATTLE FOR PRESTIGE

While the study of Latin and Greek as classical languages had an established and respected pedagogical history as mass schooling systems began to develop in the nineteenth century, the teaching of modern languages was considered non-scholarly and unprofessional. Despite calls for expansion and professionalization of the teaching of modern foreign languages throughout the nineteenth century in response to growing links in commerce and travel through Europe and the United States, the place of modern languages in American education was far from assured. Against the background of faculty psychology,[7] it was widely believed that Latin grammar was in its essence logical and that study of its structures trained the mind in logical thought. When the curriculum recommendations of the Committee of Ten were released in 1893, faculty psychology had already passed its apex and was under attack from newer psychological theories. Nevertheless, the concept of "mental training" was firmly rooted in the curriculum of U.S. colleges and universities, which held great influence over the high school curriculum. The Committee's report reemphasized the value of Latin and Greek for all students, regardless of their post-high school plans, while allowing some place for modern language study as acceptable substitutes if taught properly.[8] Under these circumstances, modern language advocates were faced with two options: side with those educational reformists pushing for a non-college-preparatory high school curriculum and argue that modern languages were more practical and useful in an industrializing society; or, side with traditional humanists advocating a college-preparatory high school education as the best life training for all students and argue that modern language (grammar) was just as valuable as Latin for

6

such training. Some managed to walk the line and simultaneously argue both sides of the coin.

By the turn of the century, modern languages appeared to be winning the battle for enrollment numbers, although by which argument it is difficult to say. Titles such as "How Can We Make the Classics More Attractive to the High School Student?" and "Do Latin and Greek Need Something Done for Them in the High School?" and "The Decline of Greek" appear by 1905 in *The American Journal of Education*, testifying to the growing popularity of German and the decline of Latin and Greek. Between 1900 and 1910, however, it is clear from a review of the same journal that the argument over the proper model for modern language study was still very much in play. The proponents of a grammar-translation curriculum, with reading ability and general mental development as its main goals, railed against any utilitarian training as both frivolous and unattainable:

French is no more "practical" than Greek. Even under the most favorable conditions, the linguistic attainment of ordinary scholars are absolutely worthless from the commercial standpoint. And were they much higher than they are, what would be the native youth's chance of success in competition with the hosts of bilingual hyphenated Americans? . . . The French (or German) reading should be so chosen as to supplement the scholar's literary work in English; it should all be of a character to arouse and cultivate the artistic sense, and at the same time afford the substantial meat upon which growing minds ought to feed. (Grandgent 1904, 462, 466–67)

Nevertheless, the utilitarian, commercial value of foreign language study in combination with the "oral methods" popularized by Berlitz made strong converts, especially among Spanish teachers looking to attract students:

As Chicago has become more and more the center of large and varied business interests, the demand for Spanish correspondents has increased. The need must be met. There are our interest in Cuba, in the Phillippines, in Mexico, to be considered. . . . But it is contended that Spain has never taken the prominent part in the history of civilization that Germany or France has; she has no such mass of literature; has tried no great educational experiments; has not delved so deeply into the secrets of science. . . . [Nevertheless] Spain is waking up in these later years to a new realization of herself and her past, and the great part she played in the exploration and settlement of the new World, and in that older history which extends far back into the days before ever Greece and Rome had reached the zenith of their power. (Dracass 1908, 539, 541–42)

Dracass here makes a deft play, claiming a contemporary commercial and political value superior to both German and French while simultaneously claiming a "great culture" more ancient even than that of Greece or Rome, hidden and awaiting discovery.

While arguments for the value of modern foreign language study based on great cultures and commercial/political utility both survived, the curriculum did not necessarily differ based on belief in one rationale or the other. The curriculum model most readily available to teachers of German, French, and Spanish was the one utilized in the teaching of Latin, focusing on reading, grammar, and translation. Such a curriculum design ensured that interaction with living representatives of other cultures would not be the goal of classroom learning; indeed, as declared by the philologist Charles Hall Grandgent, the purpose of education was not to further interaction with "hyphenated Americans." In line with the prestige strategy, the texts chosen would most likely be those considered classics—the highest representation of the culture. Thus, students of Spanish were more likely to read *Don Quixote* than a contemporary author, and students of German, more likely to read Goethe than a contemporary newspaper.

A curriculum focus on grammar-translation and literature produced centuries ago does not tend to lead to an examination of sociocultural and political context. It certainly does not require consideration of contemporary issues involving relative first language/second language (L1/L2) status, since only those cultures considered to have produced so-called worthy texts and high culture (that is, those with prestige relative to the L1 culture) are likely to be studied. So it was that circa 1910 in the United States, 28 percent of all secondary schools offered German as a foreign language (Germany being considered to have the finest education institutions of the period), 11 percent offered French, and only 2 percent offered Spanish (the language of cultures disdained by Anglo society: Spain, Mexico, and Central American nations). While one-third of U.S. universities required two or four years of study of either French or German for entrance during this period, none required or even accepted Spanish as fulfilling the entrance requirement (Zeydel 1961).

While modern language study had one foot in each door, some advocates claiming the legacy of Greek and Latin study and others the practical advantages of learning a living language, it was the prestige strategy that prevailed. Although the practicality argument would persist as a minor theme, the dominant enrollments in German language study until 1917 meant that their vision of the profession was the one most likely to be associated with the profession as a whole—and it was not German teachers who were strongly asserting the practicality argument. Theirs was the curriculum of mental training and *Kulturkunde*, a view of language and culture as intimately linked. After German enrollments collapsed in 1917, and French and Spanish enrollments grew, the prestige strategy remained in place.

Thus, as secondary schools moved toward internal curricular tracking—college-bound students versus factory-bound students—the foreign language profession associated itself with the college-preparatory track. A curriculum based on mental training and high culture was not seen as appropriate or necessary for the student destined for a job on a factory line, in a butcher shop, or as a business clerk. As enrollments grew to a larger and larger percentage of the entire school-aged population, this path ensured foreign language classrooms both a minority of students as its enrollment base and an extremely homogeneous student population in race, class, and gender. This lack of diversity would in the future become another factor mitigating against any overt discussion and inclusion of language learning setting as a factor in foreign language education: homogeneity quickly renders such factors invisible, and that which is invisible is not discussed.

As observed by H. H. Stern (1983), U.S. foreign language curriculum is dominated by a reliance on educational psychology and linguistics. Theory and research in these two fields tends to focus on the individual as a learner, thus also reinforcing the tendency to ignore sociocultural issues. This dominance can be seen as both a product of the homogeneous classroom and a contributing factor in its persistence. (Self)restriction of foreign language education to students drawn by the prestige strategy set a dynamic in motion by which generation after generation of foreign language teachers encounter only a very specific type of student in the (French or German or Spanish) classroom. These students also become the pool for future teachers, and thus the circle is completed. The boundaries of acceptable curriculum and researchable questions are defined by the White, upper- or middle-class, college-bound student populating that classroom and the teachers asking the questions. After a time, these boundaries become invisible and the profession becomes insulated from many of the most pressing questions of more recent, large educational movements that have been driven by issues of race, class, and gender.

NATION-BUILDING AND THE COLLAPSE OF GERMAN LANGUAGE STUDY

Returning for the moment to the historical period in question: The concept of high prestige culture, meaning literate culture, was closely tied in the period of 1890–1920 to nationalism and imperialism. Modern language education was battling for its place in the high school system as the United States entered a period of heightened concern over the cultural and political stability of the nation. In addition, the United States was experimenting with a new kind of imperialism as it wrestled with the "problem" territories acquired from Spain in the 1898 war. The addition of over 17 million new immigrants to the United States between 1900 and 1917, most of whom were Catholic and from countries considered racially inferior, brought anxiety over the nature of a *united* United States to a level not experienced since the Civil War. A key focus point in the debates over the nature of the American nation and culture became language, and both modern language education and advocates of linguistic pluralism would eventually be caught in a political and cultural vice.

During a period of nation-building, a key process is creating the illusion of a larger shared community—Anderson's (1983) "imagined community," one that we see ourselves as part of although composed of individuals we will never meet—within the geographical and political boundaries of the nation-state. Any number of elements can be present in such nation-building and they vary

9

from setting to setting. Since the required symbolic elements (real or manufactured), such as ethnic homogeneity, a long historical attachment to a particular geographical territory, shared mythologies, or ancient art and literature, were not available for purposes of creating the imagined community as was the case in many European settings, the United States had traditionally relied on such concepts as rugged individualism, the yeoman farmer, a belief in the nation's "manifest destiny" in the New World, and a prevailing Anglo–Protestant culture.

While language had not been a focus point for nation-building during the Revolutionary period in the United States, it was such during this later period of cultural stress. By 1900, the above-mentioned conceptual structures were breaking down under new conditions of industrialization and urbanization, and the large influx of non-White, Catholic immigrants from southern and eastern Europe. Under these conditions, language became an especially critical element in the re-creation of the American nation by the dominant majority, serving as both a rallying cry and proxy for religious and political contests.[9] Americanization programs during this period always contained English language education as their first and key component, in no small part as a means of breaking up so-called language islands and their sociopolitical communities. In addition to the perceived threat of functioning social networks, the English language in and of itself was believed to carry such ideas as democracy and capitalism, thus making encouragement (or coercion) to speak English particularly important to those who felt America's true culture and nature were being invaded by radicalism and Bolshevism.[10]

The more tightly the concept of a unified, national language—established by the dominant Anglo subculture as English, though not quickly or without strife—became linked to nation-building, the more dangerous the idea of educating children in a foreign language, or using a non-English language as a medium of instruction, came to be viewed in the United States. This conflict was heightened during the mid- to late-nineteenth century by the added element of religious division and conflict, since Irish immigrants and many of the German immigrants arriving to the United States were Catholic. Fearing Protestant proselytizing in public schools, they tended to create their own parochial schools which often used the children's native language as a medium of instruction, especially in the elementary school years. Ross's (1994) analysis shows that the arguments over what language would be the medium of instruction in private and public K–12 schools was tied to fears of a separate parochial schooling system whose existence might threaten the financial stability of the emerging public system and whose curriculum would not aid in the building of a unified, *American* culture and nation.

The conflict between language as symbol of nationhood and language pluralism in the schools came to a head in 1917 when, within months of the United States' entrance into World War I, German language teaching in the United States came close to a complete collapse (see, for example, Benseler et al. 1988; Fishman 1966; Ross 1994; Wiley 1998). Although non-English-language medium schools had been slowly declining for decades, a significant number still existed in 1917, with a large presence in the German-American settlement areas of the Midwest. The war became a catalyst allowing Americanization groups to eliminate all German (or other) language medium schools, and to attempt the elimination of all modern foreign language study, thereby purging "traitorous" foreign teachers and their pernicious influence. Indeed, some Americanization proponents attempted to erase the very *use* of languages other than English from all public life. Iowa had the distinction of being the first state to forbid the use of any foreign language in a public place including churches, sidewalks, trains, and the telephone (Bubser 1988). It was not the last state to do so. Book burnings, the destruction of churches and private schools associated with German language teaching or use, the occasional tarring and feathering of German teachers, and even lynchings were reported across the country.[11] Numerous states codified bans against the use of any foreign language as a medium of instruction in public schools and even in private schools—a direct attack on the parochial systems, especially Lutheran and Catholic schools. Other laws forbid the teaching of any foreign language below the eighth grade, by which time students were thought to be less vulnerable to the pernicious alien influence of a foreign tongue.

Ross (1994), Nollendorfs (1988), and Kloss (1966, 1971a) all show that German language teaching became inextricably linked in the minds of many Americans with support for the Kaiser and German imperialism. The study of German *Kulturkunde* was seen as further evidence of such traitorous support. The association of German language study with this interpretation of civilization and culture in the classroom continued long after the World War I era, and was described by Maxim Newmark in 1948:

In its broader sense realia denotes the traits, manners, customs, institutions, etc. of a people whose language is being studied. In this meaning it would coincide with the terms "foreign civilization" or "culture," e.g., the psychological and social complex characterizing an ethnic unit as conditioned by history, geography and climate, and expressed in its art, folklore, music, philosophy and social and political ideals. In the field of Germanics, the term *Kulturkunde* and, more specifically, *Deutschkunde*, would apply to this broader sense. (436)

Kulturkunde was mirrored in the larger society by an extensive network of German-American cultural institutions. As described by Bergquist (1983), in the 1890s the phenomenon of the "professional ethnic" appeared, as did numerous German-American associations and a large German-language press. These activists worked to maintain a viable German culture in the United States in the face of a dramatic drop in the number of new immigrants from Germany: "Out of this grew an intellectual attitude that was characterized both by an unnecessary defensiveness and by an unwarranted air of superiority. Historical and literary studies made extravagant claims for the supremacy of German culture and its contribution to American life" (9). The combination

Table 1.1
Public High School Students Studying Foreign Language

	German	*French*	*Spanish*	*Latin*
1914	33.2%	12.0%	3.7%	50.8%
1921	1.2%	28.1%	20.5%	50.0%

Source: Based on Watzke 2000, 318

of pre-1917 support for Germany's war effort by ethnic associations, such as the National German-American Alliance and by much of the German-language press, and classroom study of *Kulturkunde* (especially study of philosophical and political thought), seemed to many a plot to subvert the Allied war effort and contributed to a general paranoia that saw a propagandist in every German classroom.

The impact on German language teaching was severe. Whereas in 1914 over 33 percent of high school students were studying German, by 1921 the situation was bleak. While French and Spanish had acquired many of the students who had abandoned German—now being studied by only 1 percent of high school students—modern language advocates feared that French and Spanish would not be able to hold those numbers. Virtually all language study at the K–8 level had been eliminated and the cultures represented by French and Spanish did not have the prestige value of German, until 1917 the modern language most likely to displace Latin in the high school curriculum (see Table 1.1).

As noted by E. O. Wooley in his 1944 review of German instruction in the United States, "not all prospective students of German entered other language classes, hence the exodus from German [after 1917] meant a net loss in modern language enrollments" (reprinted in Newmark 1948, 73). How would the profession stabilize its future in an atmosphere which saw the study of any living language as inherently dangerous to the moral and patriotic development of children?

"OUR PATRIOTIC DUTY": AMERICANIZING
FOREIGN LANGUAGE STUDY

By 1920 the implications of the connection between all modern language teaching or study and the terms *unpatriotic* and *un-American* began to be seen. Rather than replacing German language study with the study of other modern languages, many incoming students were simply not enrolling. The overall trend in declining enrollments prompted a joint statement by the Modern Language Association and the National Federation of Modern Language

Teachers, a heretofore unusual show of unity among teachers of different languages. Published in several journals, the quote here appears as reprinted in *The American Journal of Education* in October 1920:

Resolved, That, in view of the fact that many more Americans than hitherto will go to foreign countries in diplomatic service, in commercial enterprises, and on economic, scientific, education, and other missions . . . it is urgently desirable that a much larger number of Americans than hitherto be trained to understand and to use the languages of the foreign countries with which we shall become most closely associated; . . . That the study of modern foreign languages should in general be begun earlier and continued longer than is now usually the case. . . . The modern languages offered in secondary schools should be French, German, and Spanish, the selection of the first language to depend on local conditions. . . . Less modern language is now being studied than before the war. To remedy this situation, we urge (a) that the quality of modern-language teaching should be improved, and (b) that all modern-language teachers should feel their cause to be a common one, and should recognize that a division into separate language camps is particularly deplorable. (776–78)

In 1920, however, the public's mood was unlikely to be altered by the restatement of the practical value of modern language study. It was clear to some modern language advocates that what was needed was an Americanization program for their curriculum. Nollendorfs' (1988) examination of one leader in German language education and my own examination of the writings of the president of the American Association of Spanish Teachers, Lawrence A. Wilkins, show that specific decisions of this type were made.

Wilkins, an influential leader who also served as head of modern language programs for the City of New York, advised Spanish teachers to show that foreign language education was an *American* activity, to separate their activities from the unpatriotic behavior of German language teachers, and to show Americans that the larger goals of national defense and the national economic development were served by Spanish language teachers. His opposition to the survival of German language study was unequivocal. In a 1918 article entitled "Spanish as a Substitute for German for Training and Culture" printed in *Hispania*, he outlined his reasons for that opposition:

The cultural value of any language lies very largely in the literature written in that language. . . . But Germany has so sadly changed since Goethe's day. . . . Until the middle of the past school year, I felt it would be unwise to have German removed from our schools, chiefly for the value inherent in the older and worthier German literature. I realized that my stand was not a very tenable one, and as time passed, I saw more clearly the weakness of that view. Finally I appeared with others before the [New York City] Board of Superintendents and asked that they discontinue the teaching of German in the high schools (it with other foreign languages had already been removed from the elementary schools), by allowing no more beginning classes in that language to be formed beginning with September, 1918. . . . The German language, the German literature, German art, German universities, German science, German culture and the entire German civilization have been vastly over-rated here and in other lands. We have had far too much teaching of German in our schools. It was fast becoming the second language of our nation. And I personally believe that it was taught chiefly for the purposes of furthering propaganda originating in Berlin. (Wilkins 1918, 207–8)

Wilkins' assessment of the status of German as a second language in the United States was an overstatement and his opinions were certainly not shared by all modern language teachers, many of whom wrote defending the teaching of German and the great works of German literary culture. But it was the political power of the German-language press, fears of German "radicalism," and the wildly exaggerated stories of German spies and sabotage which were at issue, not the value of German literature.

Wilkins presented an alternative: Spanish teachers would fulfill their patriotic duty by teaching the language of Pan-Americanism. His presidential address to the Second Annual Association meeting in 1919 was reprinted in *Hispania*:

For the teachers of Spanish comprehend clearly that theirs is in essence a patriotic duty at all times. . . . They have also the vision to see . . . an America stretching from our own land to the utmost bounds of Patagonia, Pan-America, a spiritual union of the English-, Spanish- and Portuguese-speaking peoples of twenty independent republics. . . . The attitude of superiority toward Spanish-American things and peoples so often assumed in the past by our business men, bankers, and even diplomats, is giving way to an attempt to understand those things and people. (37)

Dr. Wilkins' advice to foreign language teachers echoed the sentiments of much of the public, even among the highly educated: foreign language education should be continued, with the proviso that it alter its focus.

In 1918, Professor Frank Barnes of Union College undertook a survey of leading businessmen, and university professors and administrators not associated with foreign language teaching, the results of which were printed in *The Modern Language Journal*. Many of the responses were similar to that of R. M. McElroy of the National Security League, who expressed that German language teaching was valuable and should not be completely eliminated from the schools, so long as the work was "carefully supervised and guarded against anything in the way of propaganda" and so long as "certain phases of German political thought and social thought [are] not offered to our students" (Barnes 1918, 194). The feeling of many influential foreign language educators was not much different. Professor Calvin Thomas of Columbia University, advocating an "English-only" school policy for immigrant children and limited access to foreign language study for "American" youth, wrote in 1920: "Let us think steadily of the children and of what is going to be good for them—and not very much of propagandists who wish to magnify their specialty or to exploit their political and literary prejudices" (9). And Charles Handschin, the influential author of methods textbooks and Secretary of the National Federation of Modern Language Teachers, wrote in 1923:

Because of the possibility that students may be taught to be enthusiastic Frenchmen, Germans, or Spaniards, a word of caution is also necessary. The war has taught us that numerous American teachers have become partisans of the foreign civilization. . . . If it means that teachers are, or become, so engrossed by the supposed superiority of the foreign civilization as to magnify it above the American, it is reprehensible. The study of the foreign civilization may very properly be used as a socializing force, provided . . . that American ideals are never lost sight of, and that, if certain American institutions and customs must be criticized, this be done not in a belittling spirit, but in the spirit of opening the learners' eyes to the necessity of improving them. (82)

Under such a rubric, foreign language study becomes part of nation-building and nationalist expansion. The implications of this strategy would be long-term and profound. In part, it put the profession in the ticklish position of doing cross-cultural analysis while extolling the culture of the United States as, in the end, supreme. In addition, study of material considered hazardous to impressionable children and youth would have to be avoided; all study must work toward the creation of an American culture and loyal American citizens. Finally, all practically oriented language instruction should be in the service of American economic and political goals abroad.

Thus, any language teacher discussing political or philosophical ideas classified as foreign, or incorporating "too much" intercultural or cross-cultural analysis, especially if it would involve a critical view of the United States' actions on the world scene, was open to accusations of unpatriotic, un-American, and corrupting behavior. Under such conditions, curriculum design is constrained by what is seen as acceptable within a patriotic framework of education. A one-way analysis of culture dominates—the gaze of the American tourist or the businessman upon the foreign culture—and cannot be balanced by a more complex analysis that looks at both the macro- and micro-politics of intercultural engagement. For the much put-upon practitioner, it must have been easier to simply avoid walking such a minefield and return to the safe territory of grammar-translation using prestigious texts of earlier centuries.

What were the long-term ramifications of the push by some foreign language education leaders to adopt a "patriotic" foreign language curriculum? What echoes of the past do we still hear? What constraints, what invisible boundaries, still confine us today? While globalization is on every agenda, the fact remains that our profession has come of age in the era of nationalism, and the post–Cold War world has not cast off that era just yet. As we know well, cultural attitudes do not change so quickly.

From one perspective, if we examine the enrollment trends over the past eighty years, it does not appear that Wilkins' arguments for new types of Americanized language instruction were very successful. The implications of his proposals for a Pan-American curriculum in Spanish could have led to a "Spanish for Business" or "Practical Spanish" curriculum which was encouraged or required for all high school students, with a prestige Spanish curriculum reserved for the college-bound. However, as participation in high school

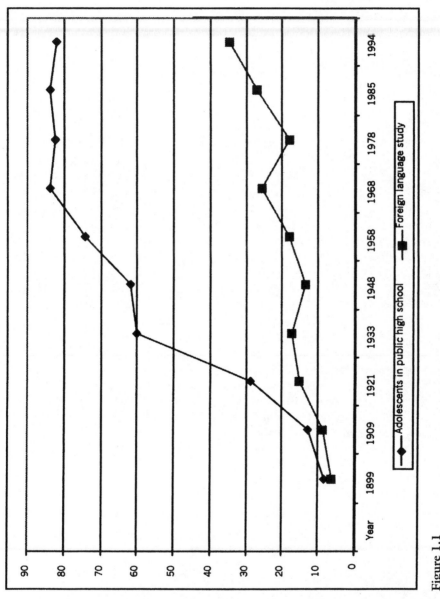

Figure 1.1
Adolescent Participation (by percentage) in Public High Schools and Foreign Language Study

became more and more common for American youth—from 28.8 percent in 1921, to 60.2 percent in 1933 and 74.3 percent in 1958—the discipline of foreign language study did *not* diversify its course offerings, thereby creating differentiated curricula for the emerging tracking system, as did other subject areas such as English and mathematics, as depicted in Figure 1.1 (Watzke 2000).

Instead, the prestige strategy continued to dominate all foreign language curriculum design, with French attracting the largest number of students under the banner of high culture, punctuated by occasional national crises and calls for a practical language curriculum (e.g., post–World War II concerns about intelligence operations or the Sputnik era of the early 1960s). Consequently, foreign language continued to be associated with the college-bound track and to attract a smaller and smaller proportion of the growing high school population. How and why this path was followed between 1920 and 1960 is a subject for further research, but I would venture at this point that the generation of teachers active in the profession in 1917 had learned two lessons well: do not espouse the virtues of the modern German (or French or Spanish) nation, and do not make the classroom a site of political contention. In 1970, John H. Fisher discussed the perceived connection between language and national loyalty, and the need for foreign language teachers to negotiate this tricky territory. Evidencing both lessons at a 1977 symposium on the history of the German language in the United States, George Schulz-Behrend noted:

First assumption: language equals political loyalty. Whoever spoke German was loyal to the Kaiser; later he was a Nazi. Second assumption: language equals culture, with a capital C. Third assumption: English equals Americanism, up to and in excess of 100 percent. . . . [M]any immigrant parents have reasoned that if the choice is between maximum proficiency in one language or partial proficiency in two, then the child should definitely be a monolingual English speaker, thus avoiding any of the psychological problems of bilingualism, *not to mention its political implications* [emphasis added]. (Kloss 1971b, 169–70)

If these are the sociopolitical roots of our profession; and if these roots dictate a curriculum which is apolitical and which is inherently inimical to the enactment of a true "5 Cs" curriculum as proposed by the national *Standards for Foreign Language Learning* (1996); and if we accept that both demographics and globalization will soon render this type of curriculum irrelevant; then, how do we chart a new course while still living in (perhaps the end-times of) a world dominated by nationalism?

CHANGING COURSE: A NEW PURPOSE IN THE TWENTY-FIRST CENTURY?

The absence of extensive discussion of such sociological factors as language learning setting and relative L1/L2 status reflect a confluence of historical processes and events: the submergence of the political nature of curriculum design in general; the focus in foreign language education on languages associated with high prestige; a narrow, homogeneous student population; and the impact of the ideology of nationalism. The absence of such discussion has in and of itself affected foreign language curriculum design; perhaps most importantly, it has impeded the profession from examining the true reasons behind and implications of the de facto banning of foreign languages from elementary schools (the sequence starting point for second language study in virtually all other countries).[12] Instead, we have tended to be obsessed with finding the magic method or approach that will allow us to produce competent students (regardless of the definition of competent) in the unrealistically short time period allowed in a two- or four-year high school or two- or four-semester university sequence.

All educational institutions and academic disciplines are to some degree affected by the timing of K–16 structural development in the United States: the expansion of K–12 education, compulsory attendance laws, and the growth of postsecondary institutions all took place within the context of intense nationalist sentiment, racist ideologies, the rise of the United States as "world policeman," colonial acquisitions, industrialization, and major battles over domestic social policy. If foreign language, more so than other disciplines, is still trapped by the implications of that period, it is because the very nature of our work puts us at the intersection of many of those sociopolitical battles. It is not a place we can escape, nor is it necessarily one we have eschewed. This does *not* mean, however, that it is not a place in which we can negotiate, navigate, and begin to refashion. We can, and practitioners' interest in the proficiency movement indicates a profound desire on the part of many to renegotiate the boundaries within which we operate.

To renegotiate these boundaries, however, will require taking risks. The question is: Are we willing to take the risk of abandoning old strategies—the traditional views of our own purpose—upon which we have relied for so many generations? And if we abandon them, how will we replace them?

While there are no easy answers to such questions, I submit, first, that we must go to the heart of our historical dilemma, confront the political implications of our work and the public's sensitivity to it, and find a way to reenter the elementary and middle school classroom. We must focus on ways to extend the sequence of modern language study by openly arguing that achieving any real proficiency in a language requires a long sequence of study. Second, as demanded by Lorraine Strasheim (1975) and F. André Paquette (1969) more than a generation ago, we must take the lead and openly argue that it is *not* un-American to be bilingual or to learn a second language. Finally, we must pursue vigorously the openings presented to us by current conditions by abandoning the prestige strategy—*and* the practicality strategy—and fashion a new purpose for our profession that includes education of all K–12 students.

Extending Sequences

Any meaningful change in our purpose and curriculum will be defeated by the incredibly short sequences viewed as normal in the United States. While we cannot lightly dismiss the historical, political, and sociological forces which have all but eliminated foreign language study below the high school level, and which has constrained it to a predominantly two-year experience in high school, this does not mean that we are incapable of changing these norms. The fact that a few students can achieve higher levels of proficiency within very short sequences must no longer be our guidepost—these students are the exception and cannot guide planning. And even those students, we must admit, only rarely achieve that proficiency without a study-abroad experience, currently available only to a privileged few. No magic method, approach, or philosophy can change this.

What it will require is a long-term commitment—a twenty-year plan—to bring about longer sequences, and a coordinated advocacy effort to take advantage of the openings presented to us at this point in history. One state which is taking advantage of those openings is New Jersey, where standards for world languages have been developed for all K–12 children and are now being implemented. When the state held community focus groups in 1992 to seek input in creating content standards as a part of its strategic plan for statewide systemic reform, parents, business leaders, and community members brought forward their concerns about student preparedness for a more and more tightly knit world community. Over the next four years, World Languages standards for all children, grades K–12, were developed and subjected to public hearings; they became final in 1996, thanks in part to an intensive effort to secure the support of state legislators and Governor Christine Todd Whitman. Janis Jensen, World Languages Coordinator for the state of New Jersey, summarized what she sees as the sociopolitical conditions which have allowed for such a sweeping program: first, a statewide standards movement; second, parents' awareness of a world grown smaller, in large part due to the leaps in technology over the past 10–20 years, and in part due to the diversity of the state's population; third, parents' awareness of early childhood development research due to media coverage and popular publications; and finally, the proficiency and communicative teaching movements in foreign language education.[13] While multiple elements are involved in implementing such a dramatic expansion of language sequences, one element highlighted by Jensen are the parent/community workshops being held across the state. She estimates that workshops on the World Languages standards will reach 50 percent of all parents in New Jersey within three years. At these GAINS (Gaining Achievement in the New Standards) workshops, parents and community members are given information about the new World Languages standards and their implementation, and are engaged in interactive activities enabling them to experience firsthand what it is like to be in a standards-driven world language classroom. They are also shown a video of a communicative classroom—something that makes a great impression on parents who have unpleasant memories of "drill and translate" classrooms from their high school years. Jensen also notes that workshop leaders talk bluntly about the need for longer sequences: "We openly discuss the fact that it takes a long time to reach proficiency in a language, and that it is simply unrealistic to expect anyone to learn to speak a language after only two years of study. Most parents embrace this idea; it just seems like common sense to them" (interview with author).[14]

The sociopolitical, financial, and structural conditions which created space in New Jersey for a true, K–12 sequence of foreign language study should be studied carefully over the next few years. Will it work? How will issues of curricula, materials, teacher education, teacher shortages, crowded schedules, and the profession's inexperience with a wide range of students be dealt with? Will parents pressure local school districts to make a world languages curriculum a reality in every school? How will the often sensitive issue of language choice be dealt with? How could New Jersey's model be imitated and adopted, or adapted to different circumstances across the country? What specific states would be the most likely successful sites for reproduction of a (hopefully) successful New Jersey model? If New Jersey and just a few other states were able to make such programs work, the prospects for nationwide change would greatly improve: in the decentralized American educational system, large-scale change is often accomplished by state leaders observing successful innovations and then imitating them.

Taking a Stand on Language and Patriotism

Foreign language educators have traditionally been less active than others in responding to language politics, often leaving such work to TESOL (Teaching of English to Speakers of Other Languages) educators. We must begin to examine the connections between the modern language classroom, the ESL (English as a Second Language) classroom, "English-only" attitudes, anti-immigrant attitudes, and language rights, as well as our *own* attitudes about patriotism, nationalism, and the role we play in the politics of language.

Abandoning Strategies that Don't Work

It is an old sales pitch that the study of foreign languages means access to cultural understanding (primarily through literature study), or to power in international business or political relationships (primarily through oral- or proficiency-oriented models). The problem with both of these approaches is that our enrollment numbers over the past forty years clearly indicate that they do not attract a majority of school-aged students to our classrooms. This is because, first, literature has been further and further de-centered as a means of accessing knowledge throughout this century; while it is still relevant, it is not considered a primary means of intellectual development as in the past. Second, no country needs a very large pool of national security experts. And finally, English-speaking Americans are not fooled by the rhetoric of language study for successful economic competition: everything around them says that, as the language of a dominant sociopolitical and military force, *theirs* is the language of power and will be so into the foreseeable future (see, for example, Skutnabb-Kangas 2000; Tollefson 1991). And as noted above, the students that these approaches *have* traditionally appealed to—middle- and upper-class Anglos—will be a shrinking percentage of the school-aged students in this country. We must find new approaches that have broader appeal and convince parents that modern language study is part of a core educational experience, not just part of the "college-prep" track or a means to (unprovable) economic gains.

MAKING IT WORK: NEW VISIONS AND MULTILEVEL COORDINATION

In closing, I would like to outline four strategic conditions that I believe will be required to effectuate long-term change that will move the profession toward viability in the twenty-first century. First, *the participation of all foreign language educators and scholars is needed if a push for extended sequences is to succeed.* The university-level debates in our profession have recently been dominated by what I perceive to be a misdirected focus: what and how to teach a minority of students. In part and most recently, this debate is set against shrinking budgets, the elimination of tenure-track lines, and the general corporatization of American higher education. This debate focuses on the wrong end of the survival chain. In contrast, much valuable time and energy has been spent by ACTFL (American Council on the Teaching of Foreign Languages) over the past few years to position modern language as one of the K–12 "basics" and to establish standards by which performance, or proficiency, can be judged. An admission by both high school teachers and university scholars that we cannot produce students who perform to the higher levels of those standards without extended sequences would be a powerful tool in legislative and public relations battles to make modern language study one of the required basics of American education. High school and postsecondary foreign language advocates publicly state that modern language study is no different than the study of mathematics or reading: *all* children are capable of learning, but performance standards are meaningless without the opportunity to learn over long periods of time.

Second, *we need to continue—and accelerate—the process of re-conceiving foreign language curricula.* We must envision curricula that are not at their base designed for business, travel, or literary analysis. If we think of extended sequences as vertical growth, a re-conceived curricula is horizontal growth. Extended K–12 sequences, designed for *all* children, will require new kinds of curricula that are age appropriate, free of race and class presumptions, and supranationalist. Some European examples, such as discussed by Byram and

Risager (1999) may be of help, in addition to the New Jersey World Languages model discussed above. I do not believe, however, that we must be in complete agreement or have fully fashioned such curricula in order to begin the push for extended sequences. Curriculum development is in part organic, a bottom-up process as much (or more so) than a top-down process. While we continue to debate and await consensus on, for example, the "right" Spanish curriculum for middle-school students in a predominantly Black inner-city school, another generation slips by. And so does another year in which we can ill-afford to ignore the demographic changes coming our way. Instead, we must find a way to strike a balance between grassroots, teacher-developed curricula and curricula development which takes into account the best of pedagogical research and international models, and then find ways of effectively disseminating information on successful projects.

Third, *it is difficult, if not impossible, for a profession to effectuate this type of change without a coordinating body.* Communication during a paradigm shift is crucial. Many state language coordinator positions have been eliminated over the past ten years; we need to recover and reinvigorate those positions. At the national level, our profession has numerous organizations (e.g., American Council on the Teaching of Foreign Languages, Association of Departments of Foreign Languages, Joint National Committee on Languages, and the language-specific organizations); the challenge is to develop a larger, active membership among modern language educators at all levels, and to establish a more sophisticated and efficient intra-professional communication and public advocacy system.

And finally, before we can begin, we must have *a vision of our new purpose in an extended sequence of study.* If we were able to build down from the now-typical two-year high school foreign language experience, moving into the middle school as a universal requirement, and then into the fourth through sixth grades as part of the experience of all young children, what would be our vision? It is this vision which must be communicated to the public, to legislators, to federal funding bureaus, before we will be able to move forward. On this there must be widespread consensus. To be successful in altering the public's perceptions and historically-rooted views, it must be a new vision that can be stated simply and clearly, and answer the question: Why do all children need an extended foreign language experience?

The changes required of our profession are possible. The only question truly in play is whether or not traditionalism and fear will prevent us from taking advantage of the openings presented to us. There is still time to change. But the clock is ticking.

ACKNOWLEDGMENT

Interdisciplinary work is particularly dependent on the courtesy and generosity of fellow scholars. I would like to thank all those who have provided support and advice on the research associated with this work, especially L. Kathy Heilenman. I would also like to thank those who assisted with insightful comments and editing of this chapter: Terry A. Osborn, David Bills, Jolene M. Stritecky, Sue K. Otto, John L. Watzke, and an anonymous reviewer. In addition, I would like to thank Janis Jensen for generously giving of her time by providing oral interviews and information on New Jersey's World Languages program. All interpretation and errors remain, of course, the sole responsibility of the author.

NOTES

1. See, for example: Über Grosse and Voght (1990), Barnett (1991), James (1991), Zipser (1992), McConeghy (1992), Henning (1993), Melton (1994), Kramsch (1995), Byrnes (1995, 1997), Bernhardt (1995a, 1995b), Petrey (1995), D'Agruma and Hardy (1997), García (1998), Siskin (1998), Jedan (1998), Hale (1999), Knox (1999), Welles (1999) Swaffar (1999), Ossipov (2000), Ulrich (2000), and Voght (2000).

2. For a discussion of the foreign language classroom culture as reinforcing and contributing to students' conceptualization of foreignness, see Osborn (2000).

3. In addition to shifts in racial demographics, the age demographics of the United States will undergo a regional shift due to macro-economic restructuring and sites of immigration over the past thirty years. The nation's children will predominantly live in the South and West according to most estimates. For one set of geo-demographic projections, see Frey (1996).

4. For updated statistics and analysis on the substantial increase in child poverty in the United States between 1978 and 1998, see reports by the National Center for Children in Poverty, Mailman School of Public Health of Columbia University. The NCCP website has information on obtaining these reports http://cpmcnet.columbia.edu/dept/nccp/. Specific releases of interest are listed in the Bibliography section of this chapter.

5. See Renner (1993) for an examination of evidence that minority participation in postsecondary education has not kept pace with their proportion of the U.S. population, despite affirmative action programs—many of which are now being dismantled.

6. The most recent demonstrations of this continued battle are the voices of William Bennett and Alan Bloom, who have called for a return to a rigorous humanities-oriented education for all children, in competition with the widespread "back to basics" movement, a call for practical skills education and rigorous testing of those skills.

7. Faculty psychology was based on the concept of the human mind as divided into various "faculties," such as memory or higher reasoning. The study of certain subjects was believed to provide "mental discipline," or strengthening of a particular faculty (e.g., mathematics strengthened the mind's logical faculty). For a description of the beliefs surrounding faculty psychology, its opponents, and the selection of school subjects at the turn of the century, see, for example, Kliebard (1995).

8. For extensive reviews of the Committee of Ten, see Kliebard (1995), and Krug (1964); for a review of modern foreign language study within the context of educational reform movements, see Watzke (2000).

9. For extensive discussion of nationalism and the psychosocial elements of nation-state development, see, for example, Paasi (1995); Hobsbawm (1990); Gellner (1983); and Smith (1979). For further discussion of the intertwining of Americanization, language, and religious strife during the Progressive era, see Wiley (1998).

10. For histories of Americanization programs in the United States, see especially Carlson (1987); see also Cortés (1976), and Meyer (1981).

11. For more on the repression of civil rights of and violence against immigrants, German-Americans, labor activists and other so-called radicals during this period, see, for example, Peterson and Fite (1957); Chambers (1980); Zinn (1980); and Preston (1994).

12. Historical reviews of foreign language education by Müller (1989), Rivers (1983), Stevick (1980), Kelly (1969) and Titone (1968) tend to give passing and brief reference to sociopolitical issues impacting the field, but no analysis, as typified by these comments:

Objections to the teaching of German and other languages in the elementary schools were raised by state and territorial officials [in the 19th century], often on the grounds that the practice was un-American. . . . However, programs persisted and grew, despite the controversies, until the United States entered World War I. At that time there was a strong reaction against everything German, especially the language, and much elementary school instruction in all foreign language was eliminated. (Curtain and Pesola 1988, 13)

No further discussion of the elimination of this entire section of the profession is given. As noted in this chapter, perhaps the connection between foreign languages and un-American behavior has become so embedded in American consciousness that even we in the field have come to see it as a natural reality rather than as a sociohistorical and political process.

13. Janis Jensen, personal communication, August 10, 2000.

14. Janis Jensen, personal communication, August 10, 2000. For more information on the New Jersey World Languages program, an excellent website is maintained at lobalteachinglearning.com. To read the New Jersey World Languages curriculum framework, see the state's education webpage devoted to standards and curriculum framework descriptions at www.state.nj.us/njded/frameworks/index.html. Randers-Pehrson (2000) also provides an overview of the program in his *Foreign Language Annals* article.

BIBLIOGRAPHY

Anderson, B. 1983. *Imagined communities*. London: Verso.

Apple, M. 1986. 1979. *Curriculum and ideology*. New York: Routledge and Kegan Paul, Ltd.

———. *Teachers and texts: A political economy of class and gender relations in education*. New York: Routledge.

Apple, M. and L. K. Christian-Smith, eds. 1991. *The politics of the textbook*. New York: Routledge.

Barnes, F. C. 1918. Shall German be dropped from our schools? *The Modern Language Journal* 2: 187–202.

Barnett, M. A. 1991. Language and literature: False dichotomies, real allies. *The ADFL Bulletin* 22 (3): 7–11.

Benseler, D. P., W.F.W. Lohnes, and V. Nollendorfs, eds. 1988. *Teaching German in America: Prolegomena to a history*. Madison: University of Wisconsin Press.

Bergquist, J. M. 1983. German-America in the 1890s: Illusions and realities. In *Germans in America: Aspects of German-American relations in the nineteenth century*, ed. E. A. McCormick, 1–14. New York: Columbia University Press.

Bernhardt, E. B. 1995a. Teaching literature or teaching students? *The ADFL Bulletin* 26 (2): 5–6.

———. 1995b. Reply to Claire Kramsch. *The ADFL Bulletin* 26 (3). 15–16.

Bubser, R. 1988. Speaking and teaching German in Iowa during World War I: A historical perspective. In *Teaching German in America: Prolegomena to a history*, ed. D. P. Benseler, W.F.W. Lohnes, and V. Nollendorfs, 206–15. Madison: University of Wisconsin Press.

Byram, M. and K. Risager. 1999. *Language teachers, politics and cultures*. Clevedon, England: Multilingual Matters, Ltd.

Byrnes, H. 1995. Response to Claire Kramsch. *The ADFL Bulletin* 25 (3): 13–14.

———. 1997. Governing language departments: Is form function? *The ADFL Bulletin* 29 (1): 7–12.

Carlson, R. A. 1987. *The Americanization syndrome: A quest for conformity*. Rev. ed. London: Croom Helm.

Chambers, II, J. W. 1980. *The tyranny of change: America in the progressive era, 1900–1917*. New York: St. Martin's Press.

Cortés, C. E., ed. 1976. *Aspects of the Mexican-American experience*. New York: Arno Press.

Crookes, G. 1997. What influences what and how second and foreign language teachers teach? *The Modern Language Journal* 81: 67–79.

Curtain, H. A. and C. A. Pesola. 1988. *Languages and children: Making the match*. Reading, MA: Addison Wesley Publishing Company.

D'Agruma, G. and J. T. Hardy. 1997. Foreign languages and cross-cultural knowledge: A survey of their importance as perceived by human resources departments of Ohio's international businesses. *Foreign Language Annals* 30: 38–48.

Dahl, A. G. 1999. Piquing the interest of African American students in foreign languages: The case of Spelman College. *The ADFL Bulletin* 31 (2): 30–35.

Dracass, C. 1908. Spanish in the secondary school. *American Journal of Education* 16, 538–42.

Educational Research Service. 1995. Demographic factors in American education. Arlington, VA: Educational Research Service. ERIC Doc. No. ED379773.

Finn, J. D. 1998. Taking foreign languages in high school. *Foreign Language Annals* 31: 287–306.

Fisher, J. H. 1970. Languages and loyalty. *The ADFL Bulletin* 2 (1): 13–16.

Fishman, J. A., 1966. *Language loyalty in the United States*. The Hague: Mouton.

Fishman, J. A., R. L. Cooper, and A. W. Conrad, eds. 1977. *The spread of English*. Rowley, MA: Newbury House Publishers.

Frey, W. H. 1996. Immigration, domestic migration, and demographic Balkanization in America: New evidence for the 1990s. *Population and Development Review* 22: 741–63.

García, E. 1998. Spanish, French, and German: An Edwardian pattern for a postmodern world. *The ADFL Bulletin* 30 (1): 9–11.

Gellner, E. 1983. *Nations and nationalism*. Oxford: Basil Blackwell.

Grandgent, C. H. 1904. French as a substitute for Latin. *The American Journal of Education* 12: 462–67.

Hale, T. A. 1999. Francophone African literature and the hexagon: Building bridges for the new millennium. *The French Review* 72: 444–55.

Handschin, C. H. 1923. *Methods of teaching modern languages.* New York: World Book Company.

Harris-Schenz, Beverly. 1990. Helping with the bootstraps: The mentor's task. *The ADFL Bulletin 22* (3): 18–21.

Heilenman, L. K. 1993. Of culture and compromises: Publishers, textbooks, and the academy. *Publishing Research Quarterly*, Summer 1993: 55–67.

Henning, S. D. 1993. The integration of language, literature, and culture: Goals and curricular design. *The ADFL Bulletin* 24 (2): 51–55.

Hobsbawm, E. J. 1990. *Nations and nationalism since 1780.* Cambridge: Cambridge University Press.

James, D. 1991. From the editor. *The ADFL Bulletin* 23 (1): 1–3.

———. 1996. Teaching language and literature: Equal opportunity in the inner-city university. *The ADFL Bulletin* 28 (1): 24–28.

Jedan, D. 1998. Shifting enrollment patterns: Departmental perspectives. *The ADFL Bulletin* 30 (1): 15–18.

Joseph, J. E. 1988. New French: A pedagogical crisis in the making. *The Modern Language Journal* 72: 31–35.

Karabel, J. and A. H. Halsey, eds. 1977. *Power and ideology in education.* New York: Oxford University Press.

Kelly, L. G. 1969. *Twenty-five centuries of language teaching.* Rowley, MA: Newbury House Publishers.

Kliebard, H. M. 1995. *The struggle for the American curriculum, 1893–1958.* 2d ed. New York: Routledge.

Kloss, H. 1966. German-American language maintenance efforts. In *Language loyalty in the United States: The maintenance and perpetuation of non-English mother tongues by American ethnic and religious groups*, ed. J. A. Fishman, 206–52. The Hague: Mouton and Co.

———. 1971a. German as an immigrant, indigenous, foreign and second language in the United States. In *The German language in America: A symposium*, ed. G. G. Gilbert, 106–27. Austin: University of Texas Press.

———. (Discussion chair). 1971b. German pedagogy and the survival of German in America: Discussion. In *The German language in America: A symposium*, ed. G. G. Gilbert, 164–78. Austin: University of Texas Press.

Knox, E. C. 1999. Between cultural studies and "cultural competence." *The French Review* 72: 669–75.

Kramsch, C. 1995. Embracing conflict versus achieving consensus in foreign language education. *The ADFL Bulletin* 26 (3): 6–12.

Kron, R. 1901. *German daily life: A reader.* New York: Newson and Company.

Krug, E. A. 1964. *The shaping of the American high school.* New York: Harper and Row Publishers.

Langenscheidt. 1974. *Langenscheidt's encyclopaedic dictionary of the English and German languages, Part II* (German-English). Berlin: Langenscheidt.

Lide, F. 1993. The dynamics and visibility of foreign language programs. In *The dynamics of language program direction*, ed. D. P. Benseler, 65–90. Boston: Heinle and Heinle.

Lindenberger, H. 1998. Must we always be in crisis? *The ADFL Bulletin* 29 (2): 5–9.

McConeghy, P. M. 1992. The new paradigm and international education: Of babies and bathwater. *The ADFL Bulletin* 23 (3): 34–41.

Melton, J. M. 1994. Foreign language interdisciplinary programs and alliances: Some observations. *The ADFL Bulletin* 26 (1): 19–24.

Meyer, S. 1981. *The five dollar day: Labor management and social control in the Ford Motor Company, 1908–1921.* Albany, NY: State University of New York Press.

Moore, Zena T. 1998. Successful teaching strategies: Findings from a case study of middle school African Americans learning Arabic. *Foreign Language Annals* 31: 347–57.

Müller, K. E., ed. 1989. *Languages in elementary schools.* New York: The American Forum.

National Center for Children in Poverty. 1999a. *Young children in poverty: A statistical update.* http://cpmcnet.columbia/dept/ccp/99uptext.html.

———. 1999b. New census data show that child poverty rate continues to lag behind other key economic indicators. http://cpmcnet.columbia/dept/ccp/cps99pr.html.

Newmark, M. 1948. The functions of realia. In *Twentieth century modern language teaching: Sources and readings,* ed. M. Newmark, 436–38. New York: The Philosophical Library.

Nollendorfs, C. L. 1988. The First World War and the survival of German studies: With a tribute to Alexander R. Hohlfeld. In *Teaching German in America: Prolegomena to a history,* ed. D. P. Benseler, W.F.W. Lohnes, and V. Nollendorfs, 176–96. Madison: University of Wisconsin Press.

Osborn, Terry A. 2000. *Critical reflection and the foreign language classroom.* Westport, CT: Bergin and Garvey.

Ossipov, H. 2000. Who is taking French and why? *Foreign Language Annals* 33:157–65.

Paasi, A. 1995. *Territories, boundaries, and consciousness: The changing geographies of the Finnish-Russian boundary.* New York: J. Wiley and Sons.

Paquette, F. A. 1969. A measure of hope. *Foreign Language Annals* 2: 432–35.

Paulston, C. B. 1994. *Linguistic minorities in multilingual settings: Implications for language policies.* Amsterdam/Philadelphia: John Benjamins Publishing Company.

Peterson, H. C. and G. C. Fite. 1957. *Opponents of war, 1917–1918.* Madison: University of Wisconsin Press.

Petrey, S. 1995. French studies/cultural studies: Reciprocal invigoration or mutual destruction? *The French Review* 68: 381–92.

Preston, Jr., W. 1994. *Aliens and dissenters: Federal suppression of radicals, 1903–1933.* 2d ed. Chicago: University of Illinois Press.

Randers-Pehrson, M. 2000. New Jersey: A model for world language education. *Foreign Language Annals* 33: 453–56.

Renner, K. E. 1993. On race and gender in higher education: Illusions of change. *Educational Record* 74 (4): 44–48.

Ricento, T. 1998. National language policy in the United States. In *Language and politics in the United States and Canada,* ed. T. Ricento and B. Burnaby, 85–112. Mahwah, NJ: Lawrence Erlbaum Associates.

Rivers, W. M. 1983. *Speaking in many tongues.* 3d ed. New York: Cambridge University Press.

Ross, W. 1994. *Forging new freedoms: Nativism, education and the Constitution, 1919–1927*. Lincoln: University of Nebraska Press.

Schermerhorn, R. A. 1977. *Comparative ethnic relations*. New York: Random House.

Schlesinger, I. M. 1991. The wax and wane of Whorfian views. In *The influence of language on culture and thought*, ed. R. L. Cooper and B. Spolsky, 7–44. New York: Mouton de Gruyter.

Siskin, H. J. 1998. The invalid revalidated: Caring for the language of Molière. *The ADFL Bulletin* 30 (1): 18–24.

Siskin, H. J., M. A. Knowles, and R. L. Davis. 1996. Le Français est mort, vive le Français: Rethinking the function of French. In *Patterns and policies: The changing demographics of foreign language instruction*, ed. J. E. Liskin-Gasparro, 35–72. Boston: Heinle and Heinle.

Skutnabb-Kangas, T. 2000. Linguistic human rights and teachers of English. In *The sociopolitics of English language teaching*, ed. J. K. Hall and W. G. Eggington, 22–44. Clevedon, UK: Multilingual Matters, Ltd.

Smith, A. 1979. *Nationalism in the twentieth century*. Oxford: Martin Robertson.

Standards for foreign language learning: Preparing for the twenty-first century. 1996. Yonkers, NY: National Standards in Foreign Language Education Project.

Stern, H. H. 1983. *Fundamental concepts in language teaching*. Oxford: Oxford University Press.

Stevick, E. W. 1980. *Teaching languages: A way and ways*. Rowley, MA: Newbury House Publishers.

Strasheim, L. A. 1975. We're *all* ethnics: Hyphenated Americans, professional ethnics, and ethnics by attraction. In *The culture revolution in foreign language teaching*, ed. R. C. Lafayette, H. B. Altman, and R. Schulz, 1–18. Skokie, IL: National Textbook Company.

Swaffar, J. 1999. The case for foreign languages as a discipline. *The ADFL Bulletin* 30 (3): 6–12.

Thomas, C. 1920. Good and bad reasons for studying modern languages in school. *The Modern Language Journal* 5: 1–11.

Titone, R. 1968. *Teaching foreign languages*. Washington, DC: Georgetown University Press.

Tollefson, J. W. 1991. *Planning language, planning inequality: Language policy in the community*. New York: Addison Wesley Longman, Inc.

Tschirner, E. 1996. Scope and sequence: Rethinking beginning foreign language instruction. *The Modern Language Journal* 80: 1–14.

Tyack, D. B. 1974. *The one best system: A history of American urban education*. Cambridge, MA: Harvard University Press.

Über Grosse, C. and G. M. Voght. 1990. Foreign languages for business and the professions at U.S. colleges and universities. *The Modern Language Journal* 74: 36–47.

Ulrich, J. N. 2000. Putting language before business: The business case study in the foreign language classroom. *Foreign Language Annals* 33: 230–36.

Valdés, Guadalupe. 1991. Minority and majority members in foreign language departments: Toward the examination of established attitudes and values. *The ADFL Bulletin* 22 (3): 1–14.

Voght, G. M. 2000. New paradigms for U.S. higher education in the twenty-first century. *Foreign Language Annals* 33: 269–77.

Walters, P. B. 1992. Who should be schooled? The politics of class, race, and ethnicity. In *The political construction of education: The state, school expansion and economic change*, ed. B. Fuller and R. Rubinson, 173–88. New York: Praeger.

Watzke, J. L. 2000. The history of foreign language and secondary education reform: Prospects for achieving standards-based goals. Ph.D. diss., University of Iowa.

Weiss, G. 1988. From New York to Philadelphia: Issues and concerns of the American Association of Teachers of German between 1926 and 1970. In *Teaching German in America: Prolegomena to a history*, ed. D. P. Benseler, W.F.W. Lohnes, and V. Nollendorfs, 215–27. Madison: University of Wisconsin Press.

Welles, E. B. 1999. From the editor. *The ADFL Bulletin* 30 (2): 1–3.

Wilberschied, L. and J. Dassier. 1995. Increasing the number of minority FL educators: Local action to meet a national imperative. *The Modern Language Journal* 79: 1–14.

Wiley, T. 1996. Language planning and language policy. In *Sociolinguistics and language teaching*, ed. S. McKay and N. Hornberger, 103–47. Cambridge, England: Cambridge University Press.

———. 1998. World War I era English-only policies. In *Language and politics in the United States and Canada*, ed. T. Ricento and B. Burnaby, 211–41. Mahwah, NJ: Lawrence Erlbaum Associates.

Wilkins, L. A. 1919. The president's address. *Hispania* 2: 36–40.

———. 1918. Spanish as a substitute for German for training and culture. *Hispania* 1(4): 205–21.

Wooley, E. O. 1948. Five decades of German instruction in America. In *Twentieth century modern language teaching: Sources and readings*, ed. M. Newmark, 67–79. New York: The Philosophical Library.

Zeydel, E. H. 1988. [1961]. The teaching of German in the United States from colonial times through World War I. In *Teaching German in America: Prolegomena to a history*, ed. D. P. Benseler, W.F.W. Lohnes, and V. Nollendorfs, 15–54. Madison: University of Wisconsin Press.

Zinn, H. 1980. *A people's history of the United States*. New York: HarperCollins Publishers.

Zipser, R. 1992. Building a full-service foreign language department: Some strategies and interdisciplinary initiatives. *The ADFL Bulletin* 23 (3): 28–33.

2

The Entangled Future of Foreign Language Learning

Stephen W. Kercel, S. Alenka Brown-VanHoozer, and W. R. VanHoozer

MATHEMATICS AS A FOREIGN LANGUAGE

Although not algorithmically computable, the processes of learning and language can be represented with self-referential mathematical structures, which are more difficult to use than number-based systems since their predictions are incomplete. "Algorithmic" has a specific meaning in computer science as a systematic process with five attributes (Knuth 1973, 4–6): (1) Algorithms terminate after a finite number of steps, (2) Each step is unambiguously defined, (3) Algorithms have zero or more input data, (4) Algorithms have one or more output data, and (5) Algorithms must be effective. "Effectiveness" is conventionally taken to mean a process that can be converted into an operational procedure called the Universal Turing Machine (Rosen 1999). Such a process is also said to be computable.

A process that lacks any of these five attributes is known as an incomputable process. Such a process cannot be described by a list of numbers and therefore cannot be described algorithmically. This is typical of many self-referential processes. Incomputable processes differ from recursive algorithms in that recursive algorithms have a defined bottom level of recursion, whereas incomputable processes refer to themselves endlessly.

Human behavior includes many instances of this sort of self-reference or "bottomless recursion." The Meta Model (model of a modeling process) in Neuro-Linguistic Programming (NLP) is a means to identify deletions, distortions, and generalizations and provide more complete linguistic descriptions of subjective (and usually unconscious) experience markers. And, yes, we have considered the possibility that once a model has been determined to be recursive, this categorization establishes a static label of the process, but even that consideration is subject to perspective and, therefore, endless recursion can follow.

To appreciate the problems posed by self-reference, consider the deceptively simple proposition $\phi(x) = \phi(x)$. It appears to say nothing and, yet, everything simultaneously. On one hand, it says that as a definition of $\phi(x)$, it does not inform us how $\phi(x)$ differs from any other entity, such as $\psi(x)$. In fact, it appears to illustrate the futility of defining an entity by circular reference. On the other hand, $\phi(x) = \phi(x)$ is a profound truth regarding every entity; it is a condensed statement of Aristotle's Law of Non-contradiction (Adler 1978). It states that a thing is what it is or is congruent with itself.

This self-referential proposition is the foundation axiom of our system of rational thinking, according to Aristotle. It is more than self-referential; it is self-evident. The Law of Non-contradiction cannot be validated from any more fundamental proposition. However, no counter example has ever been produced to contradict its validity. Paradoxically, any effort to logically prove it false starts from the assumption (usually implicit and unacknowledged) that it is true.

"Scientific" traditionalists are uneasy about self-reference because it can lead to such paradoxes. However, the simple evasion of disallowing self-reference is deeply unsatisfying for several reasons. First, our system of logic is based on the self-evident self-referential proposition, $\phi(x) = \phi(x)$; disallowing this foundation principle from the Universe of Discourse hardly appears to be a sound way to begin a logical process. Second, we can use language to discuss a paradoxical system of logic, and third, disallowing self-reference results in a system of logic that is even too impoverished to discuss mathematics.

Although mathematicians are loath to admit it, self-referential, or impredicative, propositions are both admissible and necessary in mathematics (Kleene 1950). An impredicative definition is one in which the object being defined participates in its own definition. It is subtly but crucially different from a circular definition. As already noted, a completely circular definition provides no feature to distinguish between the object being defined and the remainder of the Universe of Discourse. An impredicative definition must include some constraint (in addition to identity) on the relationship between an object and itself, and in that constraint is contained its distinguishing feature.

Hence, mathematicians and scientists prefer to avoid self-referential mathematical structures. They often lead to embarrassing paradoxes. Thus, the simplest, and conventionally accepted, way to evade the dilemma is to exclude all self-referential propositions from the epistemological Universe of Discourse, and to ignore its distinction from the ontological Universe.

The key point of this digression is that logic is founded on self-reference or impredicativity. The risk of self-reference is that it can lead to paradoxes. A blanket taboo against self-reference to avoid paradox is too simplistic. An epistemological Universe of Discourse that disallows self-reference is too impoverished to allow meaningful discussion of the ontological Universe, where self-referential structures (including mind, learning, and languages) abound.

Such exclusion of self-reference limits our comprehension and flexibility in realizing language to be an expression of our experience based on our internal representation systems coupled with external minimal cues. Minimal cues are those micro-to-macro (and or vice versa) level physiological behaviors that are equivalent to verbal expressions. If these minimal cues are not coupled with the linguistic representations of language (which is how foreign language is taught today), the learning process for comprehending language becomes more difficult, frustrating, and tedious than need be. Language is learned and spoken from the unconscious and "in time" instead of "between" or "through" time. Thus, foreign language should be taught in a manner similar to the experience of a child, at the unconscious.

SEMANTIC REFERENCE

Since this chapter is a cross-disciplinary discussion in terms of learning, languages, and mathematical structures, we feel it necessary to define specific words that we will address in this chapter for semantic cohesion. For example, "users are not conscious that that term 'concept' has elementalistic implications of 'mind' or 'intellect' taken separately, which then become verbal fictions. . . . What is called 'concept' amounts to nothing more or less than a verbal formulation, a term which eliminates the false-to-fact implications" (Korsybski 2000, lxii).

Semantic reference simply states that words have different meanings dependent on one's experience of "reality." Can language, particularly its semantics or meaning, be explored scientifically? We say that it can, but the tools of traditional science are not up to the task. A strictly objective (reductionistic) description is insufficient to describe a phenomenon as subjective (irreducible) as semantics.

Reductionism includes the notion that a process can be completely described by a list of numbers. However, the notion of reductionism is broader than this, encompassing both numbers and other objects that can be put into correspondence with numbers (Rosen 2000). Suppose that x is a natural system or referent, and $P(x)$ is a proposition that asserts that some property of x is true. Rosen argues that an essential attribute of reductionism is that any such proposition can be algorithmically constructed by "ANDing" $P_i(x)$ where i ε $\{1, \ldots, N\}$, N is a natural number, and there are N true subproperties of x that are described by N independent propositions. Since infinity is not a number, this description limits a reducible system to a finite list of properties. This algorithm constitutes a list of conditions, each necessary, and all sufficient to establish the logical validity of P(x). In Rosen's (2000) words, "every property P(x) of x is of this character" (131).

Computable, algorithmic, and reducible are three equivalent terms describing a model of a mechanism. A mechanism is a system whose operation unfolds without purpose. Incomputable, non-algorithmic and irreducible are three equivalent terms describing a model of a different kind of system, in Rosen's parlance, a complex system (Rosen 2000, 306–7). Unfortunately, "complex" is so widely used for so many different concepts that it seldom conveys any useful meaning. A more descriptive term for Rosenesque complexity is "Endogenous Systems," the endogeny stemming from the fact that they are self-referential and incomputable though logically tractable. Endogeny is largely ignored by the practitioners of traditional science, who prefer to limit themselves to the exploration of mechanisms.

The endogenous process of most interest to readers of this chapter is language, described by Chomsky as a process of liberation from conceptual, logical, or discursive rationalism. Language not only articulates, connects, and infers, it also envisages, and the intuitive grasping of language is the primary act and function of that one and single power which is called reason. For it is then that we may pass from the passive acceptance of sense-data to a fresh, constructive, and spontaneous insight into the universe (Chomsky 1993). Except for the notion of "passivity," Chomsky fairly captures the idea of language. However the "sense-data" are an active state in our language development. It is these "sense-data" that provide the minimal cues demonstrated by the individual at the unconscious, and influenced by social constraints that are embedded into the formal language. When learning a language, one does not simply learn the words, phrases, and grammar, but also the minimal cues of the culture embedded in the language better known as "non-verbals."

A more fundamental endogenous mental process than language is learning. Learning is a process that can be observed, coded, and made congruent with a model for application of teaching others. It is generated from strategies constructed by our mental representation systems (RS). "Representation systems are the "atoms of cognition" whose function is to shape our mental models of reality. . . . The manner in which these RS are structured (in sequence) forms a strategy, or a series of strategies" (Brown-VanHoozer, Kercel, and VanHoozer 2000, 2205; see also Brown-VanHoozer 1999). These learning strategies are constructed at the unconscious, and are foundations of our more complex decision-making strategies leading to behavior patterns at a conscious level. Language provides a means of feedback through which RS are expressed in our experiences or behavior.

At an even higher level of endogeny, consciousness is the process by which we are aware of events and objects in reality, and are deliberately involved in attending to them. Unconsciousness is the process by which we attend to events and objects in reality without being aware of them. "Consciousness is not a 'force' that controls our behavior. It is simply an indication of which of our mental/neurological activity has the highest signal" (Dilts 1983, 17–18). Thus, unconscious processes outstrip conscious processes in all of their perceptual, conceptual, emotional, and response capabilities. Unconscious processes encompass everything that conscious processes overlook, ignore, or reject, plus everything that the conscious processes encompass as well.

THE SCIENCE OF LEARNING

From the perspective of neurophysiology, cognitive behavior is irreducible to a list of lists of numbers. This being the case, no list of lists of numbers, no matter how big, can model behavior. To discuss cognition on any level deeper than merely tabulating empirical observations, some logical description of it must be found that is not limited by the mathematical laws governing the relationships between lists of numbers.

Rather than the old cliche "Seeing is believing" the cognitive process actually works the other way around, "Believing is seeing." The brain sees what it believes it sees. In fact, if the brain cannot construct a meaningful model from sensory input, it often ignores it (Caulfield 1999). This is based on the preferred representation system (visual, auditory, or kinesthetic) that an individual relies on to connect with reality. In other words, the preferred RS is that system we favor or value most in forming our perception of the world.

According to Korsybski (2000), notions such as time and space are Aristotelian structures of language, implying through structure, a split of what in actuality can not be separated. "In a non-Aristotelian system we do not use elementalistic terminology to represent facts that are non-elementalistic. We use terms like 'semantic relations,' 'psychosomatic,' 'space-time,' etc., which eliminate verbally implied splits, and consequent misevaluations" (Korsybski 2000, lxii). In knowing this we can begin to understand how we comprehend language "in," "through," and "between" time with space minimized to a miniscule distance within each. It is this time variance (in, through, and between) in conjunction with the unconscious that language is learned, and paired with universal grammar that the authors consider to be the minimal cues RS. It is speculated this is the process by which individuals learn distinct rules of diverse languages.

In human minds, sensory information is abstracted into percepts via an elegant automatic process at the unconscious. We can consciously abstract these percepts into symbolic concepts, and use them for learning, memory review and recall, meaning of language, knowledge, belief systems, and behavior modification.

We transform sensory based input into meaning with the three basic RS, and the entangled interactions between them. This actualization of knowledge is accomplished through a feedback process characterized as test-operate-test-exit (TOTE), originally formulated by Miller, Galanter, and Pribram (as cited in Dilts 1994). The "operate" consists of applying the sensation(s) to

35

various combinations of the representational models. The "test" is the question of whether or not the knowledge feels right, and updating the models if it feels wrong. The kinesthetic-emotive representation system performs the test, and it keeps feeding back into the TOTE process until it either feels right or diverts in a different direction (Brown-VanHoozer 1999). To "exit" the TOTE loop means to use the newly abstracted knowledge to proceed toward some internally defined goal or final cause (Dilts 1994). We perceive the result of the final test of the TOTE process as a comforting and satisfying feeling of knowing (Damasio 1999).

For example, in autism the sensory wetware is present and produces the right markers (chemical and electrical signals), though due to a neurological malfunction, the representation systems do not construct sensible percepts from them. As a result the typical autistic child lives a life of unremitting "terror" (Sacks 1995). With proper medication and training, autistics learn how to construct RS in the sequences most appropriate for their situation, exclusively "thinking in pictures." Verbal language is a pure abstraction into which high-functioning autistics have learned to translate their visual concepts. This may be due to the fact that visual representation contains no emotions, smells, tastes, or sounds. The visual RS is a quiet state from which the other representation systems must be introduced, a state from which one can access information in a manner that is quiet and unhampered by continuous sounds or feelings. However, there must be some encroachment of the other RS to remain sane.

The highly developed visual representation systems of autistics overstimulate the neurological "fight or flight" response, while the other representation systems (auditory and kinesthetic) are easily overwhelmed by sounds, touches, tastes, and smells. As a result, the daily life of the autistic adult is only slightly less frightening than that of the autistic child (Sacks 1995). It is not surprising that if the abstraction of sensations into "knowing" feels right, then a meaningless jumble of sensations may feel terribly wrong. This is a similar awareness that is found in the learning of foreign languages.

We can utilize the RS to model both success and failure, and show that all learning is propagated by a feeling (or intuition). Process words (e.g., love, friendship, anger, curiosity) used to describe feelings can be modeled employing the RS. This can also be done for understanding how one successfully learns foreign languages.

As humans, we use digital communications (streams of discrete symbols) or language to teach formal languages; however, formal language is too discrete to express the total depth of experience, or to assure clarity in communication. Thus, foreign language learning must include both discrete and analog communication. It is the analog (continuous) communications (non-verbals), such as body and eye movements that are essential for conveying meaning.

Since analog communication occurs at a more primitive level than digital, it reveals more about the internal mental state of the subject. It is at this level of observation that we begin to determine how the models of learning are constructed. Consider the simple diagram below of a learning strategy.

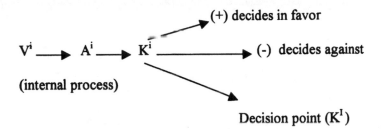

The diagram above suggests that an internal picture of a task has been accessed due to some external stimulus. This is compared against an internal sound or dialogue (test-operate); then concluded based on an internal feeling (test-exit).

It is at the unconscious that we all learn our native language. Learning languages consciously with minimal external and internal feedback is only a production in sounds. To learn different languages one must assume the position of a child. Speak only the language being learned, learn by using the nondominant hemisphere (the unconscious), and mimic the language (verbally and nonverbally) as a toddler and child would. The speed and fluency at which the language is learned will be tremendous. The learning curve will be shorter, and less frustrating for the student.

THE SCIENCE OF LANGUAGE

A child's language "grows in the mind," and is context specific. The representations used in traditional science presume context independence, and are inadequate for describing language. "The symbolic systems created in the scientific enterprise differ radically from natural languages in their fundamental formal properties, as in their semantic purposes" (Chomsky 1993, 29). In linguistics, there is a relationship between context and content. For example, a phoneme only has meaning in a spoken word, in context with other phonemes. A word only has meaning in an utterance. An utterance only has meaning in a relationship. If there is no context, then there is no communication. Thus, even upon its context-dependent face, it is apparent that the processes of language are non-algorithmic.

Bateson (1972) also notes the crucial distinction between being right and not being wrong. If we are trying to guess the missing characters in a garbled message, we do not algorithmically explore and eliminate all the wrong possibilities. We use redundancy to focus directly on the right possibility (based upon individual perception). This is precisely how radiotelegraph operators reconstruct Morse code messages based on partial information. By similar process, an individual learns foreign languages.

To appreciate how redundancy works in language, consider that meaning is the essence of any communication, and is dependent upon an isolated symbol, phrase, or sentence structure in conjunction with analog cues. From the perspective of A talking to B, suppose that A has a specific message on his pad. No new information is added about the message by inspecting B's message pad after he receives the message from A. However, what the message means depends on a complex equivalence of what is being seen, felt, or heard (the digital/analog communications) by B.

If you receive the message "It is raining," one presupposes that (1) one hears the rain, (2) one sees the rain (3) one hears thunder and/or sees lightening associated with rain, (4) one is drenched or dampened with water, (5) one sees the outdoors dampened with water, and so on. The word "rain" conveys both the symbolic message, and the ontological fact that raindrops may be descending. The universe is informed by such messages.

The meaning is not the string of symbols or the referent, instead it is in the correspondence between them (the nonverbals). Note that the meaning is nonlocal. It is not located in either the string of symbols or the referent. It is entangled, or a consequence of the relationship between the symbols and the referent. The fact that one is not aware of where the meaning resides does not make it any less real. The nonlocality of meaning is regarded as a perplexing problem by traditional thinkers in communications and neurophysiology.

However, there is no need for perplexity; what is needed is to allow for the possibility of self-reference. Nonlocal behavior is characteristic of self-referential systems. Furthermore, self-reference leads to creative behavior. Chomsky (1972) sees this level of complexity as the core problem of human language, which he describes as possessing the following qualities: (1) Having mastered a language one can understand indefinitely many expressions that are outside one's experience; (2) Through language, one is able to produce novel but appropriate expressions that can be understood by others; and (3) The normal use of language is a creative activity.

Language has irreducible properties. Rules relating syntactic structures to representation of meaning are not well understood, and highly controversial. Chomsky (who presupposes that scientific and reductionistic are equivalent concepts) admits that the contributions of grammar and context to meaning may be inseparable. This is a radical departure from traditional reductionism, which asserts that parts are always separable.

Despite the irreducible properties of language, it is possible to learn something about them from reductionistic strategies. "Abstracted study" of language ignores context. It considers formal structures (syntax, deep structure, surface structure, semantics) and relations between them. Chomsky considers that this is a legitimate hypothesis, although its presuppositions are not self-evident. (In fact, by his own recognition of the context dependency of language, he himself discredits the presuppositions.) The hypothesis is that linguistic competence is separable from how language is used. As in other forms of reductionism, its power is based on its ability to solve a certain class of problems. Since this strategy can solve some linguistic problems, it is hoped by some that it can solve all linguistic problems.

Chomsky admits that the use of language is not explainable or understandable by this reductionistic strategy. Consequently, he fears that it may be infeasible to study significant problems of language communication. His fear would be well founded if theoretical modeling were to stay limited to the reductionist strategy. Thus, even from a reductionist starting point, Chomsky allows the possibility that new intellectual tools might be needed, and might be feasible.

Why should a language teacher or educational theorist have the slightest interest in the above discussion? The short answer is that, as the next section reveals, conventional strategies of foreign language learning are woefully inadequate. The objective of this chapter is to point the way to how a useful alternative might be discovered. We claim that in the absence of a scientific understanding of how language and learning operate, no serious improvement over conventional methods is likely to be discovered. We have just shown that traditional reductionist science is inadequate to provide the needed understanding. Therefore, to find a more effective strategy for foreign language learning, we must have an understanding of the complex descriptions of the language and learning processes.

LANGUAGE LEARNING IN THE NEAR-PRESENT

By briefly examining approaches and theories that have guided foreign language education in the past in light of our discussion, one can see the constraints placed on the endeavor. Contemporary approaches to foreign language learning appear to be reactions against the much reviled Grammar Translation method (see Richards and Rodgers 1986). In its favor, Grammar Translation has a successful track record of approximately a thousand years of teaching students to read and write in classical languages. There are numerous objections to Grammar Translation. Conversational skills come late in the process. It appears to have scant theoretical support. Perhaps the most damning indictment in this era of the "student as customer" is that it is not fun.

The search for alternatives has tended to move theorists into one of two camps. One camp supposes itself to be in keeping with the traditional notions of science. Two approaches put forward by the "scientific" camp are the Oral Approach and Situational Language Teaching (Hornby 1950). In attempting to reconcile the contradiction between Behaviorism and functionality, these approaches fail in both cases since Behaviorism ignores self-reference, but functionality is defined in terms of self-reference.

Another "scientific" pedagogical strategy is the Natural Approach (Krashen and Terrell 1983). Though its theory of learning is claimed to be scientific because it is backed by many studies, in fact, the theory of learning seems to make a number of assumptions and then attempts to find data to support them. In particular, the Affective Filter Hypothesis reveals only a superficial understanding of how mental filters actually operate (see Knight 1999).

The Audiolingual method may have claim as the most scientific of all, since it is based on a strictly reductionistic theory of language, and a Behavioristic theory of learning. This is supposed to be the pure science of language learning, with artistry and subjectivity completely extracted (Carrol 1966). Yet, experience has shown the severe limitations of such an approach.

British theorists reacted by repackaging Situational Language Teaching with some developments from Chomsky and from cognitive theory, transforming Situational Language Teaching into Communicative Language Teaching (Hymes 1972). An American reaction to recent developments was Total Physical Response. It asserts that a "detailed cognitive map" can be constructed and then abstraction integrated later. How the cognitive map is to be constructed without abstraction, though, is unclear (Littlewood 1984). These "scientific approaches" are, predictably, heavily reductionistic and therefore, in fact, ignore some of the key principles of scientific inquiry. As a result, the impact of all of these approaches in facilitating successful language learning experiences is significantly curtailed.

In more recent developments, the "scientific" strategies of language learning are viewed as occupying a continuum from empiricism to rationalism (Hadley 2000). At one end of the continuum are Behaviorism and Connectionism. It is a bit startling to see Behaviorism still being seriously discussed among language experts, considering that Chomsky punctured the theory nearly a half-century ago. Connectionism, yet another algorithm, is quite trendy; everybody seems to like neural nets. However, brain research by Freeman (1999) and others shows that brain activity is irreducible. Remarkably, even some people who like computational theories of brain activity feel compelled to admit that computation cannot possibly explain cognitive processes (Fodor 2000).

The shortcomings of most of the theories at the rationalist end of the continuum have been addressed elsewhere in this chapter. The one theory that surpasses all the others in withstanding comparison with reality is Chomsky's Universal Grammar. However, even Chomsky himself realizes that it is too reductionistic to be a complete description of language, and is but the seed of some greater theory yet to come (Chomsky 1972).

The other camp of language theorists correctly objects that the foregoing reductionist strategies reduce the humanity out of language learning altogether. The subject is after all human languages, and the learners are human beings. These theorists argue, seemingly reasonably, that a more humanistic strategy should be more effective. Lamentably, these humanistic strategies overlook some of the key aspects of human behavior.

Consider the example of the Silent Way (Gattegno 1976). It is a problem solving strategy characterized by Benjamin Franklin's aphorism "involve me and I learn." It incorrectly assumes that synesthesia (the transformation of sensory experience from one representation system to another) works the same way in every student. The other fatal flaw is that it naively posits that the student will become independent, autonomous, and responsible. The disappointing reality is that with rare exceptions the student has no interest in learning a foreign language. The typical student perspective is that meeting an academic foreign language requirement is an onerous burden to be discharged with the bare minimum of effort or involvement.

Another attempt at a humanistic strategy is Community Language Learning (Curran 1972). It treats language learning as a sort of mock psychotherapy. Its goals of self-esteem and self-actualization are laudable. However, except in the most remarkable instances, the student is operating at a much lower level in the hierarchy of needs. The goal of practically all students is learning to survive. Furthermore, the theories of language and learning at the foundation of this strategy ignore how the brain/mind system actually works.

A superficial examination of mental states has also led to Suggestopedia, or the science of nonconscious or nonrational approaches (Lazanov 1978). It uses music and rhythm to facilitate memorization. However, memorization is not understanding or comprehension. Despite its appeal to humanism, its memorization of lookup pairs suggests a starkly reductionistic theory of learning. Suggestopedia poses some reasonable questions, but offers rather weak answers.

The humanistic strategies ignore some of the key discoveries about human behavior. They are unscientific, denying the notion of discoverable principles of language or learning. However, the objection that humanistic theorists raise is valid. Traditional reductionistic science is dehumanizing, and yields little insight into human language or learning. Does this mean that language learning is condemned to a stalemate, endlessly flailing back and forth between the latest technological gimmick and the currently fashionable humanistic sentimentality? Absolutely not.

The basis for a revolutionary strategy of language learning exists. Vygotsky (1986) has shown experimentally that language and thought have a complex entangled relationship (see especially pages 253–54). This relationship is irreducible to numbers, and consequently intractable by the currently popular reductionistic version of science. However, the science of endogenous systems encompasses the entangled processes of life and mind. Recent discoveries in mathematics have resolved ancient paradoxes (Barwise and Moss 1996). They have the power to provide the description for a causally-based scientific explanation of complex human behavior, including the operation of language and learning.

CONCLUSIONS

When science is unhampered by the constraints of reductionism, it is capable of comprehending human behavior. Although not algorithmically computable, the processes of language and learning can be represented with self-referential mathematical structures. These structures may be more difficult to use than number-based systems, and their predictions may be incomplete: however, despite their incompleteness, they afford a useful rational description of the processes of life, mind, learning, memory, and language.

We find that the human mental processes of learning and language are neither algorithmic nor irrational. They are tractable (albeit incompletely) with self-referential mathematical models. This is particularly true of the indispensable emotional process reflected in "the feeling of knowing." Any strategy of language learning that ignores these realities will be inherently awkward, frustrating, and time consuming. Thus, the successful language learning strategies of the future will not be found in either of the contemporary educational camps. Instead, they will be based on rational models of learning and language similar to those known in engineering and in medicine as endogenous systems.

Conventional language learning strategies do not take these realities into account. Those that favor reductionism abstract the humanity out of the task of language learning. Those who favor humanism are blissfully unaware that the human mind, including its capacity for learning and language, operates under discoverable laws.

The basis for a revolutionary strategy of language learning exists. Vygotsky has shown experimentally what Chomsky had derived from theory, that language and thought have a complex entangled relationship. This relationship is irreducible to numbers, and consequently intractable by the currently popular reductionistic version of science. However, the science of endogenous systems encompasses the entangled processes of learning and language. The mathematics of non-well-founded structures makes it possible to draw inferences on irreducible processes, and to fill the gap that Chomsky fears cannot be filled. By applying the principles introduced in this chapter, the methods of language learning that will emerge within the next generation will astonish the world with their effectiveness.

ACKNOWLEDGMENT

The authors gratefully acknowledge the assistance of Florence Reeder of the MITRE Corporation and Lucia Huang of Florence Public School District One, South Carolina, for their invaluable review and comments. This chapter is based in part on research performed at Oak Ridge National Laboratory, which is operated by UT-Battelle, LLC, for the U.S. Department of Energy under Contract No. DE-AC05–00OR22725, and at Argonne National Laboratory, which is operated by the University of Chicago for the U.S. Department of Energy under Contract No. W-31–109–ENG-38. This chapter is also based in part on research performed by Human Dynamics, LLC[tm].

BIBLIOGRAPHY

Adler, M. J. 1978. *Aristotle for everybody*. New York: MacMillan.

Barwise, J. and L. Moss. 1996. *Vicious circles: On the mathematics of non-wellfounded phenomena*. Stanford, CA: Center for the Study of Language and Information.

Bateson, G. 1972. *Steps to an ecology of mind*. Chicago: University of Chicago Press.

Brown-VanHoozer, S. A. 1999. Models of reality. In *Proceedings of the Artificial Neural Networks in Engineering Conference (ANNIE 99)*, ed. C. H. Dagli, A. L. Buczak, J. Ghosh, M. J. Embrechts, and O. Ersoy, 199–205. New York: ASME Press.

Brown-VanHoozer, S. A., S. W. Kercel, and W. R. VanHoozer. 2000. The model-based mind. In *Proceedings of SMC 2000: IEEE International Conference on Systems, Man, and Cybernetics*, 2204–9. Piscataway, NJ: Institute of Electrical and Electronic Engineers.

Carroll, J. B. 1966. The contributions of psychological theory and educational research to the teaching of foreign languages. In *Trends in Language Teaching*, 93–106. New York: McGraw-Hill.

Caufield, H. J., S. U. Egarievwe, J. L. Johnson, M. Schamshula, and R. Inguva. 1999. Perception, attention and consciousness in human artifacts. In *Proceedings of the Artificial Neural Networks in Engineering Conference (ANNIE 99)*, ed. C. H. Dagli, A. L. Buczak, J. Ghosh, M. J. Embrechts, and O. Ersoy, 237–246. New York: ASME Press.

Chomsky, N. 1972. *Language and mind*. San Diego, CA: Harcourt, Brace and Jovanovich.

———. 1993. *Language and thought*. Wakefield, RI: Moyer Bell.

Curran, C. A. 1972. *Counseling-learning: A whole person model for education*. New York: Grune and Stratton.

Damasio, A. R. 1994. *Descartes' error*. New York: Putnam.

———. 1999. *The feeling of what happens*. New York: Harcourt Brace.

Dilts, R. B. 1983. *Roots of neuro-linguistic programming*. Cupertino, CA: Meta Publications.

———. 1994. *Strategies of genius*. Capitola, CA: Meta Publications.

Fodor, J. 2000. *The mind doesn't work that way: The scope and limits of computational psychology (representation and mind)*. Cambridge, MA: MIT Press.

Freeman, W. J. 1999. The neurodynamics of intentionality is the basis of intelligent behavior. In *Proceedings of the Artificial Neural Networks in Engineering Conference (ANNIE 99)*, ed. C. H. Dagli, A. L. Buczak, J. Ghosh, M. J. Embrechts, and O. Ersoy, 185–91. New York: ASME Press.

Gattegno, C. 1976. *The common sense of teaching foreign language*. New York: Educational Solutions.

Hadley, A. O. 2000. *Teaching language in context*, 3d ed. Boston: Heinle and Heinle, 2000.

Hornby, A. S. 1950. The Situational Approach to language teaching. A series of three articles in *English Language Teaching*, 4: 98–104, 121–28, 150–56.

Hymes, D. 1972. On communicative competence. In *Sociolinguistics*, ed. J. B. Pride and J. Holmes, 269–93. Harmondsworth, UK: Penguin.

Kleene, S. C. 1950. *Introduction to Metamathematics*. Amsterdam: van Nostrand.

Knight, S. 1999. *NLP solutions*. London: Nicholas Brealey Publishing.

Knuth, D. E. 1973. *The art of computer programming*, 2d ed., Vol. 1. Reading, MA: Addison Wesley.

Korsybski, A. 1948. *Science and sanity*, 3d ed. Lancaster, PA: Science Press.

————. 2000. *Science and sanity*, 5th ed. Brooklyn, NY: Institute of General Semantics.

Krashen, S. D. and T. D. Terrell. 1983. *The Natural Approach: Language acquisition in the classroom*. Oxford: Pergamon.

Lazanov, G. 1978. *Suggestology and the outlines of Suggestopedy*. New York: Gordon and Breach.

Littlewood, W. 1984. *Foreign and second language learning: Language acquisition research and its implications for the classroom*. Cambridge, UK: Cambridge University Press.

Richards, J. C. and T. S. Rodgers. 1986. *Approaches and methods in language teaching*. Cambridge, UK: Cambridge University Press.

Rosen, K. 1999. *Discrete mathematics and its applications*, 4th ed. Boston: WCB/McGraw-Hill.

Rosen, R. 2000. *Essays on life itself*. New York: Columbia University Press.

Sacks, O. 1995. *An anthropologist on Mars*. New York: Vintage.

Vygotsky, L. 1986[1934]. *Thought and language*, translated by A. Kozulin. Cambridge, MA: MIT Press.

3

"Knowing" and "Learning" a Foreign Language: Epistemological Reflections on Classroom Practice

TIMOTHY REAGAN

As a foreign language educator, I am often asked how many languages I know, and what the best way to learn a foreign language is. Both of these questions are well-intended and, for those who ask them, presumably reasonable. And yet, I dread these two questions because providing an answer is so complex and difficult. The first assumes that "knowing" a language is pretty much an either-or matter; one either "knows" French or one doesn't. To a monolingual person, of course, such a dichotomy is both obvious and clear-cut; for the bilingual or multilingual individual, though, matters are a bit more uncertain. What does it really mean to "know" a language? Is native competence what is required, or simply an ability to carry on a conversation in the language in a relatively fluent manner? Or are we, rather, concerned with knowledge *about* the language and its structure? For instance, I was once asked by a nonnative speaker of English to explain the second conditional; as a native speaker of English, I was completely at a loss, since I had no idea at all what the "second conditional" (or even the "first conditional," for that matter) referred to.[1] In everyday speech, of course, "knowing" a language usually means being able to communicate in it rather than either native competence or knowing about the language, but even here, there are problems. I can communicate in French relatively fluently in some contexts and about some topics, while in other contexts and with other topics, I may easily find myself struggling to understand and be understood. What does this say about my knowledge of French?

The second question, about the best way to learn a foreign language, is also somewhat problematic. On the surface, it appears to be a simple question about what the empirical educational and pedagogical evidence suggests. And yet, it is really far from simple. There is, of course, a simple answer: the best way to learn any language is probably as a child immersed in the language. Indeed, this is a virtual guarantee of effective language learning, but it is also the least satisfying response to the question, since the focus of the question is really intended to be on language learning rather than on language acquisition.

In fact, one of the significant challenges that faces us as foreign language educators is attempting to understand what, exactly, we mean both by "knowing" a language and by "learning" a language. Underlying all pedagogical practice, ultimately, are questions of epistemology. The way in which we think about "knowledge" and what it means "to know" are directly and necessarily linked to all aspects of how we teach. In foreign language education, this can be seen clearly, for example, in the well-documented relationship between behaviorist learning theory and the audio-lingual method (see Bernhardt 1998; Chastain 1976, 109–29; Littlewood 1984, 17–21). Recently, a number of academic disciplines, led by scholars in mathematics, but including those in the sciences, literacy, and language arts, have begun to undergo a significant change in the epistemology which underlies their pedagogical practice (for science education, see, e.g., Fensham, Gunstone, and White 1994; Mintzes, Wandersee, and Novak 1997; Tobin 1993; for mathematics education, see, e.g., Davis, Maher, and Noddings 1990; Steffe, Cobb, and von Glasersfeld 1988; Wood, Cobb, and Yackel 1995; for literacy and language arts, see, e.g., Cooper 1993; Kamii, Manning, and Manning 1991; Nelson 1996; Spivey 1997). The change in epistemology that we are talking about is that of the growing popularity and credibility of constructivist approaches to learning theory. Constructivism as an epistemology is, as we shall see, far from uniform, and is also far from new, dating back at least some sixty years to the work of Jean Piaget (1976, 1979, 1986, 1993, 1996), and, on at least some accounts, as far back as the work of eighteenth-century German philosopher Immanuel Kant (see Boulter 1997; Spivey 1997, 6). Constructivism has, nonetheless, been relatively slow to impact significantly educational thought and practice in many areas, and is only now beginning to come into its own in educational discourse (see Fosnot 1996a; Grennon Brooks and Brooks 1993). Although to some extent arguably implicit in many contemporary discussions about communicative language teaching, and while certainly quite relevant for foreign language practice, constructivist approaches to epistemology and learning theory have only recently, and relatively rarely, been explicitly examined in terms of their implications for foreign language teaching and learning (see Blyth 1997; Craig 1995; Kaufman and Grennon Brooks 1996; Kumaravadivelu 1994; Nyikos and Hashimoto 1997; Williams and Burden 1997). In this chapter, an attempt will be made to encourage foreign language educators to consider seriously the potential contributions of constructivism to foreign language teaching and learning, first by providing a broad overview of the core assumptions and concepts of constructivism, and then by exploring the ways constructivism can inform and promote effective pedagogical practice in the foreign language context.

CONSTRUCTIVIST EPISTEMOLOGY: AN OVERVIEW

> Constructivism is not a theory about teaching. It's a theory about knowledge and learning. Drawing on a synthesis of current work in cognitive psychology, philosophy, and anthropology, the theory defines knowledge as temporary, developmental, socially and culturally mediated, and thus, non-objective. Learning from this perspective is understood as a self-regulated process of resolving inner cognitive conflicts that often become apparent through concrete experience, collaborative discourse, and reflection.
>
> —Fosnot 1993, vii

Although constructivism has gained considerable attention in the educational literature in recent years, there is no consensus of what is actually meant by the term (see Duffy and Jonassen 1992; Forman and Pufall 1988; Kafai and Resnick 1996; Nicaise and Barnes 1996; Phillips 1995, 1996; Schwandt 1994; Steffe and Gale 1995). As Virginia Richardson has noted, "One cannot think of constructivist teaching . . . as a monolithic, agreed-upon concept. . . . There are fundamental theoretical differences in the various constructivist approaches" (1997b, 3). Indeed, as the quote which opens this section of the chapter indicates, there is even debate about whether constructivism is best understood as an epistemology, an educational philosophy, a pedagogical approach, a theory of teaching, or a theory of learning (see Kaufman and Grennon Brooks 1996, 234). Arguably the best articulation of the nature of constructivism in the educational literature is that of Catherine Fosnot, who compellingly suggests that:

Constructivism is a theory about learning, not a description of teaching. No "cookbook teaching style" or pat set of instructional techniques can be abstracted from the theory and proposed as a constructivist approach to teaching. Some general principles of learning derived from constructivism may be helpful to keep in mind, however, as we rethink and reform our educational practices. (1996b, 29)

Such a view of constructivism essentially confirms its status as an epistemology—a theory of knowledge and learning, rather than as a theory of teaching (see von Glasersfeld 1993, 23–24).

As an epistemology, constructivism entails the rejection of traditional transmission-oriented views of learning, as well as behaviorist models of learning. Instead, emphasis is placed on the individual learner's construction of his or her knowledge. Beyond this, constructivism assumes not only that learning is constructed, but also that the learning process is a personal and individual one, that learning is an active process, that learning is collaborative in nature, and

47

that all learning is situated (see Merrill 1992, 102). In other words, what constructivism offers is a radically different view of the nature of the learning process—a view that is grounded in a rejection of what von Glasersfeld has called the "domination of a mindless behaviorism" (1995a, 4). This view includes a number of general principles of learning, including:

- Learning is not the result of development; learning *is* development. It requires invention and self-organization on the part of the learner.

- Disequilibrium facilitates learning. "Errors" need to be perceived as a result of learners' conceptions and therefore not minimized or avoided. . . . Contradictions, in particular, need to be illuminated, explored, and discussed.

- Reflective abstraction is the driving force of learning. As meaning-makers, humans seek to organize and generalize across experiences in a representational form.

- Dialogue within a community engenders further thinking. The classroom needs to be seen as a "community of discourse engaged in activity, reflection, and conversation" . . .

- Learning proceeds toward the development of structures. As learners struggle to make meaning, progressive structural shifts in perspective are constructed—in a sense, "big ideas". . . . These "big ideas" are learner-constructed, central organizing principles that can be generalized across experiences and that often require the undoing or reorganizing of earlier conceptions. This process continues throughout development. (Fosnot 1996b, 29–30)

It is important to stress here that constructivist epistemology is more than simply an *alternative* to other epistemological approaches; rather, it entails a rejection of some of the core assumptions that have been shared by western epistemology for some two and a half millennia (see Gergen 1982, 1995). As von Glasersfeld has argued, "the crucial fact [in understanding constructivism is] that the constructivist theory of knowing breaks with the epistemological tradition in philosophy" (1995a, 6), which is why it has been labeled not merely postmodernist, but *postepistemological* by some writers (see Noddings 1990).

Thus far in this chapter, we have discussed constructivism as a single entity, although trying to keep in mind Richardson's warning that it is far from monolithic. It has become fairly commonplace in discussions of constructivism to distinguish between what are often taken to be two fundamentally distinct, competing *types* of constructivism (see Cobb 1994, 1996; Magadla 1996). The first type of constructivism, radical constructivism, is fundamentally an epistemological construct that has been most clearly and forcefully advocated in the work of Ernst von Glasersfeld (1984, 1989, 1993, 1995a, 1995b, 1996). Radical constructivism has its philosophical roots in Piaget's genetic epistemology (Piaget 1979; Sinclair, Berthoud, Gerard, and Veneziano 1985), and is essentially a cognitive view of learning in which "students actively construct their ways of knowing as they strive to be effective by restoring coherence to the worlds of their personal experience" (Cobb 1996,

48

34). Radical constructivism is premised on the belief that an individual's knowledge can never be a "true" representation of reality (i.e., in an observer-independent sense), but is, rather, a construction of the world that s/he experiences. In other words, knowledge is not something that is passively received by the learner; it is, quite the contrary, the result of active mental work on the learner's part. From a radical constructivist perspective, knowledge is not something that can merely be conveyed from teacher to student, and any pedagogical approach that presumes otherwise must be rejected.

The alternative to radical constructivism is social constructivism, which has as its primary theoretical foundation the work of Vygotsky (1978, 1986; see also Moll 1990). Social constructivism, while accepting the notion that the individual does indeed construct his or her own knowledge, argues that the process of knowledge construction inevitably takes place in a sociocultural context, and that therefore knowledge is in fact *socially* constructed. As Driver et al. have argued with respect to science education, "it is important . . . to appreciate that scientific knowledge is both symbolic in nature and also socially negotiated . . . The objects of science are not phenomena of nature but constructs that are advanced by the scientific community to interpret nature" (1994, 5).

The tension between radical and social constructivism, between the personal and the social construction of knowledge, although important philosophically, is in practice actually amenable to resolution (see, e.g., Cobern 1993; Confrey 1995). As Paul Cobb has asserted, "the sociocultural and cognitive constructivist perspectives each constitute the background for the other" (1996, 48), and von Glasersfeld has recognized that "we must generate an explanation of how 'others' and the 'society' in which we find ourselves living can be conceptually constructed on the basis of our subjective experiences" (1995a, 12). Perhaps the most reasonable way to articulate the common, shared elements of radical and social constructivism is to talk about learning as "socially mitigated but personally constructed," a formulation that allows us to move away from the strong bifurcation of radical and social constructivism, and also allows us to move on to a discussion of the implications of constructivist epistemology for teaching practice.

CONSTRUCTIVIST APPROACHES TO TEACHING

Constructivism is not, and cannot be conceptualized as, a pedagogical theory or approach per se, but certain characteristics of the constructivist-based classroom can be identified. For example, Grennon Brooks and Brooks (1993) and Kaufman and Grennon Brooks (1996) have identified eight characteristics that have been observed in constructivist classrooms:

- Use raw data and primary sources, along with manipulative, interactive, and physical materials.

- When framing tasks, use cognitive terminology, such as *classify, analyze, predict, create*, and so on.

- Allow student thinking to drive lessons. Shift instructional strategies or alter content based on student responses.

- Inquire about students' understandings of concepts before sharing your own understandings of those concepts.

- Ask open-ended questions of students and encourage students to ask questions of others.

- Seek elaboration of students' initial responses.

- Engage students in experiences that might engender contradictions to students' initial hypotheses and then encourage a discussion.

- Provide time for students to construct relationships and create metaphors. (Kaufman and Grennon Brooks 1996, 235)

These characteristics function both as descriptive and normative attributes: They have been observed in practice, and can be (and have been) used for evaluation purposes. It is important to note here that "Many of these attributes are not unique to constructivist teaching but are representative of good teaching in general" (Kaufman and Grennon Brooks 1996, 235)—a point that would seem to confirm von Glasersfeld's claim that, "Constructivism does not claim to have made earth-shaking inventions in the area of education; it merely claims to provide a solid conceptual basis for some of the things that, until now, inspired teachers had to do without theoretical foundation" (1995a, 15). Furthermore, although it is true that "constructivist principles of learning do not automatically engender principles of teaching . . . [since] learners construct meaning on their own terms no matter what teachers do" (Winitzky and Kauchak 1997, 62), it is also true that:

Constructivist theorists would maintain . . . that learning is better or more effective when teachers use constructivist teaching methods, like culturing and keying bacteria as opposed to lecturing about bacteria. Constructivist teaching typically involves more student-centered, active learning experiences, more student-student and student-teacher interaction, and more work with concrete materials and in solving realistic problems. . . . Nevertheless, students still create their own meanings based on the interaction of their prior knowledge with instruction, and the meanings they make may not be the ones the teacher had in mind, no matter how constructivist the instruction. . . . Teachers create constructivist learning experiences for students based necessarily on what they, the teachers, find salient. But what is salient to the teacher is not necessarily so to the learner. (Winitzky and Kauchak 1997, 62–63)

With this caveat in mind, we now turn to an examination of the implications of constructivist epistemology for foreign language education.

IMPLICATIONS OF CONSTRUCTIVIST EPISTEMOLOGY FOR FOREIGN LANGUAGE EDUCATION

Constructivism has a wide range of implications for language educators, both in terms of its significance for research and its relevance for pedagogical practice. With respect to the former, studies of the social nature of language learning and acquisition are increasingly grounded in constructivist epistemological positions. Writing about developments in bilingual education, for instance, Christian Faltis has noted that "a shift toward the constructivist, social nature of learning and language acquisition is also increasingly evident in new research efforts" (1997, 194). Similarly, the veritable explosion in discourse studies is ultimately, albeit often implicitly, linked to constructivist approaches to understanding, whether one is concerned with academic discourse (see Achard 1993; Bourdieu, Passeron, and de Saint Martin 1994), classroom discourse (see Bartolomé 1998; Craig 1995; Measures, Quell, and Wells 1997; van Lier 1996; Woods 1996), or scientific discourse (see Boulter 1997). Indeed, Gunnarsson has gone so far as to suggest that:

The complexity of the construction of knowledge has been focused on by scholars dealing with scientific discourse. Proceeding from ideas within the social constructivist tradition, they have developed a methodology for the purpose of understanding how science is created through discourse. . . . [T]he social construction of scientific facts [has been described] as an antagonistic struggle among scientists, leading to a deliberate diminishing of the results of others and a leveling up—to a generalized level—of one's own results. Scientific facts are regarded as mere works; rhetoric determines what become scientific facts. (1997, 111)

The implications of such a view of the nature and role of scientific discourse for the classroom are significant:

It is the growing recognition of the significance of the social construction of conceptual understanding in science that has coincided with the development of a suitable methodology for investigating social situations involving talk. Science is now often seen within science education research as intimately constructed, through discourse, within communities of knowers. The following themes in research and discourse in science teaching and learning arise from the synthesis of constructivism and sociolinguistic methodology and can be seen in the major work in progress:

- The *complexity* of classroom discourse which has complex interactions with the ways teachers teach, the resources they use and with the particular phenomenon of science being studied;

- *Communities* in science and science classrooms having characteristic discourse patterns;

- *Collaboration* in classroom settings allowing the authentic practice of science and the development of appropriate discourse;

- *Critiques* of science, its methodology, its boundaries, its status, and its language as a cultural construct. (Boulter 1997, 242)

Such research foci emphasize, not surprisingly, the social construction of language and discourse, but there is room as well for concern with the personal or individual construction of language. One powerful way in which we can conceptualize the personal construction of language has to do with the linguistic notion of idiolects: "The unique characteristics of the language of an individual speaker are referred to as the speaker's *idiolect*. English may then be said to consist of 400,000,000 idiolects, or the number equal to the number of speakers of English" (Fromkin and Rodman 1993, 276). In other words, a transmission-based view of language learning is simply incompatible with the final outcome of such learning, since each individual speaker (whether native or nonnative) in fact constructs his or her own understanding of the target language, which will, in turn, be modified and can be evaluated by comparison with other speakers of the language. This is not, of course, to minimize in any way the key role played by interaction in the process of language learning. As Katherine Nelson has noted,

Competence in constructing and using culturally defined categories of entities (objects, events, properties, etc.) has been shown to involve a number of different linguistic components, including superordinate labels and the vocabulary of inclusive hierarchies. These verbal components can account for aspects of conceptual development previously held to be perceptually based (*e.g.*, grouping along lines of shape similarity) or logically based (*e.g.*, set relations). The verbal contributions to the development of cultural categories are integrated with experientially derived categories. . . . The coordination and integration processes involved in the assembling of cultural taxonomies . . . exemplify the more general problem encountered during the preschool years of reconfiguring individual experientially based representations established independently of linguistic input to accommodate knowledge systems displayed in language. This reconfiguration cannot be accomplished through individual constructive processes alone, but requires implicit and explicit collaboration with knowledge bearers. . . . (1996, 332)

Although Nelson's focus is on language acquisition in early childhood, the same general claim would apply to foreign language learning with respect to the complementary and interactive roles of the individual and the social construction of language. This brings us to the implications of constructivist epistemology for foreign language pedagogy.

In the context of the foreign language classroom, the application of constructivist epistemology would necessarily undergird virtually all classroom practice. As Williams and Burden have explained,

The literature on language teaching provides comprehensive accounts of different language teaching methodologies and is rich with ideas and techniques for teaching a language. However, what has become increasingly clear to us is the fundamental importance to teachers of an understanding of what is involved in the process of learning to inform and underpin our teaching of the language. Teachers' own conceptions of what is meant by learning, and what affects learning will influence everything that they do in the classroom. At the same time, in order to make informed decisions in their day-to-day teaching, teachers need to be consciously aware of what their beliefs about learning and teaching are. (1997, 1–2)

This is, as far as it goes, true not only of foreign language teaching, but of all teaching. To be sure, foreign language pedagogy does indeed have many common features with other sorts of teaching—but it is also distinct in some key ways. Successful foreign language learning entails far more for the learner than merely learning content and skills. Gardner has suggested that "Languages are unlike any other subject taught in a classroom in that they involve the acquisition of skills and behaviour patterns which are characteristic of another community" (1985, 146), while Crookall and Oxford argue that "Learning a second language is ultimately learning to be another social person" (1988, 136). It is this need for the learner to reconstruct one's personal identity that is at the heart of foreign language learning, and it is in this process of reconstruction, rather than merely in terms of learning vocabulary and grammatical forms, that constructivist epistemology may be most useful.

Williams and Burden, in an effort to summarize and consolidate the implications of constructivism for foreign language learning, have identified the following basic propositions that they believe to be essential for language teachers to understand:

There is a difference between learning and education.

Learners learn what is meaningful to them.

Learners learn in ways that are meaningful to them.

Learners learn better if they feel in control of what they are learning.

Learning is closely linked to how people feel about themselves.

Learning takes place in a social context through interaction with other people.

What teachers do in the classroom will reflect their own beliefs and attitudes.

There is a significant role for the teacher as mediator in the language classroom.

Learning tasks represent an interface between teachers and learners.

Learning is influenced by the situation in which it occurs. (1997, 204–8)

One example of a constructivist approach to foreign language teaching is provided by a teacher in an introductory Spanish class whose lesson focuses on the use of the verb *gustar* to indicate likes and dislikes.[2] The class begins with the teacher presenting the following short passage in Spanish, in which *gustar* is used in a number of different ways:

A mi me gusta bailar, pero a Ana no le gusta bailar. Mi hermana le gustan las flores, pero a mi padre no le gustan las flores. Mis hermanos le gustan la música americana. A mi me gustan todos los tipos de música. Juan y Diana les gusta hablar frances. Kelly y yo nos gusta hablar español. ¿Qué te gusta tu?

Utilizing pictures and dramatic techniques, the teacher ensures that the students understand the meaning of the passage, although they have yet to learn the specifics of the use of *gustar*. The teacher then begins to elicit class input using the basic forms of *Me gusta* +singular object (as in *Me gusta el vino*). After several students have produced correct forms of this type, the teacher then introduces a plural object (*Me gustan las flores*), and asks a student, *¿Te gustan las flores?* Using additional elicitation techniques, the teacher moves around the room, by this point alternating both the first and second person forms and the singular and plural forms, as well as gradually introducing negative forms (*No me gustan las flores*). Students are now encouraged to converse in pairs, in a round-robin fashion, asking questions and giving answers. The teacher provides input only as needed, generally using stress to indicate a student error and encourage student self-correction. During this activity, the teacher also introduces the *Me gusta* + infinitive form (*Me gusta bailar*), and then encourages students to use constructions of this type to indicate activities that they enjoy. At this point, the teacher might also introduce the third person form (*Le gusta el chocolate*) and have students discuss the likes and dislikes of other students in the class, based on the information obtained in the earlier part of the class. By the end of the class, students have begun to master the use of the verb *gustar*; additional practice and further development of the use of *gustar* will be needed, of course, but students should already be in a position to offer a reasonably accurate description of how *gustar* is used—and should be able to do so without ever having explicitly encountered a formal explanation of the grammatical rules involved.

Similar approaches can be used to teach virtually any linguistic structure, semantic relationship, or lexical item in the target language, as well as helping students to develop their own personal competence in (and hence construction of) the target language broadly conceived. In fact, I believe that a compelling case could be offered for the claim that the greater the difference between a particular structure or vocabulary item in the learner's mother tongue and the target language, the more appropriate and effective a constructivist approach to language learning may prove to be. This point is similar to that made recently by Widdowson:

[W]e now know much more than our predecessors about what makes language real for its users, and we know what learners have to do if they are to aspire to be foreign language users themselves. My main point is that this heightened understanding about language, communication, community, and social identity has also to be applied to the contexts of the classroom and the realities and identities of language learners. To do this is really only to recognize, as our predecessors have done, that what we are teaching is not language as experienced by its users but a *foreign* language which, as a subject, has to be designed for learners. (1998, 332)

Thus, *telling* students about the difference between the verbs *ser* and *estar* in Spanish (a distinction that is, in fact, rather more complex than generally sug-

ТЫ И ВЫ   [1828]

Пустое *вы* сердечным *ты*
Она, обмолвясь, заменила
И все счастливые мечты
В душе влюбленной возбудила.
Пред ней задумчиво стою,
Свести очей с нее нет силы;
И говорю ей: как *вы* милы!
И мыслю: как *тебя* люблю!

Figure 3.1
"Thou and You"

gested in foreign language classrooms in any case)[3] might well be less useful than simply having them employ the verbs and gradually come to know, in part as a result of teacher correction, when each is appropriate.

Another example in which we can see a constructivist approach to foreign language teaching is provided in a second year (or even more advanced) Russian course, after students have mastered some of the grammatical basics of the language and have a small but growing vocabulary. The teacher could revisit student understandings of the formal versus familiar distinction (analogous to the *tu/vous* distinction in French) by presenting students with Pushkin's short poem "Thou and You" (see Figure 3.1) in which this distinction is the central focus of a love poem. The poem reads as follows:

> The empty *you* by the warm *thou*
> She, with a slip of the tongue, substituted
> And all lucky daydreams
> Excited the soul in love.
> Before her in thought I stand,
> I don't have the strength to take my
> Eyes off of her;
> And I say: how nice of *you!*
> And think to myself: how I love *thee!* (My translation)

The typical student understanding of the illustrated distinction is fairly simplistic, with students mastering the singular/plural distinction reasonably well but not really internalizing the significance of the informal/formal semantic relationship. This is, of course, understandable since the distinction is alien to English speakers. Pushkin's poem, however, *requires* that one understand this semantic relationship, and provides a tool that can be effectively utilized in a classroom setting to help students construct a more meaningful and productive understanding of the distinction.

In both of the instances that have been discussed here, while explicit and directive teaching is certainly possible, the alternative of teacher modeling and individual student construction of the linguistic target has much to commend it.

CONCLUSION

Constructivist epistemology has clear implications for classroom practice, the curricula, student evaluation, and, indeed, virtually all aspects of the teaching/learning process (see Henning 1995; Zietsman 1996). Although not explicitly discussed in this chapter, constructivist epistemology also has the potential to impact in significant ways the preparation of foreign language educators (see Condon, Clyde, Kyle, and Hovda 1993; Rainer and Guyton 1994; Richardson 1997a) and the challenge of preparing such educators to engage in reflective and analytic classroom practice (see Norlander-Case, Reagan, and Case 1999; Parker 1997; Reagan, Case, and Brubacher, 2000; Richards 1998; Richards and Lockhart 1994; Zeichner and Liston 1996). The ultimate purpose of taking constructivist epistemology seriously in foreign language education, though, is to help teachers learn to empower students to acquire language more effectively.

NOTES

Much of this chapter is derived from Reagan (1999).

1. For readers who share my puzzlement, the first conditional involves the form *If + present simple + will* (as in, "If I don't go to class, I won't pass the exam"), while the second conditional involves the form *If + past simple + would* (as in, "If I could do the work, I would pass"). The difference between the first and second conditional has to do with the probability of the hypothetical event; the first conditional refers to a situation that is both real and possible, while the second conditional involves situations that are unlikely to occur.

2. I am grateful to Jamie Bernetich for sharing this lesson (*Las cosas que nos gustan*) with me.

3. For instance, it is commonly taught that *estar* is used to describe a characteristic that is not inherent (as in *Estoy cansado*). As a generalized rule, this works reasonably well, but one is then faced with trying to explain why *muerto* [dead] (as in *Está muerto*) requires *estar* but *feliz/desgraciado* [happy/unhappy] require *ser* (as in *Soy feliz*), and so on. For a fairly typical example of the way in which the *estar/ser* distinc-

tion is presented in beginning Spanish textbooks, see Schmitt and Woodford (1997, 278–82.)

BIBLIOGRAPHY

Achard, P. 1993. *La sociologie du langage.* Paris: Presses Universitaires de France.

Arndt, W. 1972. *Pushkin threefold: Narrative, lyric, polemic and ribald verse.* Dana Point, CA: Ardis Publishers.

Bartolomé, L. 1998. *The misteaching of academic discourses: The politics of language in the classroom.* Boulder, CO: Westview Press.

Bernhardt, E. 1998. Sociohistorical perspectives on language teaching in the modern United States. In *Learning foreign and second languages: Perspectives in research and scholarship,* ed. H. Byrnes, 39–57. New York: Modern Language Association.

Blyth, C. 1997. A constructivist approach to grammar: Teaching teachers to teach aspect. *The Modern Language Journal* 81: 50–66.

Boulter, C. 1997. Discourse and conceptual understanding in science. In *Encyclopedia of language and education, vol. 3: Oral discourse and education,* ed. B. Davies and D. Corson, 239–48. Dordrecht, The Netherlands: Kluwer.

Bourdieu, P., J. Passeron, and M. de Saint Martin. 1994. *Academic discourse.* Translated by T. Teese. Stanford: Stanford University Press.

Brèe, G. 1984. The place of languages in the precollegiate humanities curriculum. In *The humanities in precollegiate education: Eighty-third yearbook of the National Society for the Study of Education, Part II,* ed. B. Ladner, 57–73. Chicago: University of Chicago Press.

Chastain, K. 1976. *Developing second-language skills: Theory to practice.* 2d ed. Chicago: Rand McNally.

Cobb, P. 1994. Where is the mind? Constructivist and socioculturalist perspectives on mathematical development. *Educational Researcher* 23 (7): 13–20.

———. 1996. Where is the mind? A coordination of sociocultural and cognitive constructionist perspectives. In *Constructivism: Theory, perspectives, and practice,* ed. C. Fosnot, 34–52. New York: Teachers College Press.

Cobern, W. 1993. Contextual constructivism: The impact of culture on the learning and teaching of science. In *The practice of constructivism in science education,* ed. K. Tobin, 51–69. Hillsdale, NJ: Lawrence Erlbaum Associates.

Condon, M., J. Clyde, D. Kyle, and R. Hovda. 1993. A constructivist basis for teaching and teacher education: A framework for program development and research on graduates. *Journal of Teacher Education* 44 (4): 273–78.

Confrey, J. 1995. How compatible are radical constructivism, sociocultural approaches, and social constructivism? In *Constructivism in education,* ed. L. Steffe and J. Gale, 185–225. Hillsdale, NJ: Lawrence Erlbaum Associates.

Cooper, J. 1993. *Literacy: Helping children construct meaning.* 2d ed. Boston: Houghton Mifflin.

Craig, B. 1995. Boundary discourse and the authority of knowledge in the second-language classroom: A social-constructivist approach. In *Linguistics and the education of language teachers: Ethnolinguistic, psycholinguistic, and sociolinguistic aspects (Georgetown University Round Table of Languages and*

Linguistics 1995), ed. J. Alatis, C. Straehle, B. Gallenberger, and M. Ronkin, 40–54. Washington, DC: Georgetown University Press.

Crookall, D. and R. Oxford. 1988. Review essay. *Language Learning* 31 (1): 128–40.

Davis, R., C. Maher, and N. Noddings, eds. 1990. *Constructivist views on the teaching and learning of mathematics*. Reston, VA: National Council of Teachers of Mathematics.

Driver, R., H. Asoko, J. Leach, E. Mortimer, and P. Scott. 1994. Constructing scientific knowledge in the classroom. *Educational Researcher* 23 (7): 5–12.

Duffy, T. and D. Jonassen, eds. 1992. *Constructivism and the technology of instruction: A conversation*. Hillsdale, NJ: Lawrence Erlbaum Associates.

Faltis, C. 1997. Bilingual education in the United States. In *Encyclopedia of language and education, vol. 5: Bilingual education*, ed. J. Cummins and D. Corson, 189–97. Dordrecht, The Netherlands: Kluwer.

Fensham, P., R. Gunstone, and R. White, eds. 1994. *The content of science: A constructivist approach to its teaching and learning*. London: Falmer Press.

Forman, G. and P. Pufall, eds. 1988. *Constructivism in the computer age*. Hillsdale, NJ: Lawrence Erlbaum Associates.

Fosnot, C. 1993. Preface. In *The case for constructivist classrooms*, ed. J. Brooks and M. Brooks, vii–viii. Alexandria, VA: Association for Supervision and Curriculum Development.

———, ed. 1996a. *Constructivism: Theory, perspectives, and practice*. New York: Teachers College Press.

———. 1996b. Constructivism: A psychological theory of learning. In *Constructivism: Theory, perspectives, and practice*, ed. C. Fosnot, 8–33. New York: Teachers College Press.

Fromkin, V. and R. Rodman. 1993. *An introduction to language*. 5th ed. Fort Worth, TX: Harcourt Brace Jovanovich.

Gardner, R. 1985. *Social psychology and language learning: The role of attitudes and motivation*. London: Edward Arnold.

Gergen, K. 1982. *Towards transformation in social knowledge*. New York: Springer-Verlag.

———. 1995. Social construction and the educational process. In *Constructivism in education*, ed. L. Steffe and J. Gale, 17–39. Hillsdale, NJ: Lawrence Erlbaum Associates.

Grennon Brooks, J. and M. Brooks. 1993. *The case for constructivist classrooms*. Alexandria, VA: Association for Supervision and Curriculum Development.

Gunnarsson, B. 1997. Language for special purposes. In *Encyclopedia of language and education, vol. 4: Second language education*, ed. G. Tucker and D. Corson, 105–17. Dordrecht, The Netherlands: Kluwer.

Henning, E. 1995. Problematising the discourse of classroom management from the view of social constructivism. *South African Journal of Education* 15 (3): 124–29.

Kafai, Y. and M. Resnick, eds. 1996. *Constructivism in practice: Designing, thinking, and learning in a digital world*. Mahwah, NJ: Lawrence Erlbaum Associates.

Kamii, C., M. Manning, and G. Manning, eds. 1991. *Early literacy: A constructivist foundation for whole language*. Washington, DC: National Education Association.

Kaufman, D. and J. Grennon Brooks. 1996. Interdisciplinary collaboration in teacher education: A constructivist approach. *TESOL Quarterly* 30 (2): 231–51.

Kumaravadivelu, B. 1994. The postmethod condition: (E)merging strategies for second/foreign language teaching. *TESOL Quarterly* 28 (1): 27–48.

Littlewood, W. 1984. *Foreign and second language learning: Language acquisition research and its implications for the classroom.* Cambridge. Cambridge University Press.

Magadla, L. 1996. Constructivism: A practitioner's perspective. *South African Journal of Higher Education* 10 (1): 83–88.

Measures, E., C. Quell, and G. Wells. 1997. A sociocultural perspective on classroom discourse. In *Encyclopedia of language and education, vol. 3: Oral discourse and education*, ed. B. Davies and D. Corson, 21–29. Dordrecht, The Netherlands: Kluwer.

Merrill, M. (1992). Constructivism and instructional design. In *Constructivism and the technology of instruction: A conversation*, ed. T. Duffy and D. Jonassen, 99–114. Hillsdale, NJ: Lawrence Erlbaum Associates.

Mintzes, J., J. Wandersee, and J. Novak, eds. 1997. *Teaching science for understanding: A human constructivist view.* San Diego: Academic Press.

Moll, L., ed. 1990. *Vygotsky and education: Instructional implications and applications of sociocultural psychology.* Cambridge: Cambridge University Press.

Nelson, K. 1996. *Language in cognitive development: The emergence of the mediated mind.* Cambridge: Cambridge University Press.

Nicaise, M. and D. Barnes. 1996. The union of technology, constructivism, and teacher education. *Journal of Teacher Education* 47 (3): 205–12.

Noddings, N. 1990. Constructivism in mathematics education. In *Constructivist views on the teaching and learning of mathematics*, ed. R. Davis, C. Maher, and N. Noddings, 7–18. Reston, VA: National Council of Teachers of Mathematics.

———. 1995. *Philosophy of education.* Boulder, CO: Westview Press.

Norlander-Case, K., T. Reagan, and C. Case. 1999. *The professional teacher: The preparation and nurturance of the reflective practitioner.* San Francisco: Jossey-Bass.

Nyikos, M. and R. Hashimoto. 1997. Constructivist theory applied to collaborative learning in teacher education: In search of ZPD. *The Modern Language Journal* 81: 506–17.

Parker, S. 1997. *Reflective teaching in the postmodern world: A manifesto for education in postmodernity.* Buckingham, UK: Open University Press.

Phillips, D. C. 1995. The good, the bad, and the ugly: The many faces of constructivism. *Educational Researcher* 24 (7): 5–12.

———. 1996. Response to Ernst von Glasersfeld. *Educational Researcher* 25 (6): 20.

Piaget, J. 1976. *Psychologie et epistémologie.* Paris: Editions Gonthier.

———. 1979. *L'epistémologie génétique.* 3d ed. Paris: Presses Universitaires de France.

———. 1986. *Logique et connaissance scientifique.* Paris: Gallimard.

———. 1993. *Le jugement et le raisonnement chez l'enfant.* 8th ed. Paris: Delachaux and Niestle.

———. 1996. *La construction du réel chez l'enfant.* 6th ed. Neuchatel, France: Delachaux and Niestle.

Rainer, J. and E. Guyton. 1994. Developing a constructivist teacher education program: The policy-making stage. *Journal of Teacher Education* 45 (2): 140–46.

Reagan, T. 1999. Constructivist epistemology and second/foreign language pedagogy. *Foreign Language Annals* 32 (4): 413–25.

Reagan, T., C. Case, and J. Brubacher. 2000. *Becoming a reflective educator: How to build a culture of inquiry in the schools.* 2d ed. Thousand Oaks, CA: Corwin Press.

Richards, J. 1998. *Beyond training: Perspectives on language teacher education.* Cambridge: Cambridge University Press.

Richards, J. and C. Lockhart. 1994. *Reflective teaching in second language classrooms.* Cambridge: Cambridge University Press.

Richardson, V., ed. 1997a. *Constructivist teacher education: Building a world of new understandings.* London: Falmer Press.

———. 1997b. Constructivist teaching and teacher education: Theory and practice. In *Constructivist teacher education: Building a world of new understandings,* ed. V. Richardson, 3–14. London: Falmer Press.

Schmitt, C. and P. Woodford. 1997. *Bienvendios: Glencoe Spanish 1.* New York: Glencoe (McGraw- Hill).

Schwandt, T. 1994. Constructivist, interpretivist approaches to human inquiry. In *Handbook of qualitative research,* ed. N. Denzin and Y. Lincoln, 118–37. Thousand Oaks, CA: Sage.

Sinclair, H., I. Berthoud, J. Gerard, and E. Veneziano. 1985. Constructivisme et psycholinguistique génétique. *Archives de Psychologie* 53 (204): 37–60.

Spivey, N. 1997. *The constructivist metaphor: Reading, writing and the making of meaning.* San Diego: Academic Press.

Steffe, L., P. Cobb, and E. von Glasersfeld. 1988. *Construction of arithmetical meanings and strategies.* New York: Springer-Verlag.

Steffe, L. and J. Gale, eds. 1995. *Constructivism in education.* Hillsdale, NJ: Lawrence Erlbaum Associates.

Tobin, K., ed. 1993. *The practice of constructivism in science education.* Hillsdale, NJ: Lawrence Erlbaum Associates.

van Lier, L. 1996. *Interaction in the language curriculum: Awareness, autonomy and authenticity.* London: Longman.

von Glasersfeld, E. 1984. An introduction to radical constructivism. In *The invented reality: How do we know what we believe we know?,* ed. P. Watzlawick, 17–40. New York: Norton.

———. 1989. Cognition, construction of knowledge, and teaching. *Synthese* 80 (1): 121–40.

———. 1993. Questions and answers about radical constructivism. In *The practice of constructivism in science education,* ed. K. Tobin, 23–38. Hillsdale, NJ: Lawrence Erlbaum Associates.

———. 1995a. A constructivist approach to teaching. In *Constructivism in education,* ed. L. Steffe and J. Gale, 3–15. Hillsdale, NJ: Lawrence Erlbaum Associates.

———. 1995b. *Radical constructivism: A way of knowing.* London: Falmer Press.

———. 1996. Footnotes to "The many faces of constructivism." *Educational Researcher* 25 (6): 19.

Vygotsky, L. 1978. *Mind in society: The development of higher psychological processes.* Translated by M. Cole, V. John-Steiner, S. Scribner, and E. Souberman. Cambridge, MA: Harvard University Press.

———. 1986[1934]. *Thought and language.* Translated by A. Kozulin. Cambridge, MA: MIT Press.

Widdowson, H. G. 1998. Skills, abilities, and contexts of reality. *Annual Review of Applied Linguistics* 18: 323–33.

Williams, M. and R. Burden. 1997. *Psychology for language teachers: A social constructivist approach.* Cambridge: Cambridge University Press.

Winitzky, N. and D. Kauchak. 1997. Constructivism in teacher education: Applying cognitive theory to teacher learning. In *Constructivist teacher education: Building a world of new understandings,* ed. V. Richardson, 59–83. London: Falmer Press.

Wood, T., P. Cobb, and E.Yackel. 1995. Reflections of learning and teaching mathematics in elementary school. In *Constructivism in education,* ed. L. Steffe and J. Gale, 401–22. Hillsdale, NJ: Lawrence Erlbaum Associates.

Woods, D. 1996. *Teacher cognition in language teaching: Beliefs, decision-making and classroom practice.* Cambridge: Cambridge University Press.

Zeichner, K. and D. Liston. 1996. *Reflective teaching: An introduction.* Mahwah, NJ: Lawrence Erlbaum Associates.

Zietsman, A. 1996. Constructivism: Super theory for all educational ills? *South African Journal of Higher Education* 10 (1): 70–75.

4

Responding to Literature in the Foreign Language Classroom: Aesthetic Dimensions of Fluency

PHILIP M. ANDERSON AND TERRY A. OSBORN

LITERARY STUDY AND THE LANGUAGE CLASSROOM

Increasingly, the barriers between various "disciplines" of language study are eroding. Language specialists in the schools can no longer afford to be merely experts in native English, English as a Second Language (ESL), or foreign language teaching exclusively, since useful insights may be drawn from each discipline. These connections, in fact, seem necessary in a transnational world where the distinctions between native and foreign language begin to seem quaintly colonial. In any case, pedagogical issues and problems for language teaching, whether they be native, foreign, or ESL, are probably more alike than different for the practicing teacher. Attention to the specific perspectives each tradition brings to language teaching can only benefit the practitioner in the long run (see Garfinkel 1982), and the students will reap the added sophistication for learning and using the language.

Teachers of English have frequently supplied pedagogical insight for the teaching of English to nonnative speakers. Indeed, it can be argued that one goal for the ESL student is to understand English in the same way as the native speaker, and to a large extent, to employ the same literacy practices. As for writing proficiency, one composes in the same way whether one has learned the language as a native, or one has learned it as a second language. Some teachers even aspire to see that nonnative speakers of a language do not learn to read or write in a fundamentally different way than native speakers—in essence acting upon the presupposition that a fluent language user employs strategies and approaches to a text that should be the same regardless of language background.

Further, they correctly assume that a writer of a language is not truly literate unless he or she writes fluently and engagingly.

Conversely, ESL pedagogy has been helpful to native English teaching with its insights into the taken-for-grantedness of native language instruction, which frequently attempts to avoid the formal, didactic study of the structure of language and the problematic condition of vocabulary study and spelling. ESL pedagogy reminds the teacher of native speakers that the shift from an oral to literate state in the second language (L2) assumes cultural learning as well as linguistic acquisition, an insight customarily in evidence in multicultural English classrooms in multilingual communities. This fluency obstacle is indeed doubly problematic for speakers learning a new language as a foreign language, especially within their own native speaking environment. The tendency to focus exclusively on formal knowledge of the target language, on vocabulary, and on syntax at the expense of meaning and expression, is at some level a necessity given the "non native" (or first language [L1]) context of a nonnative speaker. Contemporary trends in pedagogy notwithstanding (see Shrum and Glisan 2000, for example), the shift to communicative goals through contextualized examples and activities still fails to adequately account for some elements that can be included under fluency.

At the same time, the use of literature in the language classroom continues to offer some positive benefits to the learner (Stone 1990). Scholars have sought engaging and unique methods to tap into that power in the language classroom, ranging from genre study (Osborn 1998; Van Vliet 1992) to Holocaust studies (Lauckner and Jokiniemi 2000). In this chapter, we argue that future language classrooms within the multicultural context of the United States can effectively utilize the similarities of the native, second language, and foreign language pedagogies by applying selected pedagogical analogies, and capitalizing on the benefits of literary reading by addressing the issues of aesthetics as they relate to fluency. As Liaw (2001) concluded regarding the use of literary response in a Taiwanese university English class:

The use of literature, if taught in a response-based manner, need not be only a vehicle for language teaching but a form of aesthetic experience that enhances the enjoyment of reading in a foreign language. The approach allows for creative and critical thinking to take place in an atmosphere where there are neither threats nor any compulsion to learn the correct answer or compete for the best interpretation. Selecting materials that are of personal relevance and appropriate difficulty helps to ensure high interest and low anxiety for students reading authentic foreign language texts. (43)

The analogy we wish to employ between teaching a foreign language and English teaching relates to what English teachers deal with as a distinction between reading for "comprehension" and reading for "response." The typical experience of foreign language students in regard to decoding text tends to focus on "reading" for word-for-word comprehension, that is, what reading specialists call "reading for comprehension." Of course, as numerous scholars argue and will be explored below, the most appropriate way to read a literary text is not using a comprehension approach, but using a response approach (Langer 1982; Purves 1981; Rosenblatt 1976, 1978; see also Beach 1993, for a comprehensive overview of the research as it relates to the classroom). The response approach to reading literary texts in a foreign language class evokes extensive possibilities for enhancing the sophistication of reading in the foreign language classroom, even in the face of limited decoding "fluency."

Some English teaching practice using response insights draws on analogies with foreign language teaching, notably the notion of translation. Anderson and Rubano's (1991) *Enhancing Aesthetic Reading and Response,* for example, explores research, theory, and practice of reader response in the English classroom, and offers several points of departure. One of their key concepts is form translation, the reader responding to a literary text by translating the text into another form. One key example of "form translation" would be the writing of a poem in response to a short story. Briefly, the intention is that the student will capture the aesthetic elements in her/his response to a literary text if s/he is asked to respond in a consciously poetic form of discourse. The analogy of translation is drawn from foreign language practice. Anderson and Rubano's synthesis of reader response research also plays out a key analogy that can be applied from English teaching to foreign language teaching, which we will explore below.

Shifts in pedagogy for teaching literature to native speakers (as in English speakers learning English) have recently been legitimized by the new curriculum frameworks and state testing practices. While the tradition of reading for comprehension has remained in the curriculum, the alternative tradition of responding to literature, a key pedagogy since the 1930s following innovators such as Louise Rosenblatt, is now part of some state standards, for example the New York State Curriculum Frameworks.

LANGUAGE LEARNING AND THE AESTHETIC

There are three maxims we accept about native language learning that hold true for learning a second language[1]:

1. Literacy involves a mastery of more than one mode of language use (see, for example, Bruner 1985; Carrasquillo and Rodriguez 1996; Eisner 1985);

2. Much of language growth and development is unconscious, and much of an individual's knowledge of language use is "intuitive" (see Britton et al. 1975; Fromkin and Rodman 1998, 347–49); and

3. "Intuitive" knowledge, or what Polanyi (1962) calls tacit knowledge (i.e., "knowing more than we can say"), is the basis for much practical linguistic and cognitive functioning (see, for example, Shrum and Glisan 2000, 4–5).

For foreign language instruction to consist of more than discrete grammar exercises and the learning of formal rules of usage, we contend that instruction must strive to include key elements related to developing an intuitive sense of a language. Without this intuitive sense, or *Sprachgefühl*, there is little connection to, and certainly nothing approaching fluency in, any language for its users. And by extension, without understanding of various forms of language, and types of language use, there can be no functional literacy.

In practical terms, several recent innovations in (native) English teaching should apply directly to the transformation of foreign language instruction. The new state frameworks for school standards require multimodal forms of literacy, that is, the new standards documents generally require more than one genre or type of writing, and, probably more importantly, more than one type of reading. Within these mandates, the most important one of these new requirements is responding to literature for expressive purposes. This "expressive purpose" is curricularists' vernacular for aesthetic response. Recognizing and responding to the aesthetic elements in language is one of the keys to using it effectively, and certainly prerequisite to any near-native level of fluency.

Aesthetic response may well be a "natural" function of human existence (Eisner 1985; Langer 1953), but an aesthetic response to literature is a "natural" response to literature in any case (see, for example, Merrifield 1982). When one reads a literary text one does not normally, or initially, analyze the text, but responds emotionally and intellectually through engaging in the world represented in the text. Fluent readers are more likely to "fill in the gaps" in the text than poor readers, that is, the fluent reader engages in "creative reading" (see Iser 1989 on gaps, Padgett 1998 on creative reading). Most writers, at least outside of school, write in a literary form as a response to a text rather than to create an analytic essay. Surely, most of us wouldn't love literary texts so much if all we did was analyze them after the fact of reading: It is the experience of reading the text that attracts us fundamentally.

At this point, key concepts about native language learning need to be articulated (and possibly some misconceptions need to be dispelled). First, native language learners typically do have the advantage of language immersion that foreign language learners do not, unless of course they are living in a setting in which that language is dominant. In this case, though, foreign language learning is typically referred to as second language learning (see Eastman 1983). It is also true that the literacy function of schooling requires connections with a full range of language functions that are neither necessarily available in the culture at large, nor in an equal distribution in all students' experience. For example, though virtually every child experiences poetry through popular music or nursery rhymes (even if only on television), not every child reads or writes poetry or fiction outside of school.

Native language instruction requires practice in all forms of literate behavior that are central elements in the culture of that language. As a result, the notion of the "hidden curriculum" is germane here as well, explaining that leaving forms of literate behavior out of the curriculum delegitimizes them in the eyes of the students and, ultimately, the culture. For example, though storytelling skills are highly valued in certain regions of the United States (notably the Southeast), such oral traditions are systematically devalued as it is the written text with which our curriculum most often engages students (see Ong 1982).

The other element of native language learning that is probably beyond effective testing, certainly within the immediate future (even given the advances of magnetic resonance imaging and other innovations), is the intuitive understanding of language that guides our everyday use of it. There is ample evidence that children learn the entire grammar of their native language before starting school, that vocabulary grows faster than instruction in grade school, and (based on informal interviews with senior English majors) that high SAT verbal scores are possible without formal articulated knowledge of grammar (see Weaver 1979).

Less studied, but often obvious to bilingual and even monolingual literate people, is the role of intuitive understanding in normal everyday literacy. For example, most people sing along to popular songs without understanding even the literal meaning; most new reading vocabulary is learned through reading, that is, learned from context clues. Reading research on miscue analysis (the substitution, dropping, or adding words during oral reading), shows that the best readers do make a significant number of miscues on the literal text (simple comprehension measure on most tests) but do comprehend the text (Goodman 1970). Not only do these more fluent readers comprehend the text in spite of the miscues, they regularly bring a richer interpretation to the text.

The intuitive understanding of language appears to be as important as the articulated formal knowledge of language. This of course explains why someone could have a formal knowledge of German grammar, but not be able to function effectively in a German-speaking environment. It also explains how a native German speaker could be "illiterate." In any case, since both the oral and literary traditions require an intuitive sense of the language, the intuitive sense of a language needs to be nurtured to facilitate fluency in any language.

One central facet of language competence that requires the nurturing of the intuitive is the aesthetic or artistic functions of language. The aesthetic is sorely neglected even in native language instruction (which tends to focus on the analytical and communicative functions, for example, essays and reports), but it is neglected at peril to the language development of the students. Language development and cognitive research identifies two essential categories of language use: the paradigmatic and the narrative (Bruner 1985), or the transactional and the poetic (Britton 1976). These functions of verbal thought and language use are reciprocal: sophistication in one mode is related to sophistication in the other. Simply, sophistication in poetic modes is enhanced by the qualities of transactional, and transactional writing is enhanced by qualities of the poetic. The application of these principles to foreign language instruction follow below.

For now, to sum up the premises:

1. Much of literacy consists of tacit knowledge developed from language experience;
2. Central to tacit knowledge, and socio-psycholinguistic fluency, are aesthetic elements in language use; and
3. The aesthetic modes of language representation reinforce the quality of articulation and representation in other modes (the analytical or formal functions).

For any foreign language curriculum to meet the goals of fluency along with comparative integrity in cultural representation (Osborn in press), the aesthetic elements must be addressed. In fact, though beyond the purview of this discussion, the aesthetic may even precede the analytical modes and the literal comprehension of language—a possibility that could potentially turn language teaching as we now know it "on its head."

AESTHETIC RESPONSE TO LITERATURE

How does a teacher promote aesthetic response to literary texts? Anderson and Rubano (1991) provide an overview of the response tradition of reading literary texts, and provide several classroom activities central to the issues raised above. They trace the various currents in reader response from Louise Rosenblatt's pioneering work (1976, 1978) to more recent work in mental imaging during reading (Collins 1991; Paivio 1986). The fundamental idea that develops from Rosenblatt's work is that of "stance," a predisposition, a set of expectations, one brings to the reading of a text. Though played out in a continuum between the two, Rosenblatt posits two types of reading stances and purposes, the aesthetic and the transactional. The aesthetic is essential to the reading of literary texts, though schools frequently emphasize (or are even restricted to) transactional reading. Rosenblatt's most infamous example of transactional reading purpose aimed at a literary text is an exercise found in an elementary reading book that asked the question: "What facts does this poem teach you?" Current trends in children's literature pedagogy have addressed this problem directly, with the promotion of sustained silent reading, children's literature texts, and the use of the author's role in writing stories in response to children's literature.

One of the central arguments of Anderson and Rubano's book is that students are more likely to engage in aesthetic response to a text if they are first encouraged, or required, to adopt an aesthetic stance toward the text. One simple way to encourage the shift to aesthetic stance is to change the expectations for reading from "What's the author trying to say?" to "What do you see?" and to change the spoken and written response expectations from the analytical and mnemonic to the creative and associative. In other words, enage students with the text for the purposes of creative response, that is, aesthetic language experience and production.

One of the best ways to encourage aesthetic reading is to ask the students to engage in what Anderson and Rubano call "form translation," responding to literary prose in poetry, and vice versa. But more to the point, and a useful first step on the road to form translation, is what the Australian English educator Peter Adams calls "dependent authorship" (see Adams 1987; Anderson and Rubano, 54 ff.). Dependent authorship allows the student to engage in reproducing the style of the text without necessarily needing to engage in analytical or comprehension activities that require them to move out of the aesthetic stance. But more importantly, the student writer enters into the world of the text, enacting the necessary engagement for developing fluency and understanding.

The teacher of a foreign language may now object, "But how can the students engage in dependent authorship if they can't 'literally' translate the text?" One could ask the same question of the native speaker reading a literary text, though teachers know that the reader "learns" to read while reading, and many literary experiences are thrilling even if there is some real confusion about meaning. One only needs to think of children who have "enjoyed" adult novels: How much comprehension actually occurred when a child reads something outside her experience of life and language? Wasn't the experience unarticulated and possibly unfathomable? In any case, the interest in reading and the experience was not based on what a reading specialist would call thorough comprehension, but on the experience of the text, an experience appropriate to the experience, vicarious and linguistic, of the reader.

In any case, what we are addressing is the reading of literature, beginner or advanced, with an assumption of some rudimentary knowledge of the language at least. One characteristic that defines the advanced student in foreign language instruction is the reading of literature in the new language; and reading literature is a different task than simple comprehension and communication. Reading literature in any language is a matter of representation and engagement, and does not end with the experience of the text.

POETS AND TRANSLATION

Perhaps the best person to answer the question about translation and comprehension (accuracy) is a translator of literary texts. The Queens section of *Newsday* (New York) for September 23, 1999, contains a story about Gregory Rabassa, professor at Queens College of the City University of New York, and translator of Garciá Marquez's early works, Cortázar's *Hopscotch*, and many other classics of Spanish and Portuguese literature. The article articulates several key elements of Rabassa's translation style that are central to our concern here, the most important being his statement concerning word-for-word translations: "An accurate translation can sound like a turkey. . . . You have to get a sense of what the author's feeling and try to be the writer." The translator of a literary text, even a student in class, cannot be said to be achieving anything by a word-for-word translation: linguistic "accuracy" is not the point—human sensibility and imagery are. Translated literary texts are not transliterations, but translations, a cognitive and linguistic act that asks one to draw on one's own cultural understanding and experience of the world.

Another recent example of this issue is discussed by Seamus Heaney in the preface to his translation of *Beowulf*. He also argues that the choices a translator makes in translating literary texts extends beyond mere accuracy. For Heaney, the key for translating the Old English poem was in the rhythms of the Anglo-Saxon-isms in his childhood speech; in many instances he resisted or rejected the assisting Old English expert's "corrections" during the editorial process. In both instances, the great writers needed to situate their understanding in the aesthetics of the language and the cultural connections with the text.

So, two sorts of activities present themselves: the translation of foreign language literary texts in poetic forms (in English), and the development of aesthetic stances toward the reading and interpreting of literary texts in the foreign language. The first assists the student in responding aesthetically; the second provides an approach to the literary text in a foreign language that focuses on the literary reading and interpretation. In fact, focusing on the literal meaning first might destroy the attempt at literary reading. And, beyond dependent authorship, the focus on literary images and metaphorical representation is central to reading literature in any language. Students can never master a language they can't creatively participate in; they won't seek out the literature of any language that doesn't provide them with a satisfying literary experience.

AESTHETIC READING AND RESPONSE IN THE CLASSROOM

The practical examples in Anderson and Rubano's monograph are easy to adapt to the foreign language classroom, but an example using foreign language texts might make the larger concepts more understandable. The easiest technique for guaranteeing attention to the aesthetic elements of language is the use of "dependent authorship." The reader is presented with a poem or a short story from which the teacher has removed words, sentences, or whole paragraphs. The most rudimentary version is an adaptation of the cloze procedure from reading comprehension, in which the text has every fifth word removed from the text, though in a poetic cloze text the teacher only removes the key words representing central images or connected ideas.

Theodor Storm (1817–1888) authored a poem which evokes strong images, *Die Stadt*. This poem serves as a standard example of a literary selection presented in lower or intermediate level language classes.[2] For purposes of illustration, Osborn's English translation of the poem will be utilized:

The City

> On the gray beach, on the gray sea
> And the city lies adjacent

The fog weighs heavily on the rooftops
And through the silence roars the sea
Monotonously around the city.

No forest murmurs, no bird sings
Incessantly in May;
The wild goose with its hard cry
Only flies by in an autumn night;
At the beach the grass waves.

Yet my whole heart clings to you,
You gray city on the sea
For ever and ever, the magic of youth
Rests smilingly still on you, on you
You gray city on the sea.

As a cloze exercise, Anderson and Rubano (1991) point to this use of such a poem as dependent authorship or unarticulated response. Students can be given a list of vocabulary simultaneously all drawn from the poem, which they then attempt to match back to the original. For example,

At the _____ beach, on the gray sea
And the city lies adjacent.
The fog weighs _____ on the _____
And through the _____ roars the sea
_____ around the city.

(monotonously) (gray) (heavily) (silence) (rooftops)

With a careful selection of omitted words, the teacher can assist the students as well in looking for context clues and grammatical issues simultaneously, as evidenced by the lack of "fit" inherent in certain possible answers above. In other words, an adverb will not serve as an object of a preposition. For example, *the fog weighs heavily on the monotonously* simply cannot work. Students thus attend in this instance to multiple dimensions of accuracy as well as the aesthetic dimensions of fluency.

Another common form of dependent authorship is the "continuation" of a story, for example, adding an ending to a story from which the teacher has removed the ending. The ending might even be written in English after reading the first part of the story with the teacher's guidance. Having written the ending enhances the translation which has already taken place in that the student must "return" to the earlier reading to extend the story, though the student may move away from the "correct" (i.e., the original) ending. Assessment could be centered on anything from appropriate style to appropriate cultural representation.

An exercise used quite frequently these days in English classrooms is a form of dependent authorship that might be better called "writing within a text." Most English teachers routinely ask students to take on the role of a character, writing something in the voice of the character. In many cases, the assignment is a letter or diary entry for the character at that point in the book or in response to a key dramatic moment in the book or poem. More sophisticated teachers take Iser's notions of "gaps" in the text seriously, and ask students to provide various elements "missing" from the text. The gaps might include fuller character descriptions (reveals students' cultural and psychological understanding), more details of setting (cultural), or "off-stage" conversations and actions (aesthetic and cultural issues). Greg Rubano's assignment for Willams' *The Glass Menagerie* is a classic: Laura's brother Tom works in a factory and writes poetry on matchbook covers (no sample of which is provided by Williams). Rubano asks students to write matchbook-sized poems, and the students respond with poems that reflect either Tom's state-of-mind or the conditions under which he is working (see Anderson and Rubano 1991, 72ff.).

A more important approach for foreign language instruction is the development of image-focused reading and learning to respond to literary texts through image production. Alan Paivio's (1986) work in dual-code processing of texts, when combined with the reader response research, presents various opportunities for aesthetic response. Paivio's research demonstrated that both the verbal and visual functions of the brain were engaged during reading. Readers produce images in their minds while reading (a finding not surprising to reader response theorists and literary critics).

One way to promote mental imaging in reading is simply to ask students to read focusing on the images, but a more practical way that reinforces aesthetic reading response is to ask the students to produce their own poems using images from the reading they are doing. The work of the poet Kenneth Koch prefigured these issues represented by his poetry writing activities in *Rose, Where Did You Get That Red?* (1990). Koch asked elementary school children to "read" classic adult poetry (Shakespeare, Yeats, etc.) by extrapolating the dramatic situation of the poem (that is, the visual action in the form of a poetic trope). For example, William Blake's famous "Tiger, Tiger" poem from *Songs of Innocence and Experience* is interpreted as a dramatic situation in which the students imagine themselves meeting a fantastical creature. Relying on the intuitive and aesthetic aspects of dependent authorship, students then produce their own poems. The results tend to be startling, far beyond what one normally expects of language sophistication from such young students.

One reason for the sophistication of the poetic responses may be the use of what Bruner (1985), drawing on Vygotsky (1962), calls "cognitive scaffolding," from which dependent authorship and Koch's technique receive their pedagogical power. Cognitive scaffolding is the expert structure placed on a student task that allows the student to perform at higher levels than the student could without expert direction and structure (i.e., Vygotsky's "zone of proximal development"). In each of the examples above, the students are responding to a text within a structure (and with a stance) promoted by the teacher-selected activity. In each instance the effect is to focus the student on the aesthetic elements in the text. The setting of teacher expectations is, of course, central to all good teaching, and can be used to focus the student reader on any element of the text from cultural elements to punctuation. The failure to articulate a teacher expectation usually puts the student in the "default" mode of comprehension of searching for an ethical or moral truism.

But the other possibility for sophisticated literacy here is the cross-cultural connection of image production in reading and writing that transcends linguistic codes (historical and dialectal). The students tend to produce more sophisticated responses, even in dealing with native language texts, when they focus on the central concepts and images in the text. In the case of foreign language instruction, the writing of a poem in response to the reading of a poem that focused on the central images would likely provide a much higher level of linguistic sophistication than stopping at the simple translation of the text.

Consider again, for example, Storm's "The City." If students are given partial stanzas until the entire poem has been presented, and they are then asked for the central images, they might create a list as follows: dark, gloomy, dense, loud, repetitive, wind, and memories. From these images, then, students could create their own poems, as a form of aesthetic response. Teachers may choose to assess communicative effectiveness prior to, or even in lieu of, accuracy issues. In this way, student appreciation of and attention to the beauty of literary selections can be enhanced.

CONCLUSION

By focusing on aesthetic dimensions of literary selections through the utilization of reader response, teachers of language in the foreign language classes of the future can enable students to move beyond the literal into the literary. Translation, though often discredited as a holdover from the grammar-translation methodological error, is valuable in developing aesthetic sense because translation is, in fact, creative in nature. Translation is as much style as it is accuracy. Therefore, accuracy should be judged on style and poetic qualities, not merely on literalness. Finally, foreign language study should focus on reading, reader response, or literary study, rather than on comprehension alone, utilizing literary study to aid in the students' full acquisition of language fluency.

NOTES

1. Compare these insights from the English/Language Arts field to the insights from holistic approaches to language study and the language acquisition/learning distinction (see, for example, Richards and Rodgers, 1986).

2. This poem appeared in Walbruck and Specht's (1987) *Deutsch gestern und heute*.

BIBLIOGRAPHY

Adams, P. 1987. Writing from reading: "Dependent authorship" as a response. In *Readers, texts, teachers*, ed. B. Corcoran and E. Evans, 119–52. Portsmouth, NH: Boynton Cook Heinemann.

Anderson, P. M. and G. Rubano. 1991. *Enhancing aesthetic reading and response.* Urbana, IL: National Council of Teachers of English.

Applebee, A. 1985. Studies in the spectator role: An approach to response to literature. In *Researching response to literature and the teaching of literature: Points of departure*, ed. C. R. Cooper, 87–102. Norwood, NJ: Ablex.

Beach, R. 1993. *A teacher's introduction to reader-response theories.* Urbana, IL: National Council of Teachers of English.

Britton, J. 1976. Language and the nature of learning: An individual perspective. In *The teaching of English: 76th yearbook of the National Society for the Study of Education, Part I*, ed. J. Squire, 1–37. Chicago: U. of Chicago Press.

Britton, J., T. Burgess, N. Martin, A. McLeod, and H. Rosen. 1975. *The development of writing abilities (11–18).* Schools Council Research Studies. New York: Macmillan.

Bruner, J. 1985. Narrative and paradigmatic modes of thought. In *Learning and teaching the ways of knowing of 84th yearbook of the National Society for the Study of Education, Part II*, ed. E. Eisner. Chicago: University of Chicago Press.

Carrasquillo, A. L. and V. Rodriguez. 1996. *Language minority students in the mainstream classroom.* Bristol, PA: Multilingual Matters.

Clifford, J. 1979. Transactional teaching and the literary experience. *English Journal* 68: 36–39.

Collins, C. 1991. *Reading the written image: Verbal play, interpretation, and the roots of iconophobia.* University Park: Pennsylvania State University Press, 1991.

Corcoran, B. 1987. Teachers creating readers. In *Readers, texts, teachers*, ed. B. Corcoran and E. Evans, 41–74. Portsmouth, NH: Boynton Cook Heineman.

Eastman, C. M. 1983. *Language planning: An introduction.* San Francisco: Chandler and Sharp.

Eisner, E. 1985. Aesthetic modes of knowing. *Learning and teaching the ways of knowing: 84th yearbook of the National Society for the Study of Education*, Part I, ed. E. Eisner. Chicago: University of Chicago Press.

Evans, E. 1987. Readers recreating texts. In *Readers, texts, teachers*, ed. B. Corcoran and E. Evans, 22–40. Portsmouth, NH: Boynton Cook Heinemann.

Fromkin, V. and R. Rodman. 1998. *An introduction to language.* 6th ed. Fort Worth, TX: Harcourt Brace.

Garfinkel, A., ed. 1982. *ESL and the foreign language teacher. Report of central states conference on the teaching of foreign languages.* Skokie, IL: National Textbook Company.

Goodman, K. S. 1970. Reading: A psycholinguistic guessing game. In *Theoretical models and processes of reading*, ed. H. Singer and R. B. Ruddell. Newark, DE: International Reading Association.

Hillocks, G., Jr. 1980. Toward a hierarchy of skills in the comprehension of literature. *English Journal* 69 (3): 54–59.

Holland, N. 1975. *Five readers reading.* New Haven, CT: Yale University Press.

Hosic, J. F. 1921. *Empirical studies of school reading.* New York: Teachers College, Columbia University.

Iser, W. 1978. *The act of reading.* Baltimore: Johns Hopkins University Press.
——. 1989. *Prospecting: From reader response to literary anthropology.* Baltimore: Johns Hopkins University Press.
Kahn, E., C. Walter, and L. Johannessen. 1984. *Writing about literature.* Urbana, IL: National Council of Teachers of English.
Koch, K. 1990. *Rose, where did you get that red!: Teaching great poetry to children.* Rev. ed. New York: Random House.
Langer, J. 1982. The reading process. In *Secondary school reading: What research reveals for classroom practice,* ed. A. Berger and H. A. Robinson, 39–51. Urbana, IL: National Council of Teachers of English.
——. 1990. The process of understanding: Reading for literary and informative purposes. *Research in the Teaching of English* 24 (3): 229–57.
Langer, J., ed. 1992. *Literature instruction: A focus on student response.* Urbana, IL: National Council of Teachers of English.
Langer, S. K. 1953. *Feeling and form.* New York: Charles Scribner's Sons, 1953.
Lauckner, N. A. and M. Jokiniemi. 2000. *Shedding light on the darkness: A guide to teaching the holocaust.* New York: Berghahn Books.
Liaw, M. 2001. Exploring literary responses in an EFL classroom. *Foreign Language Annals* 34 (1): 35–45.
Merrifield, D. F. 1982. *Praktische Anleitung zur Interpretation von Dichtung.* Rev. ed. Lanham, MD: University Press of America.
Ong, W. J. 1982. *Orality and literacy: The technologizing of the word.* London: Routledge.
Osborn, T. A. 1998. Providing access: Foreign language learners and genre theory. *Foreign Language Annals* 31 (1): 40–47.
——. In press. Making connections and comparisons: Integrating foreign language with other core curricula. *NECTFL Review.*
Padgett, R. 1998. *Creative reading.* Urbana, IL: National Council of Teachers of English.
Paivio, A. 1986. *Mental representations: A dual coding approach.* New York: Oxford University Press.
Petrosky, A. R. 1985. Response: A way of knowing. In *Researching response to literature and the teaching of literature: Points of departure,* ed. C. R. Cooper, 70–83. Norwood, NJ: Ablex Publishing Corp.
Polanyi, M. 1962. *Personal knowledge: Towards a post-critical philosophy.* Chicago: University of Chicago Press.
Purves, A. C. 1973. *Literature education in ten countries.* Stockholm: Almqvist and Wicksell.
Purves, A. C. and R. Beach. 1972. *Literature and the reader: Research in response to literature, reading interests, and the teaching of literature.* Urbana, IL: National Council of Teachers of English.
Purves, A. C., with D. Harnisch, D. Quirk, and B. Bauer. 1981. *Reading and literature: American achievement in international perspective.* Urbana, IL: National Council of Teachers of English.
Richards, J. C. and T. S. Rodgers. 1986. *Approaches and methods in language teaching: A description and analysis.* Cambridge, UK: Cambridge University Press.
Rosenblatt, L. 1976. *Literature as exploration.* 3d ed. New York: Noble and Noble.

————. 1978. *The reader, the text, the poem: The transactional theory of the literary work.* Carbondale and Edwardsville, IL: Southern Illinois University Press.

Sadowski, M., E. T. Goetz, and S. Kangiser. 1988. Imagination in story response: Relationships between imagery, affect, and structural importance. *Reading Research Quarterly* 23 (3): 320–36.

Shrum, J. L. and E. W. Glisan. 2000. *Teacher's handbook: Contextualized language instruction.* 2d ed. Boston, MA: Heinle and Heinle.

Squire, J. 1964. *The responses of adolescents while reading four short stories.* Urbana, IL: National Council of Teachers of English.

————, ed. 1968. *Response to literature.* Urbana, IL: National Council of Teachers of English.

Stone, R. 1990. The motivation to study literature. *Babel* 25 (3): 18–21.

Van Vliet, L. W. 1992. *Approaches to literature through genre.* Phoenix, AZ: Oryx.

Vygotsky, L. 1962. *Thought and language.* Translated by E. Hanfmann and G. Vakar. Cambridge: MIT Press.

Walbruck, H. A. and R. H. Specht. 1987. *Deutch gestern und heute.* Teacher's ed. Saint Paul, MN: EMC Publishing.

Weaver, C. 1979. *Grammar for teachers.* Urbana, IL: National Council of Teachers of English.

Young, A. 1982. Considering values: The poetic function of language. In *Language connections: Writing and reading across the curriculum,* ed. T. Fulwiler and A. Young. Urbana, IL: National Council of Teachers of English.

5

Challenging the Monovocal Narrative: Interdisciplinary Units in the Foreign Language Classroom

DAVID GERWIN AND TERRY A. OSBORN

INTRODUCTION

Connecting with other disciplines has, until recently, not been a strong point of foreign language curriculum and instruction, at times because curriculum developers in the other core areas fail to recognize the potential contributions the field can provide. As the latest state frameworks and national standards attest, however, these interdisciplinary links construct powerful connections for students among the subjects that they study (see, for example, National Standards in Foreign Language Education Project 1996; Nebraska Department of Education 1996; Osborn in press). Indeed, as language education takes its much-coveted place among the core subjects offered in the schools, encouraging students to make these associations will prove invaluable.

Within the past decade, a growing number of scholars in the core content areas have included interdisciplinary curricula within the list of needed reforms (Diaz, Massialas, and Xanthopoulos 1999; Lonning, DeFranco, and Weinland 1998; National Council of Teachers of Mathematics 1991). During the same period, others have noted that the hurdles faced by planners in integrating the aspects of course content constitute a sizable challenge (Davison, Miller, and Methany 1995; Lonning and DeFranco 1997). Certainly within the field of foreign language education, some researchers have looked for ways to effectively move beyond traditional barriers of the classroom in terms of pedagogy and instructional content (Biron 1998; Gehlker, Gozzi, and Zeller 1999; Overfield 1997). These trends are reflected in the values articulated by the framers of the *Standards for Foreign Language Learning*:

The conscious effort to connect the foreign language curriculum with other parts of students' academic lives opens doors to information and experiences which enrich the entire school and life experience. Those connections flow from other areas to the foreign language classroom and also originate in the foreign language classroom to add unique experiences and insights to the rest of the curriculum. (National Standards in Foreign Language Education Project 1996, 49)

Discussions of history in the foreign language classroom have often been included, if only briefly, under the banner of "culture." Though we recognize that historical knowledge and culture are not synonyms, the term "culture" in this sense is usually employed by teachers and planners as a catch-all category to describe nonlinguistic or nonmechanical aspects of language instruction. As the newest standards challenge both the traditional grammatical and even solely communicative approaches to foreign language education, however, curriculum planners can extend the parameters of study in the language classroom. Simply put, some themes or topics that cannot be included under the broader banner of traditional "culture" may still prove to be appropriate and effective, given new directions in the field, and though they deviate from time-honored categories.

In this chapter we will explore one such application through the use of an interdisciplinary unit including history and language. The history as mystery approach (Gerwin and Zevin in preparation) when combined with Osborn's (in press) criteria of interdisciplinary curricula involving the language classroom will, we believe, facilitate student development of multi-perspective critical thinking skills. First, we present relevant theoretical considerations and then focus on the unit theme of *Multiple Voices: Challenging the Monovocal Narrative*. Finally, we discuss the implications of such cooperative ventures in fostering diverse evaluative frameworks.

CONSIDERATIONS FROM THE HISTORICAL DOMAIN

What is history? Why, the past of course. But the past involves everything that everyone has done from a second ago to as far back as we can get. And now that scholars have started writing environmental history it includes not only human actors, but also animals, germs, natural resources, climate—the entire biosphere. Since it is impossible to record absolutely everything, whatever we choose to study is only a tiny fraction of the whole. Our selection is a tremendous act of interpretation. Beyond simply picking what to recount, we also turn the past into a narrative. Researchers set a beginning and an end to their study, and try to wring meaning from events, meanings which are imposed on the event itself. After all of that we have a historical narrative. In a sense the portion of the past we retell as history is as much created as found.

Some writers think that recognizing the created nature of historical narrative makes the entire enterprise no more (and no less) than creating fiction; given the effort required they suggest it may not be worthwhile (Jenkins

1999). Others note that, while facts may not dictate meaning, they still restrict the stories we can tell and those stories still have power (Novick 1988). In practice, high school history teachers have always recognized the power of literature to engage students with historical events. How many students have read *The Grapes of Wrath* in English while studying the Great Depression in American history? (For one example of using literature to motivate the study of history, see Gerwin and Manolios 1999). What this sensitivity should mean, for high school students, is an end to the omniscient, depersonalized monovocal narrative of the history textbook as the sole authority in history classes. For one thing, history textbooks often get even the facts of the story wrong, and are quite out of step with the work of historians in the meanings they ascribe to events (Loewen 1995). Still, even if textbooks were factually correct and up to date, the presentation of a single narration is misleading. The necessity for high school students to build a multi-vocal narrative with an international history perspective, even within a course built around a single nation's history, provides a powerful incentive for crafting interdisciplinary curricula between history and so-called foreign language.

One way to make the multi-vocal approach to history accessible to high school students is to present history as a mystery. Such an approach is particularly useful in an interdisciplinary unit whose focus is not on the meaning of history. Mystery sounds exciting and adventurous. It is also humbling:

Deeply embedded into mystery is the notion that we are in possession of only parts or pieces of the whole, and that we need to find clues so we can understand what has happened. We do not "know it all," maybe far from it. Worse yet, we are not certain of our evidence or able to perfect our understanding, for many and varied reasons. In order to solve a mystery, even partially, the past must be brought back to life.

History, like mystery, must delve into the past for clues and motives. As historians we must search through words, documents, diaries, news stories, songs, stories, diplomatic accounts, paintings, photographs, and other sources, for evidence, for corroboration, for comprehension, for inference, and for theory. But it is we, not those who are gone, who put the clues together, and carefully, or we will make serious mistakes about the past and about ourselves. We will fail to grasp what happened and why it happened unless we open ourselves to observation, to gathering data, and to explanations that help us understand human actions and motives. (Gerwin and Zevin in preparation)

Students need only be presented with a mystery and a short reminder to weigh evidence and they are off and running. The challenge we face is crafting mystery that incorporates the many voices that the students need to hear.

SOCIAL STUDIES, CULTURE, AND GLOBAL CONNECTIONS

Though this chapter focuses on history as mystery we note that the social studies and language have independent concerns with both culture and global perspectives. These provide an important platform for collaborations between the foreign language and social studies classroom, so we briefly explore them here. The national standards in social studies consist of ten themes (sometimes referred to as "strands") that provide a framework for social studies education. Without specifying specific content (i.e., events to teach in U.S. History), the themes alert curriculum planners to considerations all social studies courses should include. Culture heads that list as the first of the ten themes, and social studies programs need to "provide for the study of culture and cultural diversity." Expansions upon this idea ask what language tells us about culture. At different grade levels students are expected to describe, explain, or predict "how information and experiences may be interpreted by people from diverse cultural perspectives and frames of reference." There is also a specific expectation that students can make similar connections between a language or literature as expressions of a particular culture and as forces that shape group behavior (National Council for the Social Studies 1994, 21, 33). Culture keeps appearing in the rest of the framework. Investigating "Time, Continuity and Change," students must encounter periods and patterns of change within and across cultures. Studying "People, Places, & Environments" requires that pupils "describe and compare how people create places that reflect culture as they design and build." A review of the other themes would establish the ubiquity of culture in the social studies curriculum (National Council for the Social Studies 1994, 21–45). Even outside the framework of the mystery/interpretative approach to teaching history, there are many possibilities for collaboration between the foreign language classroom and the social studies classroom when both include the study of culture as a primary focus instead of treating it as an add-on.

"Global Connections" constitute the ninth strand of the ten social studies themes. Students analyze patterns and relationships within and among world cultures, explore economic competition and ethnic enmities, investigate concepts of human rights, and draw upon language and literature in these investigations (National Council for the Social Studies 1994, 29). Educators advocating global perspectives in social studies are well aware that a variety of human differences lead to "subcultures within cultures" and that the United States in particular epitomizes a trend toward fewer homogeneous nations and greater cross-cultural interactions within nations. Social studies teachers with a global perspective provide students with multiple viewpoints on concepts and events, drawing upon a variety of resources including media coverage from around the world. Globally oriented teachers avoid an "us-them" dichotomy and focus instead upon developing an appreciation of diversity at home and abroad (Merryfield 1997). Social studies educators point to social studies teachers as the typical resource to whom school administrators will turn for leadership in global education (Tucker and Evans 1996). To the extent this is correct, and social studies teachers are prepared to respond, foreign language and social studies educators might well forge strong alliances in support of global education.

FOREIGN LANGUAGE DOMAIN CONSIDERATIONS

It is impossible to meaningfully separate the linguistic content of the foreign language course from its concomitant cultural components. As Kramsch (1993) asserts:

One often reads in teachers' guidelines that language teaching consists of teaching the four skills [reading, writing, listening, and speaking] 'plus culture.' This dichotomy of language and culture is an entrenched feature of language teaching around the world. It is part of the linguistic heritage of the profession. Whether it is called (Fr.) *civilisation*, (G.) *Landeskunde*, or (Eng.) *culture*, culture is often seen as mere information conveyed by the language, not as a feature of language itself; cultural awareness becomes an educational objective in itself, separate from language. If, however, language is seen as social practice, culture becomes the very core of language teaching. Cultural awareness must then be viewed both as enabling language proficiency and as being the outcome of reflection on language proficiency. (8)

Moore's (1996) research of foreign language classrooms points out that culture is still treated in the language course context as a curricular "add-on," rather than an integral course component. Within the language course, most teachers would agree, learning is recursive and involves much review and re-learning. As Osborn (in press) has argued, some cultural items included in the foreign language curriculum will be more similar to the home culture, whereas others will resemble the cultural values of the target culture,[1] and thus effective interdisciplinary units must employ themes and activities which include connective validity, comparative integrity, or both. Connective validity and comparative integrity are focused on achieving a balance among elements of disciplinary epistemology and multicultural perspectives. Themes possessing both features should simultaneously resonate as "authentic" with both academics and members of the represented culture.

CONNECTIVE VALIDITY AND THE INTERDISCIPLINARY UNIT

Connective validity suggests that the unit includes the following aspects:

1. Integration of communicative aspects in the skills of reading, writing, listening, or speaking;
2. Subjectification of the domestic (or "home") perspective; and
3. Attention to the related global or local realities of pluralism, including any role played by language diversity.

81

The integrated, interdisciplinary unit we suggest should focus on historical themes containing elements that can be investigated through sources in the foreign language classroom. Documents, videos, audio recordings, and other media are examples of such sources. The language teacher, utilizing that realia as a communicative springboard, can then plan to include activities related to reading, writing, listening, or speaking in any combination. Though all of the activities need not specifically relate to the connections in a history class, the point of connection should involve the acquisition of information in the target language as demonstrative of diverse, multi-vocal perspectives.

The unit should also include a concerted attempt to subjectify the "home" perspective. The presentation of material in neutral and natural frames supports what Giroux (1997) refers to as a "culture of positivism" and leads students to understand, fallaciously, that knowledge is apolitical and beyond the influence of culture. As discussed prior, in history courses, as well, students often feel compelled to find the one authoritative interpretation. The National Standards for History bemoan the current situation and stipulate that students must, as well, realize that historians differ both on the facts to include in a narrative, and on how those facts should be interpreted. Counteracting that tendency requires "a rich variety of historical documents and artifacts that present alternative voices, accounts, and interpretations or perspectives on the past" (National Center for History in the Schools 1996, 10). The foreign language classroom can work in tandem with the history classroom to help students understand the home perspective as one created from within a specific time and place, and to hear other voices that sought to modify or replace the dominant perspective with a new and sometimes dissenting view. In this way, students grow to understand through the subjectification of the perspective that the evidence being presented in any narrative—historical, linguistic, or otherwise—represents a consensus or dominant opinion, not always an unbiased fact.

Finally, connective validity indicates that the theme attends to the realities of global pluralism. If the theme does not relate to internationalization or cultural diversity in some identifiable way, then the connection to the language classroom is likely contrived. The theme of multi-vocal narration, however, most certainly attends to the realities of diversity both at home and abroad. As we pointed out in discussing Merryfield's (1997) work, multiple perspectives provide a key resource for teachers infusing global education into the social studies curriculum. The social studies teacher may lead the class to study broad social studies concepts (e.g., human rights), a specific historical event, current issues, an individual (e.g., Gandhi), or personal experiences (e.g., slaves) from a variety of viewpoints (190–91).

COMPARATIVE INTEGRITY AND THE INTERDISCIPLINARY UNIT

Wong (1993) has noted the following in relation to comparative approaches to literature:

A key instructional means of eliciting insight being comparison and contrast, at every turn we need to decide what to compare a marginalized literature to, and to what end If this is done from a fallacious assumption of one's impartiality, however well-intentioned, the purpose of broadening the curriculum, namely, to honor the articulation of previously suppressed subjectivities, will be seriously undermined. (112)

In a related vein, several scholars have pointed recently to the inclusion of culturally reductionist or misrepresentative elements within language curricula and texts (Brosh 1997; Osborn 1999, 2000; Reagan and Osborn 1998; Wieczorek 1994) and a similar problem in history (Davis 2000; Kolchin 2000). Comparisons of information that is cross-cultural in nature must be evaluated in an attempt to preclude the tendency toward exacerbating cultural divisiveness.

Comparative validity indicates that the unit themes or material include:

1. An *emic*, or insider's, representation of the cultural information;
2. An avoidance of bifurcatious ("we/they," for example), categorization; and
3. Articulation of multiple perspectives within the "home" culture.

These criteria can be addressed within both the history and the language classroom.

The *emic*, or insider's perspective, is essential for a unit theme or activities to possess comparative integrity. No matter how well intentioned, if the classroom activities, discussions, or presentations attempt to act as agent for representing the target cultural perspective, the resultant depictions will likely be both self-serving and reductionist as well as monovocal. As in the case of naturalistic research, it is often difficult to present the *emic*. Nonetheless, integrated and interdisciplinary units should strive for it.

The avoidance of bifurcation relates to establishing "us" and "them" categories. Though seldom so blatant, discussions of the "American" versus "foreign" perspective present the same problem in a language or history class. These categories, obviously, ignore the mosaic of diversity found globally and compromise the educational value of any interdisciplinary unit.

Finally, by noting for students the multiple perspectives within the home and target cultures, curricular planners provide a dialectical understanding of cultural mediation for the students. Simply put, no historical or cultural issue is one-dimensional nor are they monovocal. Tensions and resistance exist in all cultural matters, and exploring such facets with students is centrally important to the integrity of the unit.

VIETNAM AND HISTORY CLASS COMPONENTS

We have crafted an example of an interdisciplinary unit focused on *Multiple Perspectives: Challenging the Monovocal Narrative* which, in the history class, focuses on the conflict between the United States and Vietnam. Ackerman

(1989) has argued that such units include themes which are valid to the individual disciplines involved. Indeed, by examining the mystery of what happened in the Gulf of Tonkin and on the meaning made of the event, one can see the validity of our theme for the history classroom.

The mystery material drawn strictly from typical primary sources is in itself powerful, but the interdisciplinary unit allows classroom teachers to develop a much more interesting and compelling historical problem. The Vietnam War is such a potentially controversial topic that textbooks and school systems have taken very "neutral" approaches to Vietnam; some approaches are so bland that there have been boring classes about the Vietnam War! A mystery approach invites the controversy back in, allowing the students to investigate it, and the contribution from the foreign language classroom provides a rare, multinational perspective that helps explain why the event is so controversial.

There are many mysteries to choose from with Vietnam, but from the perspective of U.S. involvement in a major shooting war, perhaps the clearest place to begin is with the 1964 Gulf of Tonkin incident and the resolution that followed. Although U.S. involvement with Vietnam dates earlier, this is *the* resolution that authorized the American president to directly involve U.S. troops in offensive missions against North Vietnam.

Most textbooks dispense with the Gulf of Tonkin incident in about four sentences. Students learn that in early August 1964 there was North Vietnamese fire on one or two ships in the Gulf of Tonkin, and that despite some doubt about the attack taking place, the Johnson administration used this moment to respond in force, directly attacking North Vietnam with American fire. More significantly, students are told that the attack served as the trigger for a congressional resolution that gave the president a "blank check," in the form of authorization to take "all necessary measures to repel any armed attack against the forces of the United States and to prevent further aggression." Finally, textbooks inform students that the resolution passed the House unanimously and only two senators voted against it; shortly after this Johnson dramatically escalated U.S. involvement in the war.

In a history classroom we present a range of evidence regarding the event and help students determine the facts as they understand them, and construct their own interpretation of the event. The mystery approach makes a good start at challenging the monovocal narrative by replacing an authoritative account with evidence and student interpretations. In this instance, although a North Vietnamese commander does provide one item of evidence, the other eleven are drawn from exclusively American sources. Students review contemporary newspaper accounts of the incident, and official statements about the event.

The first item is a U.S. Navy film. In international waters in the Gulf of Tonkin, destroyers of the U.S. Navy are assigned routine patrols from time to time. On Sunday, August 2, 1964, the destroyer *Maddox* was on such a patrol. Shortly after noon, the calm of the day is broken as general quarters sound. In a deliberate and unprovoked action, three North Vietnam PT boats unleash a torpedo attack against the *Maddox*. At once, the enemy patrol boats are brought under fire by the destroyer. The second item examined in the history class is a statement by U.S. Defense Secretary Robert McNamara, who states, "No, it [the *USS Maddox*] has no special relationship to any operations in that area [North Vietnam]. We're carrying routine patrols of this kind on all over the world all the time."

The third item to be considered in the history class is another part of the U.S. Navy Film. Following the Sunday attack, the *Maddox* is joined by the *U.S.S. Turner Joy*. As directed by the president of the United States, the *Maddox* and *Turner Joy* resume patrol operations in the Gulf of Tonkin. On the night of August 4, North Vietnamese patrol boats strike again. Item four consists of a statement by General Phung The Tai:

On the night of August 4, the United States made public that so-called "Gulf of Tonkin incident." But the story was a fabrication, created by the U.S. National Security Council. Even as the National Security Council met, American aircraft were being sent to destroy several areas of our country. In reality, the second Gulf of Tonkin incident never happened.

The fifth item in evidence is information gleaned from *USS Maddox* and *Turner Joy* deck logs of August 2, 1964. The *Maddox* noted that three enemy (North Vietnamese) vessels approached the ship. The attacks began at 5:08 P.M. Saigon time. At 5:34 P.M. four U.S. aircraft arrived on the scene. Maneuvering to close with the *Maddox*, the USS *Turner Joy* cruised toward the northwest at speeds of twenty-five knots beginning at 4:25 P.M. By 7:28 P.M., the *Turner Joy* sighted the *Maddox*; she was fifteen miles away. The *Turner Joy* sited U.S. aircraft overhead at 7:44 P.M. Item six adds information gleaned from *Maddox* and *Turner Joy* deck logs and action reports of August 4, 1964. The *Maddox*, traveling south out of the gulf, met first three and then four "high speed contacts," at 9:59 P.M. By 12:53 P.M., the *Maddox* was clear of the attackers according to its deck logs. According to the *Turner Joy's* action report, the attack began at 10:35 P.M. The deck logs report that enemy contacts had ceased and the attack was over by 1:22 A.M.

The seventh item is a lack of photographic evidence, since photographic information does not exist for the August 4 attacks. Though no photos are able to be presented, this deficiency does count as historical evidence. Item eight is the radar evidence. The only strong radar contact made that night was at the time the *Maddox* fire control radar locked on the *Turner Joy*. Item nine consists of visual or physical evidence. No members of the crew visually sited any enemy vessels. The ship reported no physical damage.

The tenth evidentiary item includes interrogation reports of captured North Vietnamese Naval crewmen contained in the Seventh Fleet Exploitation Study. Fuel, radar, and navigation limits kept the North Vietnamese navy squadrons' operations area within 106°30′ E longitude (Tourison, 1995).

The eleventh item is official Navy history: The August 4 incident occurred near 108° E longitude. The final item is from naval records. Leaving the port of Keelung with a communications van on board, the *Maddox* was part of the Desoto Patrol program. Sent into the Tonkin Gulf to survey and gather intelligence from North Vietnam and China, the *Maddox* followed a predetermined schedule. The van, maintained by the Naval Security Group, contained electronic equipment used to gather and process Electronic Intelligence (ELINT). Designed to intercept communications and electronic emissions, the Desoto Patrol surveyed the coasts of North Vietnam and China. By emitting certain signals, the *Maddox* could make the North Vietnamese believe she was a force of ships or she could mask herself, deceiving them into thinking no ship was in the area.

Along with the van, a contingent of trained personnel were aboard the *Maddox*. Some personnel were from the Naval Security Group (NAVSECGRU) Taipei and some arrived for duty from NAVSECGRU Philippines. Those from the Philippines were able to understand the Vietnamese language and those from Taipei could translate Chinese.

Within the context of a history class we want students to work from evidence rather than facts. The deck logs of the USS *Maddox* and the USS *Turner Joy* conflict on the times of the attacks, or the times when U.S. planes flew overhead. What facts does this establish? It could mean that keeping accurate logs during combat is difficult, or a low priority. It could mean that these two ships had confused or distracted personnel. One ship could be accurate, or they both could be wrong. Students will have to figure out what "facts" the evidence creates. There are other contradictions. Secretary of Defense Robert McNamara stated that the ship was on routine patrol. The history of the DeSoto Patrols suggests a different conclusion. What are the facts? What is the truth? Historians are not certain that they can recite "the facts" of the incident, so they prefer the term "evidence." History teachers can encourage the students to debate the "facts" that they can derive from all of this material. Since nobody in the West knows with absolute certainty what happened in the Gulf of Tonkin on August 4, 1964 (if there was an attack, then one supposes that the PT boat commanders know it happened, but if there was no attack after all, then even the North Vietnamese command must at least wonder if someone wandered into the path of the ships and fired without orders), the students can reach their own conclusions.

The hope is that a puzzle such as this one gets students used to looking at an event from more than one perspective, and that understanding that truth may not rest entirely within the context of a monovocal narrative, even if presented by their own government. It provides a starting point for an investigation of the meaning of the event. Students could write about numerous related topics, including what does the event mean if there was an attack or what does the event mean if there was no attack?

Though all of the evidence considered to this point has been from American, and thus English language resources, the overarching theme of *Multiple Perspectives: Challenging the Monovocal Narrative* includes possibilities of examining evidentiary sources in other languages as well. This opportunity can become a powerful nexus to language curricula.

LANGUAGE CLASSROOM COMPONENTS

In the foreign language classroom, the teacher can choose to also highlight the Vietnam War as a touchstone. Remembering that it is the theme of *Multiple Voices*, not necessarily the specific mystery presented in the history class, that receives the focus in both classrooms. Nonetheless, depending upon the language abilities of the students, the newspaper accounts of the Gulf of Tonkin events could be given to the students in the target language, in translation, or a combination of the two. These selections satisfy the requirement of connective validity, therefore, through the integration of reading skills. At the same time, the teacher subjectifies the domestic perspective through the presentation of examples both in favor of and in opposition to American intervention. Finally, attention is paid to the global and local realities of pluralism, by including these articles related to the war.

Since Vietnam was formerly a colony of France, French sources are a logical resource, but since war impacts virtually every nation on earth, accounts should be accessible in almost any modern language taught. Students can compare two English language newspapers as they recount the event, the *New York Times* (or *Washington Post* or any other paper) published in America and the *Herald Tribune International* published in Paris. How do these two English language sources regard the event? What about the *Catholic Worker*, or *IF Stones Weekly*? Students can examine French language newspapers from Paris, Saigon, Hanoi, and New York.[2] How do these newspapers view the accounts? Students begin to experience the reality that in some issues, national boundaries do not always become the demarcation points for differences of opinion.

As a result, the criteria of comparative integrity are satisfied in that an *emic*, or insider's, representation of the information becomes evident through the lack of solely national definition to the issues. Vietnamese accounts, even if in translation, could be presented to optimize this effect. An avoidance of bifurcatious categorization is likely since the United States itself was bitterly divided over the war, a point which also naturally achieves the articulation of multiple perspectives within the "home" culture. The language classes can further develop the theme of *Multiple Perspectives* (and move beyond the topic of the Vietnam War) through the use of a number of internal debates within target cultures and countries being studied, or even through the use of literature.

A simple, yet effective approach to using literature in such a unit would be to examine the literary characteristic of the narrative situation. Two types of narration are the first-person and the third-person narrative. The first-person example is seen as a character in the story tells the story. First-person narrations often seem to pull the reader into the story by giving the biases and feelings of a character in the work, and obviously represent that perspective.

However, students commonly have a problem understanding the role of the narrator when studying literature (see, for example, Lazar 1993). To examine the narrative perspective of a literary selection, students could write their own versions written from the standpoint of different characters in the work and then contrast the author's version with their own. If the work being presented has many characters, students can rewrite the story from the perspective of one who is not the narrator of the story. Obviously, with a third-person narrator, students may rewrite the story from the perspective of any character, even if the work contains only one character. These revisions then become the basis for examining multiple perspectives. Cooperative learning groups, for example, could be assigned different characters and the results of each group's work shared, leading to a discussion of the difference in narrative perspective. Additionally, the instructor may choose to have students act out a story, portraying characters that do not appear in the story. One student could play a parent or child of one of the protagonists. The goal here is not to present the story as it actually is. Instead students should be examining the reality of multiple perspectives, in comparison to that of the narrator in the work, by contrasting it with other conceivable perspectives of narration.

The result of teaching narrative perspective in this manner is that the student learns to see the influence a narrator has on the work, rather than simply being able to identify a first- or third-person narrator. Additionally, students begin to see the impact of monovocalism on perception. By encouraging students to challenge the monovocal narrative, then, literature becomes another effective component within the language classroom in an interdisciplinary unit.

CONCLUSION

Contemporary trends in curricular development within history and language can be utilized in complementary approaches to enhance student learning. Gerwin and Zevin's (in preparation) history as mystery approach when combined with Osborn's (in press) approach have demonstrated the potential of such ventures. Language education as part of the core is ultimately more valuable as students and their teachers begin to recognize the nexus among the subjects that they study and teach.

Perhaps one of the ultimate benefits of language study in the school setting can be developing the students' ability to challenge singular, monovocal evaluative discourse. These narrow perspectives are not only hindrances to education in the broadest philosophical sense of the term, but tend to exacerbate misunderstanding within our own nation and in the course of our nation's interactions in a global forum. Interdisciplinary units, likewise, provide students concrete examples of the arbitrary nature of academic delineations in comparison to what we experience as knowledge. Such curricular innovations will, as well, facilitate opportunities for students to develop evaluative frameworks which can incorporate interpretive diversity in appropriate measure. It is just such endeavors that can form one basis of future language curriculum development in the United States.

NOTES

1. See Osborn (in press) for specific qualification of the terms *home* and *target culture*. The term home culture refers in this instance to the specific cultural context of the classroom and school. Target culture refers to the cultural aspects attributable to native speakers of the target language both in the United States and abroad.

2. If local resources permit, the teacher can even decline to identify the sources of the papers, and have the students attempt to identify them based on the tone of the comments. This will direct their attention even more forcefully to the role of the different cultures despite, in spite of, and in conjunction with, the language.

BIBLIOGRAPHY

Ackerman, D. 1989. Intellectual and practical criteria for successful curriculum integration. In *Interdisciplinary curriculum: Design and implementation*, ed. H. Jacobs, 25–38. Alexandria, VA: Association for Supervision and Curriculum Development.

Banks, J. 1997. Multicultural education: Characteristics and goals. In *Multicultural Education*, ed. J. Banks and C. Banks. 3d ed. Boston: Allyn and Bacon.

Biron, C. 1998. Bringing the standards to life: Points of departure. *Foreign Language Annals* 31 (4): 584–94.

Brosh, H. 1997. The sociocultural message of language textbooks: Arabic in the Israeli setting. *Foreign Language Annals* 30 (3): 311–26.

Carr, E. H. 1961. *What is history?* New York: Vintage Books.

Davis, D. B. 2000. Looking at slavery from a broader perspective. *American Historical Review* 105 (2): 452–66.

Davison, D. M., K. W. Miller, and D. L. Methany. 1995. What does integration of science and mathematics really mean? *School Science and Mathematics* 95 (5): 226–30.

Diaz, C., B. Massialas, and J. Xanthopoulos. 1999. *Global perspectives for educators*. Boston: Allyn and Bacon.

Gehlker, M., M. L. Gozzi, and I. Zeller. 1999. Teaching the Holocaust in the foreign language classroom. *Northeast Conference Review* 46: 20–29.

Gerwin, D. and V. Manolios. 1999. Using Stephen Crane's *Maggie* to teach the progressive era. *OAH Magazine of History* 13 (2): 33–35.

Gerwin D. and J. Zevin. In preparation. *History as mystery*.

Giroux, H. A. 1997. *Pedagogy and the politics of hope: Theory, culture and schooling*. Boulder, CO: Westview Press.

Jenkins, K. 1999. *Why history?* London: Routledge.

Kolchin, P. 2000. The big picture: A comment on David Brion Davis's "Looking at Slavery from a Broader Perspective." *American Historical Review* 105 (2): 467–71.

Kramsch, C. 1993. *Context and culture in language teaching.* Oxford: Oxford University Press.

Lazar, G. 1993. *Literature and language teaching: A guide for teachers and trainers.* Cambridge: Cambridge University Press.

Loewen, J. 1995. *Lies my teacher told me.* New York: Simon and Schuster/Touchstone Press.

Lonning, R. A. and T. C. DeFranco. 1997. Integration of science and mathematics: A theoretical model. *School Science and Mathematics* 97 (4): 18–25.

Lonning, R. A., T. C. DeFranco, and T. P. Weinland. 1998. Development of theme-based, interdisciplinary, integrated curriculum: A theoretical model. *School Science and Mathematics* 98 (6): 312–18.

Merryfield, M. M. 1997. Infusing global perspectives into the social studies curriculum. In *The social studies curriculum,* ed. E. W. Ross. Albany: State University of New York Press.

Moore, Z. 1996. Culture: How do teachers teach it? In *Foreign language teacher education: Multiple perspectives,* ed. Z. Moore. Lanham, MD: University Press of America.

National Center for History in the Schools. 1994. *Lessons from history.* Los Angeles: Social Studies School Service.

———. 1996. *Bring history alive! A sourcebook for teaching United States history.* Los Angeles: National Center for History in the Schools/University of California, Los Angeles.

National Council for the Social Studies. 1994. A vision of powerful teaching and learning in the social studies: Building social understanding and civic efficacy. In *Expectations of excellence: Curriculum standards for social studies.* Washington DC: National Council for the Social Studies.

National Council of Teachers of Mathematics. 1991. *Professional standards for teaching mathematics.* Reston, VA: Author.

National Standards in Foreign Language Education Project. 1996. *Standards for foreign language learning: Preparing for the 21st century.* Lawrence, KS: Allen Press.

Nebraska Department of Education. 1996. *Nebraska K–12 foreign language frameworks.* Lincoln, NE: Author.

Novick, P. 1988. *That noble dream.* Chicago: University of Chicago Press.

Osborn, T. A. 1999. Reflecting on *foreignness:* The challenges of a new millennium. *New York State Association of Foreign Language Teachers Annual Meeting Series* 16: 21–24.

———. 2000. *Critical reflection and the foreign language classroom.* Critical Studies in Education and Culture Series, ed. Henry A. Giroux. Westport, CT: Bergin & Garvey.

———. In press. Making connections and comparisons: Integrating foreign language with other core curricula. *NECTFL Review.*

Overfield, D. M. 1997. From the margins to the mainstream: Foreign language education and community-based learning. *Foreign Language Annals* 30 (4): 485–91.

Reagan, T. and T. A. Osborn. 1998. Power, authority, and domination in foreign language education: Toward an analysis of educational failure. *Educational Foundations* 12 (2): 45–62.

Roupp, H., ed. 1999. A jumpstart manual for world history teachers. A collection of articles presented at the Eighth Annual World History Association International Conference, June 27–July 1.

Tourison, Sedgwick. 1995. *Secret army, secret war: Washington's tragic spy operations in North Vietnam.* Annapolis, MD: Naval Institute Press.

Tucker, J. and A. Evans. 1996. The challenge of a global age. In *Critical Issues in Teaching Social Studies K–12*, ed. B. Massialas and J. Allen. Belmont, CA: Wadsworth Publishing.

Weitzman, K. 1996. The relevance of the Tonkin Gulf incidents: U.S. military action in Vietnam, August 1964. A paper presented at the 1996 Vietnam Symposium at Texas Tech: *After the Cold War: Reassessing Vietnam.*

Wieczorek, J. A. 1994. The concept of "French" in foreign language texts. *Foreign Language Annals* 27 (4): 487–97.

Wineburg, S. S. 1991. On the reading of historical texts: Notes on the breach between school and academy. *American Educational Research Journal* 28 (3): 495–519.

Wong, S. C. 1993. Promises, pitfalls, and principles of text selection in curricular diversification: The Asian-American case. In *Freedom's plow*, ed. T. Perry and J. Fraser, 109–20. New York: Routledge.

6

Enabling Teachers Through Type Theory: Nurturing the Pluralistic Persona

A. J. VOGELY

Know thyself . . . know thy learner.
Understand and respect those differences
And teach to them.

INTRODUCTION

The greatest challenge teachers face today is not technology, certification, tenure, peer-evaluation, etc., but the pluralism of the classroom. The traditional demographics of a classroom have been changing and will continue to change, possibly in ways we can not even predict at this moment, and as these changes occur the overall success rate of the students changes as well. Because of many factors, including the different reality of each student, more students are struggling to succeed in the classroom. Too often, when a student doesn't perform in the expected way, it is assumed that the student has a problem. Teachers and administrators tend to view the cause of the problem to be the student's attitude toward learning and authority, or the friends they keep, or the inability to learn. The student is not trying hard enough, not doing X, Y, or Z enough. Too often educators will say, "That kid is impossible. Nothing can be done for him/her." The student, in turn, blames the teacher, who blames the principal, who blames the student, who blames the parents, who blames the system, etc. Failure begets failure and the cycle begins.

This cycle is most troublesome. I believe that neither the teachers nor the students are "bad" or "impossible," nor that one of the two is right and the other is wrong, but that they are lacking a nonjudgmental language with which to express their own perspective and to explore the perspective of the other. In order to break the cycle of failure and blame there needs to be a common "language," shared by administrators, teachers, parents, and students alike, through which these judgments and dichotomies are eliminated. Having a nonjudgmental language with which to discuss troublesome situations would shed light on the "why and wherefore" of the conflict in a way that all might work together to define the "square one" at which everyone must begin in order to work together toward a viable solution to an all too common problem.

DEFINING THE PROBLEM

Although academic failure is a widespread problem, there is no simple, clear-cut explanation of the problem because it goes way beyond one formula of cause and effect. All of the populations involved with a school, which include administrators, staff, teachers, students, and parents, contribute to the problems present in the schools today, and all of those populations need to determine their part in the solution. The piece of the problem and the corresponding solution addressed in this chapter has to do with how can we prepare teachers so that they can understand and effectively communicate with all of tomorrow's learners. Teacher preparation programs will have to expand their focus on content area and teaching methods in order to include not only what is taught and how it should be taught, but who is teaching and how they teach, as well as who is being taught and how they best learn. It is the differences in teaching styles and learner preferences that complicate the situation.

Some teachers work on a conceptual level and spend a lot of class time speculating about, creating, imagining, doing group work on tasks that are not straightforward and leave a lot of room for interpretation. This approach is perfect for students who share the same perceptual dynamics and attitudes, but may not suit the students who need to work alone, need step-by-step instructions and detailed explanations before beginning a task, and struggle to create and speculate. In this case, both the student and the teacher end up frustrated and blame the other for not doing their part. The impact of these opposing approaches to teaching and learning have been the focus of much research that has shown that "those students who share their teacher's style will feel comfortable with the learning environment and corresponding classroom techniques. Learners whose style preference is conspicuously different from the teacher's preference may be plagued by anxiety and respond negatively to the teacher, the classroom, and the subject matter" (Oxford and Lavine 1992, 38). Oxford and Lavine call this conflict "style wars." The ability to teach to those students whose learning style conflicts with your natural teaching style has been, is, and will be a critical area of teacher preparation and teaching practices.

Thankfully, one of the innate characteristics of the brain is the desire to learn, but why does learning happen in some cases and not in others? What would be the most effective basic tool that any teacher could use in a classroom that would help all students learn, including the most challenging students? Is there a universal tool that offers a common language that all teachers could use to discuss a student or a class of students, and to determine instructional solutions they could all agree upon without resorting to negative reactions to express frustration?

A SOLUTION TO THE PROBLEM

While seeking an answer to this question, someone put Gordon Lawrence's book, *People Types and Tiger Stripes,* into my hands. I read it from cover to cover, then read it again. This type theory stuff made all kinds of sense to me. I began to read all that I could get my hands on, and experimented with type theory in my classes. After attending a Myers-Briggs Type Indicator® (MBTI) training session and becoming qualified to administer and interpret the MBTI, it was clear to me how type theory offered the clearest and most consistent guidelines for new teachers to learn about themselves as teachers and their students as learners. I saw type theory as an avenue for talking about teaching methods without judgment.

Traditionally, teachers teach one way, and expect all to learn based on that one approach. Up until now, to question that one way of teaching was totally unacceptable. It has always been up to the student to accommodate the teacher's style, not the other way around. In order to remove the dichotomy of "right vs. wrong," "good vs. bad," "effective vs. ineffective," etc., from the question of *how* to teach, I needed something that would validate the teachers' natural and most comfortable teaching style, which would teach to part of their audience, and would provide tools for them to perfect their "opposite" teaching style, which would reach the other part of their audience. Psychological type theory lent itself perfectly to my needs.

DEFINITION OF TERMS

Enabling vs. Empowering. The first word in the title of this chapter was originally "empower" rather than "enable." The word "empower" was used because of its high frequency use in articles that discuss solutions to the problems faced by teachers in the classroom. These articles talk about the need to empower the teacher to remove a student from a class, to empower the teacher with zero tolerance, and to empower the teacher as the person who would diagnose the readiness and ability of a student for learning. Again, searching for a starting point, I looked up the definition of the word "empower" and determined that it was not truly appropriate for the focus of this chapter. According to Webster, "empower" means "to give official or legal power to"; synonyms included "permit," "authorize," "sanction," and "allow," among others. The word "empower" reflects a top-down approach to solving problems, which puts the teacher in the role of "judge" rather than "arbitrator." A search for the appropriate word brought me to the word "enable." Although the word "enable" has gleaned a less than desirable interpretation in the world of psychology, it better reflects the way in which this chapter approaches the topic. The definition of enable is "to provide with the means or opportunity" and the synonyms of "enable" include the words "capacitate," "facilitate," and "prepare." I decided to reclaim the word "enable" and return to it a positive interpretation.

Teacher preparation programs must be preparing, enabling teachers to teach more, to guide more, and to depend less on control. Quality teachers will know how to enable their students to be responsible learners. But, in order to enable their students, teachers must enable themselves first. I propose that knowledge and practice of psychological type theory can accomplish just that.

Psychological Type Theory. The term "psychological type theory" refers to the work done by Isabel Myers and Katherine Briggs, which was based on the theories of Carl Jung. Although used widely in business and counseling, psychological type theory has yet to make its mark in the field of education. Consequently, few educators, let alone administrators, are familiar with its precepts. When used effectively, it has proven to be a powerful tool in teacher preparation because of the nonjudgmental language it uses to describe a person's way of perceiving and interacting with the world. Unlike traditional programs that support a teaching approach (communicative, direct, natural, audio-lingual, etc.) that may be difficult and unnatural for some, type theory lends itself to discussing a person's natural teaching style based on his or her type dynamics. Thus, the dichotomy of good or bad, effective or ineffective is eliminated, and the teacher, student, administrator, and parent have a "square one" from which to open a line of communication.

Psychological type theory has its roots in the theories of the Swiss psychologist, Carl Gustav Jung (1923). Through his research, Jung was able to define certain dynamics in the human personality, which he referred to as archetypes, that interacted to form predictable patterns of behavior. Each individual person developed these patterns in different degrees through different means but all of the behaviors sprung from the same underlying patterns. The behavior patterns Jung studied were described as opposite preferences and presented two sharply contrasting ways of behaving. Jung called these opposing patterns of behavior *Introversion* (**I**) and *Extraversion* (**E**), *Sensing* (**S**) and *iNtuition* (**N**), and *Thinking* (**T**) and *Feeling* (**F**). It was Meyers and Briggs that eventually added the fourth set of dynamics, *Judging* (**J**) and *Perceiving* (**P**). These behavior patterns were the basis for Isabel Briggs Myer's most important work, the development of the Myers-Briggs Type Indicator (MBTI). The MBTI was designed to determine how these behavioral choices might combine to represent an individual's type by ascertaining a profile of a person's way of perceiving and judging the world. Although their work was originally undertaken to help women involved in the war effort to find jobs they could be good at, Myer's studies soon expanded to assist ordinary people within ordinary, everyday situations. Her goal was to help people discover their natural gifts so that they could be happy in the profession of their choice. To do that, she devised a way to move beyond the old idea that there is one accepted model of a "normal person" and that we are all deviations of that ideal. Her goal was to shift the focus from striving to imitate that "ideal" to recognizing that "each of us is born with different gifts, with unique imprints of how we prefer to use our minds and values and feelings in the business of living everyday" (Myers 1985, xii). Through painstaking work and dedication, and after teaming up with her mother, Katherine Cook Briggs, the MBTI was created.

Nurture. The term "nurture" is defined in this chapter as "training that nourishes the sum of the influences modifying the expression of the genetic potentialities of an organism" (Webster 1984, 812). Jung considered the behaviors driven by type preferences to be innate, in that we are predisposed to particular behavior patterns. Thus the idea of nurturing focuses on tapping into and cultivating the nature of the teacher and the nature of the student as unique individuals.

Pluralistic Persona. The "persona" referred to in the title reflects the role the teacher is called upon to play. Webster's definition calls it "an individual's social façade or front that, especially in the analytic psychology of C. G. Jung, reflects the role in life the individual is playing" (Webster 1984, 877). "Pluralistic" is used to define "persona" because in the classroom a teacher must be able to practice "pluralism" which is defined as "a theory that there are more than one or more than two kinds of ultimate reality; a theory that reality is composed of a plurality of entities" (Webster 1984, 906).

Based on these definitions, another way to state the title would be "Providing Teachers with the Means and Opportunity to Know Who They Are and to Know Who Their Learners Are: Resulting in the Ability to Nourish the Innate Potentiality of Their Own Reality and the Reality of their Learners." In other words, how to use psychological type theory to help teachers to know their own reality, to know their learners' realities, to understand and respect the differences in their realities and to teach to them. How can psychological type theory help us to bring these two realities together?

AN OVERVIEW OF PSYCHOLOGICAL TYPE

The MBTI was originally used, and proven effective, in one-on-one counseling, then expanded into team building, organizational development, training, and career development. Acceptance by the educational community has been slow but steady, as teachers and administrators discover its value. Type theory provides us with a different way of understanding who we are, our reality, and how we interact with the world around us. It forces us into a new way of thinking about and responding to ourselves and the people around us. It also affords us the same perspective of our colleagues, administrators, parents, and, most importantly, our learners. If our goal in the classroom is to teach to all of our learners, psychological type theory must become a foundation for the way teachers think about and design curriculum as well as how they view and interact with their students.

This chapter can not even begin to do that, but it can provide an overview of how type theory applies to the classroom, that is, how these behavioral choices manifest in the way teachers teach and students learn. This will be accomplished by, first, briefly discussing the preferences in general terms and, then, how each preference manifests in the learning environment. In the discussion of the eight dynamics, I will use the following terminology I learned in a workshop with Otto Kroeger, which he created in order to prevent people from interpreting the preferences as personality traits: *Introverted Energizers* and *Extraverted Energizers, Sensing Perceivers* and *INtuitive Perceivers, Thinking Deciders* and *Feeling Deciders,* and *Judging Doers* and *Perceiving Doers.* It is important to remember that the eight dynamics do not represent traits that are measured in strength but mental habits that manifest through a behavior that is measured by degree of clarity for that preference. While reading about the preferences there are two critical perspectives to keep in mind: (1) both behaviors are practiced by everyone, but one of the two is preferred; it is never a question of "either/or"; and (2) the healthy development of these preferences and the resulting behaviors are influenced by environment, as well as other variables.

Introverted Energizers and Extraverted Energizers

The first set of dynamics, which represent the focus of Jung's research, is that of the preference of Introversion, represented by **I**, and Extraversion, represented by **E**. These dynamics indicate the source from which a person seeks their energy. Those with an introverted (from Latin meaning "inner turning") preference find their greatest source of energy within themselves. Those with an extraverted (from Latin meaning "outer turning") preference find their greatest source of energy from the world around them. Within our culture, society sees the extraverted preference as outgoing and assertive, and the introverted preference as shy and withdrawn. In schools, especially in foreign language classes, these preferences are used to evaluate class participation, which can be unfortunate for those students who prefer introversion.

What are the characteristics of a teacher with a preference for Introversion? They focus on the content they are striving to teach through highly structured activities using materials that they select for the students. Their instruction is guided strongly by the structure of the activity and a well-ordered classroom. Tolerance for noise and movement is minimal. Teachers with a preference for Extraversion are more likely to provide students with choices of materials and activities in which the response of the students can change or influence decisions about the activities. With a higher tolerance for noise and movement, group work and class projects are popular.

The learning preferences of a student with a preference for Introversion include think time to formulate an answer, therefore they prefer to volunteer answers after they have been able to think everything through, rather than be called on spontaneously. They prefer to work alone in a quiet space where they can focus their concentration without interruption. Introverted students excel at structured tasks with clear, concise directions, in which they are in complete control. Group work, role-plays, brainstorming, verbal problem-solving, highly supervised tasks, and spontaneous performances are all very trying for the introverted energizer. Often their reluctant class participation is interpreted as lack of knowledge. On the other hand, students with a preference for Extraversion prefer to think out loud and will raise their hands before they have even formulated an answer. They thrive on group work, spontaneity, role-plays, and action-oriented activities where they can share their ideas verbally. For them, hands-on tasks with variety and flexibility is the best way to learn. They have no problem with class participation and can often schmooze their way into the heart of a teacher who prefers extraversion, but often get on the nerves of a teacher who prefers introversion.

Sensing Perceivers and INtuitive Perceivers

These two dynamics represent distinct ways of perceiving and processing information and can provide important clues to the learning styles of the students. The Sensing perceiver, represented by S, focuses on details, the practical, step-by-step, factual information based on experience and perceived through the five senses. With this preference the "eyes tell the mind" (Lawrence 1997, 5). The iNtuitive perceiver, represented by N, focuses on the big picture, concepts, patterns, and possibilities by drawing on the imagination. The iNtuitive perceiver lets "the mind tell the eyes" (ibid). Both typify how we take in and process information, and also have been referred to as analytical and global learners.

The Sensing teacher tends to begin with and focus on details, facts, and concrete skills through activities that offer a narrow range of choices. Their questioning style generally seeks predictable right or wrong answers based on learned and observed facts. When the big picture is absent, the N students do not have the necessary framework into which they can plug the details and facts. The iNtuitive teacher begins with the big picture by emphasizing concepts, relationships, and implications. They often use group work, provide a wide range of choices, and expect independent and creative thinking. Their questioning style seeks synthesis, evaluation, and the students' response to relationships and implications. Often the facts become secondary to the big picture and the S students are left without the basis of observable facts that they need to process the information.

The S student is certainly capable of seeing the big picture, but only after being presented with the specifics in a clear, sequential manner. They are easily confused when confronted with seemingly unconnected bits of information from which they are expected to discover an answer. On the other hand, an **N** student sees information presented in this manner as a challenge to their creativity and original thought and can see quickly associations between the bits of information that appear unconnected to the **S** students. The **N** student thrives on exploration of a topic where inspiration is key, without being confined by facts and details. They will attend to the details only after they have been able to paint the big picture in their minds.

Thinking Deciders and Feeling Deciders

These two dynamics govern the judgment or decision-making process. It is important to note that the terms "thinking" and "feeling" when used in the context of type do not refer to the mind (intellect) and the heart (emotions). Within the arena of type both represent our logical reasoning process that we use to rationalize our decisions. The Thinking deciders, represented by **T**, call upon logic, impersonal criteria and principles, and cause and effect relationships to steer their decision-making process. The Feeling deciders, represented by **F**, call upon human values and motives, personal criteria and principles, and harmony in relationships to steer their decision-making process (Lawrence 1997, 5).

Teachers who are Thinking deciders prefer centralized instruction that focuses unwaveringly on what students are supposed to learn. They present the information through a narrow range of activities that target specific facts, concrete skills, and practical information. Their feedback generally consists of objective input about the correctness of the product, and they rarely comment on the performance of the student. They expect the student to spend most of the class time focusing on whatever the teacher is saying or doing. Quiet and order is a must. Teachers who are Feeling deciders are more likely "to praise, criticize, support and correct, in words and body language" (Lawrence 1993, 75). Decisions about activities and projects are made with the students in mind. They concern themselves not only with what it is the students must learn but how it is the students will interact with the information. The search for harmony between all components of the classroom promotes close relationships between teacher and student, subjective input from the teacher that addresses performance, and a broader range of possible ways of reaching a learning goal.

Before they can engage in active learning, the students that are Thinking deciders will have to know why they have to learn what the teacher is presenting. Not just based on logic, but also based on purpose. Why are we learning this and where does it fit into the scheme of things? These students will be the first to criticize an activity if they do not understand the purpose behind it. Their preference is to remain outside of a situation in order to view it as a detached, uninvolved observer. From that perspective they are able to maintain their objectivity and not become emotionally involved in a situation, which is often seen as being aloof and critical. They seek, and readily offer, feedback that is specific, objective, and leads to the most logical next step. On the other hand, the Feeling deciders will immediately become emotionally involved, especially with issues they care about. Harmony between themselves and their classmates and teacher is of top priority; they will always take into account other people's motives, values, and reactions. Any activity that has a human element, that is, involves personal relationships and addresses something they care deeply about, gives that activity purpose enough for the **F** students. The greatest feedback for them is to feel recognized and appreciated. Once they have been made to feel good about their work, then they can hear suggestions for improvement, but not before.

Judging Doer and Perceiving Doer

These last two dynamics were added by Myers and Briggs after many years of application and revision of the MBTI. These dynamics reflect the way we conduct our outer life and directly impact our organizational skills. The Judging Doers, represented by **J**, are more decisive than curious, and the Perceiving Doers, represented by **P**, are more curious than decisive (Myers 1985, 75). Consequently, the actions of someone with a **J** preference are considered to be focused and purposeful, while the actions of someone with a **P** preference are often considered haphazard and unfocused.

Teachers who are Judging doers are very careful planners. They organize their classes so that they can inform the student in advance when, why, and how changes might occur. The structure is predictable and includes planned flexibility. Their strong need for closure helps them provide students with specific directions that emphasize the product more than the process. The feedback they offer is precise, to the point, and centers on providing the students with a clear idea of where the weaknesses lie. Order is of top priority, which brings with it a low threshold for movement, noise, and socialization. Teachers who are Perceiving doers thrive on movement and noise, and encourage group work in which open-ended discussions and socializing occur. Although capable of planning well-organized lessons, they are ready to deviate at a moment's notice and "go with the flow" of the class dynamics. Because they value spontaneity, they resist being too structured in their directions and will encourage students to step outside the structure in order to explore other possibilities. Their feedback centers just as much on the potential they see in a student's work as in the actual work done.

Students who are Judging doers share the love of order and structure. They want to know at any moment why they are doing what they are doing and where it is leading them, as well as how they are to accomplish the task. Their need for closure motivates them to begin a project immediately and to finish it promptly, usually ahead of schedule. They rarely do things casually, without a purpose, and expect everything they do to count as something. They can never get enough feedback because it is the one thing that keeps them right on track with the assignment. Without the teacher's feedback they can spend a lot of energy fretting about doing something unnecessary. Exploration and discovery have their place only when doing research on a specific topic for a specific project. Having the end product in their hands is their goal, the process of getting there is secondary.

On the other hand, students that are Perceiving doers love the process so much that they can easily get lost in the exploration of a topic. Their natural curiosity will generate more questions than answers and will make selection of a specific topic very difficult. As well, they will struggle with deadlines and will need help staying on task, although some of them do their best work when under pressure. They will rebel against any punitive pressure and will resist compliance by withdrawing silently or reacting rebelliously. For them, the process is more important and fulfilling than the product.

Table 6.1 serves to summarize the information just presented. Remember that the information has been greatly simplified here in order to assist the reader in grasping the concepts behind type theory. As you compare the list of characteristics, consider a preference that you can relate to as a learner and think about teachers you might have had that represented your same preferences and those that represented your opposite preferences. How did your attitude toward those two teachers differ?

These descriptions only scratch the surface of psychological type. People are much more complex than a simple list of characteristics. With the four-letter type there is a preferred or dominant function and an auxiliary function, one of which will be extraverted, the other of which will be introverted. The other two functions become the tertiary and the inferior processes. All of them interact with each other in different ways at different times, depending on the external stimulus. Together they represent a relatively predictable pattern of behavior. Although complex, type theory provides one of the clearest windows into the way people perceive and judge the world around them. How would this body of knowledge translate into a teacher preparation program? For lack of other models, the next section will explain how I have successfully used type theory in a methodology course.

PSYCHOLOGICAL TYPE IN TEACHER PREPARATION

In order to incorporate psychological type into a teacher preparation program so that it becomes a way of thinking, it is necessary to go beyond just learning about it. The preprofessional teachers will need to practice with it, apply it, and revisit it constantly throughout their courses. Consequently, the entire first semester focuses on the exploration of the teacher and the learner through psychological type theory; only in the second semester does the methodology course begin to center on the content area, in this case, foreign languages. Once the preprofessional teachers are comfortable with positive

Table 6.1
Overview of Type Characteristics

Introverted Energizer	Extraverted Energizer	Sensing Perceiver	INtuitive Perceiver	Thinking Decider	Feeling Decider	Judging Doer	Perceiving Doer
Teacher							
"inner turning"	"outer turning"	"the eyes tell the mind"	"the mind tells the eyes"	seeks order	seeks harmony	careful planners	nonchalant planners
focus on content	focus on process	narrow range of choices	wide range of choices	focuses on skill and information	focuses on needs of students	does everything with purpose	sees possibilities everywhere
prefers structure	prefers choices	seeks answer based on learned facts	seeks creative answer based on implications	gives feedback on correctness first then performance	gives performance feedback first then on correctness	pursues closure	postpones closure
low tolerance for noise	high tolerance for noise					prefers defined projects	prefers open-ended projects
Student							
thinks silently	thinks out loud	needs facts presented before seeing big picture	needs big picture presented first then can plug in facts	focuses on the "why"	focuses on the "who"	needs to know *what* and *why* before beginning task	prefers to discover purpose once task is underway
rarely volunteers	volunteers readily	clear sequence critical	prefers to figure out sequence	critical observer	active participant	finishes projects ahead of time	struggles with deadlines
prefers thinking tasks	prefers action task	seeks practicality of topic	seeks inspiration from topic	needs specific objective for learning	needs personal reason for learning	predictable	unpredictable
rarely spontaneous	embraces spontaneity			seeks logic and honesty	seeks recognition and praise	plans procrastination	procrastinates easily

and negative manifestations of type and are well-versed in brain-based learning theory, both of these bodies of knowledge are applied to the concept of classroom management. We must never lose sight of the fact that what occurs within a classroom is dependent upon the dynamics between human beings, each with their own set of preferences and realities.

I use three different instruments to determine the type of each of my students: (1) the MBTI, (2) Gordon Lawrence's (1993, 2–4) self-profile, and (3) the set of overhead transparencies called "*Looking at Type*" by Earle Page (1997). This process begins with an activity I learned during my MBTI Qualifying Training that is done to sensitize my students to what is meant by "preferences." First, they write their name with their dominant hand and describe how it felt. A list is compiled and always contains words like "natural," "comfortable," "effortless," and "unconscious." Then I ask them to write their name with their nondominant hand and to describe how it felt. Invariably, the list we compile contains the words "unnatural," "uncomfortable," "difficult," and "requires conscious effort." Then, after recognizing that the degree of effort needed to write with the nondominant hand varied from person to person, I ask if there was anyone who was absolutely incapable of writing their name with their nondominant hand. No one raises their hand because they were all capable of accessing that skill. I relate that to the eight preferences. Although we are able to engage in all eight behaviors, we are more comfortable with one or the other.

Before distributing the MBTI, I ask them to sit back and close their eyes and imagine themselves putting on all of the hats that their lives require them to wear. Once they have the hats on, they imagine themselves removing one hat at a time. They must remove the mother hat, the significant other or spouse hat, the teacher hat, the sibling hat, the boss hat, the student hat, the roommate hat, and any other hat that is relative to them. They must imagine themselves without any of those hats on their heads influencing their way of thinking, and see themselves through their dominant hand, that is, picture who they are when they feel comfortable and natural. I then distribute the MBTI and, keeping the writing activity in mind, ask them to answer the questions as their "hatless" self with their dominant hand. Once everyone has completed the MBTI, it is collected and scored, and individual four-lettered type is recorded on the "Type Report Sheet." Their assignment is to complete the exercise on the beginning pages of *People Types and Tiger Stripes* by Gordon Lawrence (1993) in order to determine what he calls their "pattern of mental habits" (1).

The students come to the next class having determined their "pattern of mental habits." I begin the class with a set of transparencies (Page 1997) that go through all of the preferences with pictures and statements, and have the students record their preferred way of perceiving, thinking, and deciding, ultimately representing those preferences with the appropriate four-letter type. I then distribute the report forms with the type indicated by the MBTI and explain how to interpret them. They then compare the results of all three instruments. I briefly meet with each student to determine if they concur with the four-lettered type indicated by the three instruments and address any confusion they might have. The rest of the class is dedicated to guided exploration of the different types and their characteristics, as well as the significance of the dynamics of the functions (dominant, auxiliary, tertiary, and inferior).

Once my students understand the concepts of type theory and can speak the "language" of type, they can explore their "natural" teaching style and can compare and contrast different teaching styles within a nonthreatening construct. This kind of exploration opens the doors for dialogues about the very heart of diversity and promotes understanding and validation for each student and teacher as individuals and as a part of the collective dynamic of a classroom. The question of "right vs. wrong," "good vs. bad" and "ineffective vs. effective" are removed from the discussion of how we teach and how we learn. They also begin to understand the concept of "style wars." By understanding the behavioral preferences that cause conflicts in style, teachers can design lessons and activities that minimize those conflicts. The language of type theory validates a teacher's natural, most comfortable teaching style, and provides the knowledge and tools needed to perfect the "opposite" teaching style. When a teacher, or anyone else, begins to nurture their pluralistic persona, their ability to understand and to communicate with other people increases. How does this fit into the foreign language classroom?

TYPE THEORY AND FOREIGN LANGUAGE TEACHING

The basic nature of the foreign language classroom sets it apart from most other content-area classes in that it actively targets four skill areas: listening, speaking, reading, and writing. This skill-based focus provides students with the unique opportunity to learn how they learn, as well as new strategies they can employ to enhance that learning. The foreign language teacher is in the position to facilitate students' knowledge about the learning process in general, and their own way of learning in particular. Type theory provides a powerful tool for the teacher in that they can design lessons and tasks that address those varied preferences and can apply them in all four skill areas. Knowledge of type preferences also promotes fairer evaluation of students. Let's consider briefly the evaluation of the speaking skill as an example.

The communicative approach has long been a popular method of teaching foreign languages. This approach emphasizes verbal communication in a target language first and correctness of grammar second. INtuitive perceiving teachers embrace this approach because it views language as a system with which to communicate ideas, rather than a system of specific rules. Often teachers who embrace this approach do not provide enough specific rules and step-by-step application of those rules needed by the Sensing perceiving students in order to participate comfortably in a communicative task. The opportunity to experiment verbally with the language will excite the **N** students and frustrate the **S** students. This happens in reverse with a teacher who is a Sensing perceiver and emphasizes knowledge of the rules before communication. The **S** students will be in their element and the **N** students will feel bogged down by details. Both **S** and **N** teachers will have to give equal time to connecting the rules of language use to the context of the communicative task in order to develop speaking skills in both **S** and **N** students. If these different preferences are not accommodated, in the end, the **N** student will continue to take risks and say more, but with more errors, and the **S** students will avoid taking risks and say less, but with fewer errors. Clearly both can not be evaluated in exactly the same way.

Teachers who are Extraverted energizers value spontaneous verbalization and often base their class participation grade on the number of times a student volunteers to speak. What happens to those students that are Introverted energizers? Often **E** teachers press them to speak before they are ready and then incorrectly interpret their silence. This translates into a low participation grade. The irony is that, although not participating outwardly, the **I** students are furiously participating inside their heads. On the other hand, teachers who are Introverted energizers have difficulty appreciating the **E** student's need to process the language out loud and often interpret their verbalizations as idle talk (which it is sometimes). In order to evaluate fairly both **E** and **I** students, both the **E** and **I** teachers need to accommodate both preferences, by providing both private and public practice opportunities before beginning a speaking task.

These are but a few examples of how type theory impacts the foreign language classroom. The bottom line is that all types represent a valid perspective from which to perceive and judge the world. Just because we don't share behavioral choices with certain students does not make us right and them wrong. In order to discover their true potential, students must recognize their unique perspective and accept it as their own. As teachers, we need to recognize their unique perspectives as well before we can begin to enable them as responsible learners. The same applies to administrators and parents. This is the "square one" that is accessible to all who are capable of seeing beyond their own narrow view of the world. With type language I believe that we could have those dialogues in which all parties would begin to recognize their contribution to the problems facing education today and could begin to formulate their active contribution to the solutions.

CONCLUSION

As anything valuable and worthwhile, learning about type takes time, energy, and risk, and presents a body of knowledge that must be expanded upon daily. It does not represent a quick fix or a panacea for all classroom problems, nor is it a neat package that can be opened and closed at will. In order to use it effectively, teachers and administrators, as well as those who prepare teachers, must be trained and qualified to administer and interpret the MBTI. With practice and application, this tool can eventually become second nature.

My experience with using type theory in teacher preparation has convinced me that it can equip new teachers with the kinds of tools they will need to teach effectively in tomorrow's schools, and can provide them with the knowledge they will need to develop the kind of curriculum that will teach to all of the various learning styles represented by any group of students. Armed with this knowledge of themselves and others, these teachers are equipped to not only challenge but to lead the offense against the "style wars" by rising to the challenges of the pluralistic classroom and making a long-lasting difference.

ADDITIONAL SUGGESTED READINGS

DiTiberio, J. K. and G. H. Jensen. 1995. *Writing and personality: Finding your voice, your style, your way.* Palo Alto, CA: Davies-Black Publishing.

Ellison, L. 1993. *Seeing with magic glasses.* Arlington, VA: Great Ocean Publishers.

Fairhurst, A. M. and L. L. Fairhurst. 1995. *Effective teaching, effective learning: Making the personality connection in your classroom.* Palo Alto, CA: Davies-Black Publishing.

Kroeger, O., with J. M. Thuesen. 1992. *Type talk at work: How the 16 personality types determine your success on the job.* New York: Dell Publishing.

Mamchur, C. 1993. *A teacher's guide to cognitive type theory and learning style.* Alexandria, VA: Association of Supervision and Curriculum Development.

Tieger, P. and B. Barron-Tieger. 1997. *Nurture by nature.* New York: Little, Brown and Company.

BIBLIOGRAPHY

Jung, C. G. 1923. *Psychological types.* New York: Harcourt Brace.

Kiersey, D. and M. Bates. 1984. *Please understand me: Character and temperament types.* 2d ed. Del Mar, CA: Prometheus Nemesis Book Company.

Lawrence, G. D. 1993. *People types and tiger stripes.* 3d ed. Gainesville, FL: Center for Applications of Psychological Type, Inc., 1993.

———. 1997. *Looking at type and learning styles.* Gainesville, FL: Center for Application of Psychological Type, 1997.

Myers, I. B., with P. B. Myers. 1985. *Gifts differing.* Palo Alto, CA: Davis-Black Publishing.

Myers, I. B. and M. H. McCaulley. 1985. *Manual: A guide to the development and use of the Myers-Briggs Type Indicator.* Palo Alto, CA: Consulting Psychologists Press.

Oxford, R. L. and R. Z. Lavine. 1992. Teacher-student style wars in the language classroom: Research insights and suggestions. *Association of Departments of Foreign Languages* 23 (2): 38–45.

Page, E. C. 1997. *Looking at type: A description of the preferences reported by the Myers-Briggs Type Indicator.* 3d ed. Gainesville, FL: Center for Application of Psychological Type.

Quenk, N. L. 1993. *Beside ourselves: Our hidden personality in everyday life*. Palo Alto, CA: Consulting Psychologists Press.

———. 1996. *In the grip: Our hidden personality*. Palo Alto, CA: Consulting Psychologists Press.

Webster, M. 1984. *Webster's ninth new collegiate dictionary*. Springfield, MA: Merriam-Webster Inc.

7

Professional Renewal: The Role of Teacher Education in Multicultural America

TERRY A. OSBORN AND JACQUELINE DAVIS

Almost four decades ago Queens College of the City University of New York was the site of an innovative program designed to prepare teachers who would work in public schools with students who were "culturally deprived" (Downing et al. 1965). These teachers were in the Building Resources for Instruction of Disadvantaged Groups in Education (BRIDGE) Project to learn enhanced skills in the use of technology (primarily audiovisual equipment), reading instruction, and activity development. The program reflected one major approach to the crisis in urban education, the utilization of teacher education programs to improve education (Weiner 1993). Student teachers were advised that they would "learn more about teaching children who are handicapped because of their impoverished backgrounds" and were given suggestions for "working with culturally deprived children," including an admonition to "remember that their background of general information is meager," and to "never show that you are shocked or that you are afraid" (Storen and Edgar 1963, 59).

One assumption behind the BRIDGE Project was that there existed a significant gap between the advantages of the teachers and the disadvantages of the school children. Today, we acknowledge a similar gap, typically that between the cultural background of teachers and students, and indeed attempt to help teachers recognize this fact (though rejecting the qualitative characterizations of the past) through early field placements, the utilization of professional development models, stressing constructivist teaching methods, and reflective practice. As Weiner (1993) notes:

Just as doctors need to know how to apply epidemiological findings to clinical practice, to understand their usefulness and limitations, teachers need to understand how cultural, gender, and class differences pose risks to students and how using a range of teaching strategies can improve their chances of academic success. . . . While *all* teachers will be more effective if they know how to teach students of varying abilities and sensibilities, it is critical for the achievement of poor, minority students that their teachers have this capacity to reflect on and adapt their practice. When teaching occurs in urban classrooms, the need for preparation that develops this capability increases exponentially because school policies and structures discourage it. (112–13)

In all disciplines, these concerns are well warranted. However, it is in the field of foreign language education where these differences begin to be altered in significant ways. When language becomes the focus of the discussion, for example, the cultural similarities and differences between the students may not be as pronounced as suspected. For example, at the teacher training schools in Queens in 1928, over half of the candidates spoke two or more languages other than English, and more than two-thirds were from homes where parents were born outside the United States (Rousmaniere 1997). Over time, New York has been melting pot, salad bowl, or mosaic—but it has always included speakers of non-English languages in significant numbers. As these speakers have entered the teaching corps, the question of appropriate preparation is still of concern. More pressing, however, than the differences between prospective teachers and the students, may be the need to evaluate efforts in promoting a sense of ownership in the profession within the teacher corps we graduate. To the point, the future of foreign language education in the United States rests largely in the hands of its practitioners. As the demographics of that group continue to change and reflect increasing diversity, the largely elitist framework upon which the field is founded will be rightfully challenged. At the heart of these struggles will be the profession's new owners: the teachers.

In this chapter, we will explore the exigencies of inculcating professional renewal in a foreign language teacher education program in a highly diverse setting of the United States. The foreign language education programs in the Department of Secondary Education and Youth Services, Queens College, City University of New York consist of an undergraduate minor, a postbaccalaureate certificate program for those who already hold a liberal arts degree, and a Master of Science in Education program. From Fall 1998 through Spring 2001, we were codirectors of the programs.[1] There were approximately fifty students pursuing degrees in the program, making it one of the largest in the state. The demographics are, as one might suspect, reflective of the diversity in Queens and on Long Island.

TOWARD A CRITICALLY REFLECTIVE PRACTICE

Language teaching is a political act. Though the irrefutable nature of the endeavor lends credence to such a claim, it has only been lately that scholars of language education, notably Auerbach (1995), Brosh (1993), Kramsch (1993), Osborn (2000), Pennycook (1995), Reagan (1997a, 1997b), Skutnabb-Kangas (1988) and Tollefson (1995) have brought the issues under closer scrutiny. The growing body of evidence has led to an increased understanding that not only education in general is cultural mediation (see Apple 1996; Giroux 1997), but more specific to our unique educational sphere there exist inherent sociocultural and sociopolitical contests.

Perhaps nowhere is the power-imbued aspect of language teaching more apparent than the exceptionally diverse locale of Queens. Students at the college speak sixty-seven native languages in a community where over 120 different languages can be claimed as native. Though teachers of language in largely linguistically homogeneous areas of the United States may be able to avoid confronting power-based mediative activities, in our context such a "luxury" is impossible. Simple questions related to such topics as the "real" variety of language, vocabulary choices, immigration and cultural representation, and so on are typically questioned by students—whose knowledge may well surpass that of the teacher in many cases—and occasionally even openly challenged. This need not lead to an adversarial framework among teachers and students. Critically reflective practitioners can effectively navigate the waters of such classrooms with positive educational outcomes.

Reagan, Case, and Brubacher (2000), drawing on Van Manen (1977) and Irwin (1987), have explored three levels of reflective practice:

At this first level, reflection entails only the appropriate selection and use of instructional strategies and the like in the classroom. The second level involves reflection about the assumptions underlying specific classroom practices, as well as about the consequences of particular strategies, curricula, and so on. . . . Finally, the third level of reflectivity (sometimes called *critical reflection*) entails the questioning of moral, ethical, and other types of normative criteria related directly and indirectly to the classroom. (22)

Brookfield (1995), as well, provides a description of critical reflection that is useful in regard to foreign language classrooms:

Critical reflection is inherently ideological. It is also morally grounded. It springs from a concern to create the conditions under which people can learn to love one another, and it alerts them to the forces that prevent this. Being anchored in values of justice, fairness, and compassion, critical reflection finds its political representation in the democratic process . . . [encouraging] us to create conditions under which each person is respected, valued, and heard. (26–27)

Developing these skills in potential foreign language teachers consists of three components, the first of which is the expansion of knowledge into what Lippi-Green (1997) has termed the linguistic facts of life (for related issues, see also Andrews, 1997):

• Spoken languages change over time;

- Spoken languages are equal in linguistic terms;
- Grammaticality and communicative effectiveness are independent issues; and
- Variation is intrinsic to all spoken language. (10–29)

Second, teachers are introduced to the process of critical reflection. As Osborn (2000) explains:

Critical reflection involves challenging the boundaries of our educational thought and practice and rearranging or dissecting the constructs that we employ in an effort to understand the relations of power which underlie them. It is ideological and moral, yes, but it is also disquieting. Critical reflection should not result in lengthy, complex lists of the essential or base elements of equitable praxis in the foreign language classroom, but ideally should lead us to discover that the parameters of our theory and practice, our curriculum and instruction, our language and culture are inherently *context dependent*. The aspects of this context include social, cultural, political, economic, historical, and other categories associated with the interaction of human beings within a society. (66)

As a process, critical reflection involves analyzing behaviors or problems in the classroom with an eye toward explaining both pedagogical and power-based reasons for their existence. As teachers begin to see the nature of language teaching as cultural mediation, they move away from cultural misrepresentation, reductionism, and an inculcation of "foreignness" ideological constructs in the minds of their students (see also Reagan 1997b).

Finally, teachers grow from their skills in critical reflection to develop abilities in macrocontextualization. Again, Osborn (2000) explains:

Macrocontextualization is the process of planning and implementing language instruction by incorporating the local political, economic, and cultural factors relating to linguistic diversity with the intent of developing students' skills in understanding the role that language plays in society. Beyond current goals of simply developing marginal skills in the language, students acquire an awareness of how language issues function in their society to both empower and discriminate against various segments of people. (114)

Macrocontextualization encompasses curriculum development, instructional delivery, and ultimately evaluation as teachers learn to apply the insights afforded by critical reflection in the classroom.

One goal of critical reflection in language teacher education programs is emancipatory praxis (see, for example, Giroux 1997; Wink 2000). Emancipatory praxis assumes that teaching itself becomes a type of political activism. Certainly with the mandates of increasing central control in education, the ownership of the profession will be polarized. On the one hand, bureaucrats at some unseen top level will have significant control of the language educational plan and evaluation through standards and standardized tests. At the same time, however, teachers will continue to exercise the time-honored power described in their common adage, "When the classroom door closes, *I* am in charge." That sentiment is, in fact, a desired component when teachers are owners of the profession.

ACTION RESEARCH

Action research is a tool that has a wide variety of functions within education, sociology, and other social sciences. These functions range from activity that seeks to further democratic ideals from a critical perspective focused on societal issues at large, to more local and immediate issues in the classroom. Action research is readily usable by the student teacher, the novice teacher, the classroom teacher, as well as by higher education faculty. We will provide some overarching themes and practical applications in this section of the chapter for the public school language teacher or graduate student practitioner, and we hope to provide some ideas applicable to higher education faculty working in language teacher preparation.

Action research is both a formal and an informal way to address and examine problems in teaching or practice. It is additionally a research method that has been used for academic publications as well as a practical solution to making improvements in agriculture and industry, and for making constructive change to benefit the members of targeted groups (Noffke 1997). Action research may also fall under the broader umbrella terms of practitioner or participant research (see Jarvis 1999; Punch 1998).

While action research is a research methodology and a formal and informal way of addressing a problem in teaching, it is also much more. The Educational Research Information Clearinghouse (ERIC) thesaurus defines action research as "research designed to yield practical results that are immediately applicable to a specific situation or problem" (as quoted in Noffke 1997, 309). Drawing on Corey (1953), an early pioneer of action research, Noffke (1997) described it as "research that is undertaken by educational practitioners because they believe that by so doing they can make better decisions and engage in better action . . . [the] focus was on learning, which is central to knowledge production, but this was coupled with a strong emphasis on *doing*. The profession of teaching involved understanding one's work, but in order to *act* on that knowledge" (317). Noffke provides a review of action research literature looking at the dimensions from personal to professional and even political, asserting that action research is many things depending on the traditions and contexts from and in which it evolved, including:

- a technique for use in teacher education;
- a staff and professional development strategy;
- a springboard for societal change;
- an addition to the knowledge base by teachers;
- a collaborative effort between teachers and outside "experts";

- an effort to improve teaching practice; and
- a political agenda to bring about change for equality and democracy.

Carson and Sumara (1997), on the other hand, define action research as a "living process," or a process approach that ties into practice. What makes action research unique is the realization that this type of research interacts with elements of who and what we are as well as with what we do. While most research methodologies and techniques carry the assumption and expectation that the researcher will remain detached and objective, action research encourages the researcher to be a participant and to grow and develop as the subjects do in a study.

The traditional view of research, though, is that it is usually passed along in the form of a published report. The finished report rarely includes in-depth information about the research conditions because such analysis is not usually perceived as useful. Such conditions are part and parcel of what is meant by the living process (Carson and Sumara 1997). As public school teachers, we remember sensing that many quantitative published reports on foreign language teaching were not relevant to us because we did not work with subjects, rather we worked daily with five groups of between twenty and thirty-five individuals. Not one of these students was necessarily under control, much less part of a control group. Statistical relevance had no relevance to our classrooms, and what was an alpha factor anyway?

The teacher who reflects on ways to make the language come alive or to develop alternative assessments that will both challenge and motivate his or her students is engaged continually in a kind of action research as a living practice. Teachers who bring authentic menus in Spanish or German, for example, to share with the class or who struggle to make their courses meaningful to the heritage learners in the class are living their practice. The French teacher who brings in information from other Francophone countries to represent the wide diversity of French, who takes care to acknowledge the culture and language variety of the Haitian student in the group of nonnative speakers of French, is living practice. The Italian teacher who returns to the country of her ancestors in the summer so that she can improve and enrich her already deep understanding of the country is living her practice when she brings it back into the classroom.

As teacher educators, we are also action researchers. We are constantly alert for information, materials, research reports, helpful web sites, and ideas that we can apply to our own teaching practice or share as resources for our teacher candidates. Terry, for example, adapted a noncompetitive theme of the television show "Survivor" into a graduate course on communities of inquiry. We continually bounced ideas and concerns between each other. We shared our unique experiences and areas of expertise. We discussed ways to challenge our students meaningfully, given the context of their lives here in New York City as parents, wives and husbands, students, teachers, commuters, family members, immigrants, or as second-generation or even fifth-generation Americans.

Action research is a powerful tool for professional ownership as some accept that not only the conclusions of research are important aspects of knowledge generation and intellectual practices, but that the path of reaching those conclusions is particularly relevant to other practitioners. The details involved, the context of the research setting, and the "specific relational organization of one's living conditions" (Carson and Sumara 1997, xvi) are part and parcel of action research. It is the details of the setting, the context of the teacher and the students, that make action research particularly empowering, professionally renewing, as well as contributory to knowledge in the field. Now let's focus on *doing* action research.

Action research, again, can address a wide variety of concerns. This section is limited to its use to approach classroom teaching practice. Examples will be provided from our work in formal and informal situations, as well as examples in general to provide a clearer explanation of the practice. Action research begins with a concern, a problem, or a question about teaching practice. The action researcher then gathers data to research the problem. It is a cyclical process consisting of research, action, and evaluation, followed by additional research.

Action research problems have a broad range on the continuum from university researchers bringing about change in the student teaching practicum and creating publishable reports of their research findings, to student teachers trying to determine the best way to motivate students to study for a series of tests. Methods of disseminating action research range from academic journal publication (see, for example, Yamada and Moeller 2001), book publication, sharing the findings at a professional conference, or sharing findings with the cooperating teacher, other student teachers, or in the student teaching seminar. Action research can also be done by two or more collaborating teachers or by university researchers working in collaboration with public school teachers (Anderson and Herr 1999). The goal of action research is to bring about change in teaching practice, assessment structure, or curriculum (Richards and Lockhart 1996). Anderson and Herr (1999) state, "The most powerful practitioner research studies are those in which the practitioners recount a spiraling change in their own and their participants' understandings" (16).

One example illustrating this process is from prior work that Jacqueline conducted with Joan Kelly Hall at the University of Georgia. Hall and Davis (1995) realized that some student teachers and cooperating teachers of Spanish developed good relationships and some did not. Those relationships were very important to the student teachers that talked about them. They began the study by asking, "What kinds of relationships do student teachers and cooperating teachers develop?" With those findings they spiraled into the next year studying the question, "How can we help participants develop more meaningful relationships?" These findings were incorporated into their student teaching supervision. They presented both studies at professional conferences together, including one panel presentation incorporating the cooperating teachers and student teachers. They also published their findings. The cooperating teachers in the study became more involved in the program and regular meetings were instituted between cooperating teachers and supervisors, as well as whole group meetings that included the student teachers. These meetings remained an important element of the student teaching experience in the following years. These studies had a significant impact on all the participants and all involved in that study grew and changed.

THE CRITICAL ACTION RESEARCHER

When one sets out to conduct action research, the data collected can be as complex and formal as recording and transcribing classroom talk, to examining the discourse patterns that are in effect, or to administering a simple survey. Other data can come from conducting interviews with students or other teachers. It can be more introspective data such as writing journal entries following a particularly trying class and then examining those entries critically and reflectively. As teacher educators, we continually think of ways to improve teaching by making the courses more relevant to the students. Both of us, for example, routinely asked students for anonymous written feedback at varying points in the semester. This provides a window into the students' perceptions of the course and the teaching. Student complaints and positive comments provided data to evaluate, such as the way the course was structured, for example, not enough lecture or too much lecture, not enough group work or too much group work, not enough graded assignments or too many time-consuming assignments.

The teacher then reflects on their comments and may choose to make some adjustments in terms of reduced or refocused assignments up to even adjustments in percentages of the grade reflecting the time that the students are putting into one assignment. The teacher may explain to the students why certain elements were included in the course that they perhaps did not value. In at least one case, this was followed by a class discussion that aired some concerns and clarified elements that they were not convinced were important. While not all students were convinced that some of these elements were important, it was interesting that they became less resistant and more cheerful about doing them. This process will be continued in future teaching. The professor realized that the students did have valid insights and interests in the time they were devoting to preparing assignments and the students realized their opinions were important to adjustments in the course. In contrast, the student evaluations at the end of the semester during the first year provided information on how the teaching went, but did not help to make *changes* that would improve the ongoing semester.

After examining the data, the action researcher determines a course of action in light of the information gathered. This action, or critical activism, can indeed involve a number of modifications to curriculum, instructional delivery, evaluation, or all three. The guiding objective for determining the course of action involves not only an improvement on practice, but an orientation toward *praxis*. Emancipatory practice, or *praxis*, as critical pedagogues describe it, is appropriate given the contextual components of language education in a highly diverse setting such as Queens. The importance of returning the ownership for curriculum development to the teachers, taking into account the demographic shifts and growing awareness of the enriching qualities of diversity, is perhaps best understood in terms of the larger, global context in which it resides. As Martel (2000) points out,

there is a sense today that ideas, institutions, and political structures resting on the vertical [hierarchical] axis represent a deficit model of human organisation. Largely products and constructs of the Western world and of its political culture, like the Nation-State, products exported with Western Europe's historical world-wide displacement of its internal competitions and wars, they are not adapted to meet the budding axial shift [to collaborative/horizontal frames]. They are not structures based on peace and sharing. On the contrary, they are based on competition and even warfare. Languages, as markers of civilisations and communities, as instruments of communications, as processes of understanding are tributary and makers of ideologies. (154)

Since schools are examples of those institutions and curricula, tests, and similar components are products, we recognize that failing to bring in the practitioner's voice in a setting such as ours is, in effect, a form of psychological violence that, at a symbolic level, strives to invalidate their own experiences and perceptions. In other words, the deficit model Martel describes above, the foreignness agenda described by Osborn (2000), and the contemporary models of top-down curriculum development do much more than simply deskill the teacher (see Apple 1995). Insidiously, the systems of foreign language teacher education currently practiced attempt to replace the voice of practitioner experience with ideologically-constructed systems of official knowledge. Moreover, such activity takes place in the context of the most personal and fundamental of expressive media—language.

The action stage in terms of our praxis has included the codification of the students' own experiences in language education through the writing of language-learning biographies. We have encouraged teacher-candidates to examine their own stories, and to reflect on the stories of their students. We encourage them to challenge ideologically-based concepts such as the standard language myth, and to hypothesize possible approaches to incorporating previously marginalized voices in the language classroom. Our teacher-candidates have responded, for example, by proposing the literary works of native L2 speakers in the United States. These voices in the classroom allow for the language learning context to be about so much more than the "nuts and bolts" of linguistic code.

Following the action, the researcher then evaluates to see if there was the expected or hoped-for change. It is dynamic and the researcher is invested in the outcome. In terms of our own practice, we have noted evidence that the teachers are encouraged and empowered by the approaches we are using. Terry, for example, has authored a book that describes a process of critical reflection in language teaching. Jacqueline used this book as a text in a graduate curriculum course whose enrollment primarily consists of practicing teachers.

The students in her course were engaged in discussion of the reading material and reported that it relates to their life experiences as teachers, as nonnative speakers of English, and as students in the U.S. school system. They also reported that it ties into some suspicions they have held about the conditions under which they are expected to teach language. One student, for example, shared that she never learned her native language after migrating to the United States, due to her parents' concern that she would speak English with an accent and have difficulties integrating into the society.

Within the first two classes, these students were enthusiastic about beginning research papers applying critical reflection to a topic they had passion about. In this course, they wrote a literature review of their topic. In the following semester in their research course, they conducted action research on the same topic. The topics proposed included special education and foreign language, and gender expectations for language learning.

We, of course, recognize that another phase in the continuing research process is to disseminate the information gleaned. After completing parts of the action research, sharing the results and the process with others can lead to additional insights and other angles to approach when continuing to research the problem. As we shall discuss, we attempt to accomplish this through professional conferences, and we encourage our students to do the same. However, it is germane first to focus on one written product of our teacher education program, the portfolio.

PORTFOLIO DEVELOPMENT

Portfolio assessment has been described as a systematic collection of work focused on showing a progression of skills related to instructional objectives (O'Malley and Pierce 1996; see also Valencia 1991), and reflects the trend away from oversimplified paper-and-pencil tests in current educational practice (Aschbacher 1991; Herman, Aschbacher, and Winters 1992; O'Malley and Pierce 1996; Stiggins 1991). Portfolio development in teacher education is a tool for creating a culture of professionals examining teaching practice together. It is at the same time supportive and evaluative, momentary and transcendent, remedial and enriching even as language teaching is both complex and simple, frustrating and rewarding, finite and never-ending. Though such claims seem paradoxical, the challenges facing language educators in the future will demand a repertoire of skills that have not previously been expected of those who formerly only taught the basics of language. Standards, national assessments, instructional individualization, and becoming one of the "core" subjects are leading the profession in a very different direction than the traditional perceived role of teaching only the elite. Though paper- and -pencil tests could never measure one's teaching ability in this regard, developing, maintaining, and discussing a teaching portfolio can be part of a demonstration of readiness to teach, whether in the first week or final year of a career.

A portfolio can function as a point of contact, among teacher educators, administrators, students, parents, and teachers. A portfolio, as an emergent document, is a snapshot in time. The thousand words behind that picture are those conversations and reflections with others or alone which assist everyone involved in growing as teachers. A portfolio should not be, as an end to itself, a pass or fail test for new teachers. By itself a portfolio is a weak substitute for a comprehensive evaluation. However, a portfolio can demonstrate that a teacher possesses certain prerequisite skills important for a career in the classroom, and these skills can be refined or even redefined as the teacher herself or himself learns about this challenging and valuable undertaking we call language education.

Lee Shulman (1998), a pioneer in the use of portfolios in teaching, has defined them as follows:

A teaching portfolio is the structured, documentary history of a set of coached or mentored acts of teaching, substantiated by samples of student portfolios, and fully realized only through reflective writing, deliberation, and conversation. I think all of those parts are necessary—but I may be wrong. (37)

Dollase (1998), however, asserts that the Vermont portfolio includes a demonstration of a teacher's best work, exhibits progress, and includes notable competence in meeting state standards. He adds that many teachers use this document in the job search. Teitel, Ricci, and Coogan (1998) point to the possibility of using the portfolio as a tool to enhance the teacher's public relations, particularly with parents. Lyons (1998) does point out that portfolio development in teacher education continues to be in its infancy, and as a result, numerous conceptualizations of the portfolio have emerged.

In the program at Queens College, students use the portfolio as a touchstone document, a common symbol and process in the development of a community of teachers as learners. The approach facilitated a greater sense of continuity across the curriculum, since the complex lives of students necessitate unifying program components. Students quite rarely move through as anything resembling a cohort, and attempts to incorporate innovations which could achieve similar ends, such as professional development site models, find significant barriers related to the realities of urban life at a commuter college.

Finally, the portfolio enables us as teacher educators to help teachers realize, as Weiner (1999) suggests, that ongoing professional growth is a personal responsibility. Teaching can be a quite isolated undertaking, and language teaching certainly is unique and individualistic. The language teacher's portfolio becomes a future guide to professional development, and ultimately can lead to a greater sense of ownership in the profession, even their own practice, on the part of teachers.

BRINGING IT ALL TOGETHER: ORGANIZED PROFESSIONALS

All efforts related to guiding teachers to take responsibility for renewing and guiding the profession are to no end if the teachers keep their thoughts, innovations, successes, and failures in a single classroom. We encouraged, therefore, active participation in professional organizations such as the state foreign language organization, New York State Association of Foreign Language Teachers (NYSAFLT). Students are quite fortunate that NYSAFLT is extremely supportive of teachers sharing ideas with one another both in presentation and publication formats.

In graduate classes, therefore, we required students to prepare mock presentations which could be offered at a professional meeting. In effect, teachers become leaders who actively share their successes and insights with their colleagues. Though admittedly not every student will become active in this regard, the few who do will indubitably have an impact on the profession. This sharing, we believe, will strengthen the profession even as teachers take greater ownership.

Additionally we bring information into the classroom from practitioners. We are fortunate to have a corps of experienced and now retired classroom teachers as adjuncts for student teaching supervision. These adjuncts have among them significant experiences in both New York City schools and in the suburbs at both the high school and middle school level (we have a dual level certification program), and as foreign language assistant principals. Furthermore, some of them have worked with the New York City Board of Education, served as officers in professional language teaching organizations, published, presented at local and state professional conferences, and conducted professional development workshops. They have, additionally, significant experience as cooperating teachers and university supervisors. They also encourage our students to become active in professional organizations. Probably of most importance to the students, these adjuncts help them find their first jobs by recommending them, introducing them to prospective employers, or informing them of job openings they hear about through the professional grapevine. Adjunct instructors help with student teaching placements and we attended to their recommendations for grading student teachers, as well as the recommendations given by the cooperating teachers who work with the students.

The importance of bringing classroom "experts" into teacher preparation courses was an element found essential in prior research on the foreign language methods course (Davis 1997a, 1997b). Therefore, guest "experts" came into our fall semester foreign language teaching methods course to share information and lessen the students' anxiety about student teaching in the spring semester. These experts included supervising adjuncts, cooperating teachers, assistant principals from the schools we work with, and former student teachers from our program.

THE FUTURE OF US ALL

Some people are surprised to find that the Borough of Queens, like its Brooklyn counterpart, is actually located on Long Island. If you head over the Throgs Neck Bridge on the way to the Bronx, and take the first exit, you will see a small building with a mural on its side. Brightly colored words at the top of the mural proclaim, "Welcome to the Mainland, USA." It is a fitting thought to conclude this chapter, since some thirty-five years after the BRIDGE project was undertaken at Queens College, students in the Secondary Foreign Language Education programs are still building bridges.

Admittedly, not every section of the United States will be urban, but if demographic trends continue and the political winds do not shift toward a significant and overt oppression of linguistic diversity of the scale seen during World War I (Wiley 1998), we will see the language landscape of the country continue to change, from Long Island to the Mainland. As a result, the challenges facing language educators, along with the opportunities for viable social and curricular change, will prove laden with positive possibilities.

Teachers who are students at this institution, however, far from being "culturally disadvantaged" as the inflammatory rhetoric of the sixties described them, are the ones who, along with their counterparts nationwide, can best shape this future toward positive, equitable, and socially just constructs. Together, utilizing the tools of critical reflection, action research, and portfolio development, the practitioners and the scholars, the university and the schools, can operate in partnerships to build those bridges to the mainland. We believe that ultimately the diverse classrooms from Evinston, Florida, to Dermott, Arkansas, to Anchorage, Alaska, and all in between, will be the beneficiaries of the co-labor.

NOTES

An earlier version of this paper was presented by the authors at the annual meeting of the New York State Association of Foreign Language Teachers, October 14, 2000 in Ellenville, NY.

1. Dr. Osborn is now affiliated with the Neag School of Education, University of Connecticut.

BIBLIOGRAPHY

Anderson, G. L. and K. Herr. 1999. The new paradigm wars: Is there room for rigorous practitioner knowledge in schools and universities? *Educational Researcher* 28 (5): 12–21, 40.

Andrews, L. 1997. *Language exploration and awareness.* Mahwah, NJ: Lawrence Erlbaum Associates.

Apple, M. W. 1995. *Education and power.* 2d ed. New York: Routledge.

———. 1996. *Cultural politics and education.* New York: Teacher's College Press.

Aschbacher, P. R. 1991. Performance assessment: State activity, interest, and concerns. *Applied Measurement in Education* 4 (4): 275–88.

Auerbach, E. R. 1995. The politics of the ESL classroom: Issues of power in pedagogical choices. In *Power and inequality in language education*, ed. J. W. Tollefson, 9–33. New York: Cambridge University Press.

Brookfield, S. D. 1995. *Becoming a critically reflective teacher.* San Francisco: Jossey-Bass.

Brosh, H. 1993. The influence of language status on language acquisition: Arabic in the Israeli setting. *Foreign Language Annals* 26 (3): 347–58.

———. 1997. The sociocultural message of language textbooks: Arabic in the Israeli setting. *Foreign Language Annals* 30 (3): 311–26.

Carson, T. and D. Sumara, eds. 1997. Editors' introduction: Reconceptualizing action research as a living practice. In *Action research as a living practice*, ed. T. Carson and D. Sumara, xiii–xxxv. New York: Peter Lang Publishing, Inc.

Cochran-Smith, M. and S. L. Lytle. 1999. The teacher research movement: A decade later. *Educational Researcher* 28(7): 15–25.

Corey, S. M. 1953. *Action research to improve school practices.* New York: Teachers College Press.

Davis, J. F. 1997a. Establishing expertise and teacher identity through interactions: An oral practice in the foreign language teaching methods course. *Studies in English Education* 1(2): 133–60.

———. 1997b. Guest teachers in the methods course: Applying theory to practice to theory in teacher education. Paper presented at the 22nd Annual Applied Linguistics Association of Australia (ALAA) Congress. The University of Southern Queensland, Toowoomba, Australia.

Davis, J. F. and J. K. Hall. 1998. Building reciprocal relationships in the student teaching practicum. *The ESPecialist* 19 (1): 91–121.

Dollase, R. H. 1998. When the state mandates portfolios: The Vermont experience. In *With portfolio in hand: Validating the new teacher professionalism*, ed. N. Lyons, 220–36. New York and London: Teachers College Press.

Downing, G., R. W. Edgar, A. J. Jarris, L. Kornberg, and H. F. Storen. 1965. *The preparation of teachers for schools in culturally deprived neighborhoods.* Flushing, NY: The BRIDGE Project, City University of New York, Queens College.

Giroux, H. A. 1997. *Pedagogy and the politics of hope: Theory, culture and schooling.* Boulder, CO: Westview Press.

Hall, J. K. and J. F. Davis. 1995. What we know about relationships that develop between cooperating and student teachers. *Foreign Language Annals* 28: 32–48.

Herman, J. L., P. R. Aschbacher, and L. Winters. 1992. *A practical guide to alternative assessment.* Alexandria, VA: Association for Supervision and Curriculum Development.

Irwin, J. W. 1987. What is a reflective/analytical teacher? Unpublished manuscript, University of Connecticut, School of Education Storrs, as quoted in Reagan et al. (2000).

Jarvis, P. 1999. *The practitioner-researcher: Developing theory from practice.* San Francisco: Jossey-Bass.

Kramsch, C. 1993. *Context and culture in language teaching.* Oxford. Oxford University Press.

Lippi-Green, R. 1997. *English with an accent: Language, ideology, and discrimination in the United States.* Routledge: London.

Lyons, N., ed. 1998. *With portfolio in hand: Validating the new teacher professionalism.* New York and London: Teachers College Press.

Martel, A. 2000. Paradoxes of plurilingualism. For better? For worse? And beyond? In *Rights to language: Equity, power, and education. Celebrating the 60th birthday of Tove Skutnabb-Kangas,* ed. R. Phillipson, 151–59.

Noffke, S. 1997. Professional, personal and political dimensions of action research, in *Review of research in education, volume 22,* ed. M. Apple, 305–43. Washington: AERA.

O'Malley, J. M. and L. V. Pierce. 1996. *Authentic assessment for English language learners: Practical approaches for teachers.* New York: Addison-Wesley.

Osborn, T. A. 2000. *Critical reflection and the foreign language classroom.* Critical Studies in Education and Culture Series, ed. Henry A. Giroux. Westport, CT: Bergin and Garvey.

Pennycook, A. 1995. English in the world/The world in English. In *Power and inequality in language education,* ed. J. W. Tollefson, 34–58. Cambridge, UK: Cambridge University Press.

Punch, K. F. 1998. *Introduction to social research: Quantitative and qualitative approaches.* London: Sage Publications.

Reagan, T. 1997a. The case for applied linguistics in teacher education. *Journal of Teacher Education* 48: 185–96.

———. 1997b. When is a language not a language? Challenges to "linguistic legitimacy" in educational discourse. *Educational Foundations* 11(3): 5–28.

Reagan, T. G., C. W. Case, and J. W. Brubacher. 2000. *Becoming a reflective educator: How to build a culture of inquiry in the schools.* 2d ed. Thousand Oaks, CA: Corwin Press.

Richards, J. C. and C. Lockhart. 1996. *Reflective teaching in second language classrooms.* Cambridge, UK: Cambridge University Press.

Rousmaniere, K. 1997. *City teachers: Teaching and school reform in historical perspective.* New York: Teachers College Press.

Shulman, L. 1998. Teacher portfolios: A theoretical activity. In *With portfolio in hand: Validating the new teacher professionalism,* ed. N. Lyons, 23–38. New York and London: Teachers College Press.

Skutnabb-Kangas, T. 1988. Multilingualism and the education of minority children. In *Minority education: From shame to struggle,* ed. T. Skutnabb-Kangas and J. Cummins, 9–44. Clevedon, UK: Multilingual Matters.

Stiggins, R. H. 1991. Facing the challenges of a new era of educational assessment. *Applied Measurement in Education* 4 (4): 263–72.

Storen, H. F. and R. Edgar. 1963. *Learning to teach in difficult schools: A booklet prepared for the classes in methods of teaching in the secondary schools.* Flushing, NY: Department of Education, Queens College.

Teitel L., M. Ricci, and J. Coogan. 1998. Experienced teachers construct teaching portfolios: A culture of compliance vs. a culture of professional development. In *With portfolio in hand: Validating the new teacher professionalism,* ed. N. Lyons, 143–55. New York and London: Teachers College Press.

Tollefson, J. W., ed. 1995. 1995. *Power and inequality in language education.* New York: Cambridge University Press.

Valencia, S. W. 1991. Portfolios: Panacea or pandora's box. In *Educational performance assessment,* ed. F. L. Finch. Chicago: Riverside Publishing.

Van Manen, J. 1977. Linking ways of knowing with ways of being practical. *Curriculum Inquiry* 6: 205–08.

Weiner, L. 1993. *Preparing teachers for urban schools: Lessons from thirty years of school reform.* New York: Teachers College Press.

———. 1999. *Urban teaching: The essentials.* New York: Teachers College Press.

Wiley, T. J. 1998. The imposition of World War I era English-only policies and the fate of German in North America. In *Language and politics in the United States and Canada: Myths and realities,* ed. T. Ricento and B. Burnaby, 211–42. Mahwah, NJ: Lawrence Erlbaum Associates.

Wink, J. 2000. *Critical pedagogy: Notes from the real world.* 2d ed. New York: Longman.

Yamada, Y. and A. J. Moeller. 2001. Weaving curricular standards into the language classroom: An action research study. *Foreign Language Annals* 34 (1): 26–34.

8

Toward a Political Economy of the Less Commonly Taught Languages in American Public Schools

TIMOTHY REAGAN

Ninety-seven percent of the students of modern foreign languages in the public schools of this country are studying Spanish, French, and German. . . . In American colleges and universities, Spanish, French and German enroll approximately eighty-five percent of the students of foreign languages. . . . A rough calculation presents a startling aspect of educational practice in the United States: *At least ninety-one percent of the academic study of foreign languages is directed toward languages used by twelve to thirteen percent of humanity.*
—Walker 1989, 111, emphasis added

There is no generally agreed-upon estimate of the total number of languages currently spoken in the world. In fact, estimates of the number of languages spoken around the world vary dramatically, generally ranging somewhere between 3,000 and 8,000, with the most reasonable estimates in the neighborhood of 4,500 to 5,000 separate and distinct languages (Fromkin and Rodman 1978, 329). What is especially interesting, from the perspective of the foreign language educator, is how few of this substantial number of different languages are commonly taught in the context of foreign language education programs.[1] To be sure, although linguists stress the fundamental equality of languages, some languages are, in social, demographic, economic, and political terms, clearly more equal than others (Altmann 1997, 226–33; see also Pennycook 1994; Phillipson 1992; Wardhaugh 1987). Using simply the number of native speakers as the selection criterion, the ten largest languages in the world are, in order, Mandarin, English, Hindi, Spanish, Russian, Arabic, Bengali, Portuguese, Japanese, and French (Fromkin and Rodman 1993, 351–54). If one takes into account languages that are widely used as second languages, then the list changes somewhat, and our focus becomes the languages of wider communication (generally taken to include English, French, Spanish, Russian, Arabic, and German).

Draper and Hicks (1996) report that fewer than half of all secondary students in American public schools study a foreign language. Of the six million students in middle and secondary schools who *do* study a foreign language, approximately 65 percent study Spanish, 22 percent study French, 6 percent study German, and 3.5 percent study Latin. The remaining 3.5 percent of students study a wide variety of languages, including African languages, American Sign Language, Arabic, Chinese (Cantonese and Mandarin), Greek, Haitian Creole, Hawai'ian, Hebrew, Italian, Japanese, Korean, Native American languages, Norwegian, Polish, Portuguese, Russian, Spanish for Native Speakers, Vietnamese, and others. It is with the languages studied by this 3.5 percent of the student population, as well as those languages that are not studied at all, that this chapter will be concerned. Specifically, our concern here will be on the need for what might be called a "social grammar" of the less commonly taught languages (hereafter, LCTLs) in general,[2] and with respect to their presence (or lack of presence) in the public school curriculum. In particular, we will be concerned with trying to identify some of the factors that seem to underlie the implicit linguistic hierarchy that governs the study of the different LCTLs.

There are a number of compelling reasons for linguists, policy makers, and foreign language educators to be interested in the teaching and learning of LCTLs. First and foremost, at least in terms of making a public case for the study of the LCTLs, is what can be called the geopolitical aspect of language teaching and learning. In essence, it is in the best interest of the society to produce sufficient numbers of linguistically competent individuals to function in the various national and regional languages that are used in areas of national political, economic, and strategic concern. For example, when the U.S. government identified 169 "critical languages" that "would promote important scientific research or security interests of a national or economic kind" (Crystal 1987, 342) in 1985, it was this geopolitical aspect of language teaching and learning that was at issue.

Furthermore, the LCTLs are important in terms of our ability to understand the speech communities that use them. As Robert Bunge has observed, "Language is not just another thing we do as humans; it is *the* thing we do. It is a total environment; we live in the language as a fish lives in water. It is the audible and visible manifestation of the soul of a people" (1992, 376, emphasis in original). It would, in short, be difficult to overstate the centrality of language to worldview and both group and individual identity. As Appel and Muysken suggested in their book *Language Contact and Bilingualism*:

Language is not only an instrument for the communication of messages. This becomes especially clear in multilingual communities where various groups have their own language: e.g., the Flemish in Belgium and the Gujeratis in India. With its language a group distinguishes itself. The cultural norms and values of a group are transmitted by its language. Group feelings are emphasized by using the group's own language, and members of the outgroup are excluded from its internal transactions. (1987, 11)

There are also pedagogical lessons to be learned from the experiences of teachers and students of the LCTLs. As Roger Allen has explained with respect to teachers of Arabic, the contributions that teachers of non-Western languages:

may have for language teaching have until recently been ignored by the profession at large. It does not seem an exaggeration to claim that one of the results of the proficiency movement has been to bring the issues raised by the non-Western, less commonly taught, "critical," "exotic" languages very much to the attention of the language-teaching profession as a whole. (1992, 236–37)

Although one might argue that Allen is perhaps overly optimistic in terms of the extent to which the LCTLs have been taken seriously by most language educators in the United States, his fundamental point is nevertheless an important and valuable one. There can be little doubt that teachers of LCTLs bring with them very different sets of experiences with respect to foreign language pedagogy, and the discussion about and reflection on their experiences is almost certain to benefit both other LCTL teachers as well as teachers of the more commonly taught languages (see Ihde 1997). Beyond these lessons for foreign language education pedagogy, though, the teaching and learning of LCTLs also impacts on education in a number of other areas, amongst which are multicultural education programs, global education programs, critical language and language awareness programs (including FLEX programs at the elementary level), and, as will be discussed later in this chapter, with respect to what might be called the political component of foreign language teaching and learning.

CONCEPTUALIZING THE LCTLS

In a seminal article on the LCTLs, Walker (1989) argued that, at least in the U.S. context, there is a fundamental distinction made between the traditionally taught languages (i.e., French, Spanish, and German) and all other languages (the LCTLs). Although it is not uncommon for the LCTLs to be grouped together in this manner as something of a "miscellaneous" category (see, e.g., Brecht and Walton 1994; Crookes, Sakka, Shiroma, and Lei Ye, 1991; Everson 1993; Ryding 1989; Walker 1991), this is inevitably misleading on a number of grounds, not the least of which is the problem of grouping together radically different *kinds* of languages. Indeed, Walker has suggested that "thinking of LCTLs as a category of language is like thinking of 'nonelephants' as a category of animals" (1989, 111). In attempting to address this problem, Walton suggests that the LCTLs can be best understood as being divided in practice into three subgroups:

(1) less commonly taught European languages such as Russian, Italian, Portuguese, and Swedish; (2) higher-enrollment non-Indo-European languages, such as Arabic, Chinese, and Japanese; and (3) lower-enrollment non-Indo-European languages such as Burmese, Indonesian, and Swahili. (1992, 1)

Jordan and Walton (1987) have even gone so far as to label the second and third groups the "truly foreign languages," emphasizing their presumed difficulty for speakers of English, as well as their degree of difference from English. Jacobs (1996), in what could be considered a sort of linguistic one-upmanship, has offered an argument for the inclusion of American Sign Language in one of these categories as well. The key criterion that seems to be applied in making these distinctions is essentially the distance from English, in terms of such factors as phonology, grammar, lexicon, orthography, and spelling (see Hawkins 1981, 79–82; James 1979). Utilizing a five-point rating scale, the interlingual distance between any two languages can be determined and assigned a quantitative rating. Thus, in an analysis of the interlingual distances of English to French, German, Italian, Russian and Spanish, James (1979) determined the following global scores:

French	12
German	10 (12 if Gothic script is taught)
Italian	6
Russian	16
Spanish	7

Thus, Italian and Spanish would be relatively easier languages for an English speaker to learn than would be French or German, with Russian constituting the most difficult language for English speakers to learn of those in James' sample. It is interesting to note that these results are actually fairly consistent with the Educational Testing Service's (ETS) estimates of the classroom time required to meet various levels of linguistic proficiency in different languages (see Hadley 1993; Liskin-Gasparro 1982). Basically, the ETS estimates divide target languages into four groups, ranging from those which are most quickly acquired by English speakers to those that require the most time.[3]

Although the division of LCTLs by degree of difficulty for English speakers does have a certain amount of face validity, it does not really move us forward in terms of understanding *why* certain LCTLs are more popular than others. If interlingual distance was really all that was at stake, then we would expect languages in ETS Group I to be considerably more common than those in Group IV—and yet, that does not appear to be the case. Three of the four listed languages in Group IV (Arabic, Chinese, and Japanese) are among the more popular LCTLs, while Group I includes a large number of languages that are virtually never taught in U.S. public schools (e.g., Afrikaans, Danish, Dutch, Norwegian, Romanian, and Swedish), despite their presumed relative ease of acquisition. The problem, of course, is that decisions and choices about language are rarely made simply on grounds of ease of learning or what might be called "hierarchies of difficulty" (see DiPietro 1971, 161–64); rather, such choices are deeply grounded and embedded in social, cultural, economic, political, demographic, and ideological beliefs and attitudes. It is in order to achieve a better understanding of these extralinguistic factors that guide language choice that a "social grammar" of the LCTLs is needed.

TOWARD AN OUTLINE OF A SOCIAL GRAMMAR OF THE LCTLS

If ease of acquisition does not provide an adequate or satisfactory explanation for why some LCTLs are found in public school curricula in the United States, and others are not, then what could explain this difference? The answer, as suggested above, requires a "social grammar" of the LCTLs: a framework within which such factors as social, cultural, economic, political, demographic, and ideological beliefs and attitudes can be taken into account. A good place to begin the development of such a framework is with what Dell Hymes has identified as the six core assumptions about language in the United States. Hymes suggests that these core (and generally tacit) assumptions include the ideas that:

- Everyone in the United States speaks only English, or should.

- Bilingualism is inherently unstable, probably injurious, and possibly unnatural.

- Foreign literary languages can be respectively studied, but not foreign languages in their domestic varieties (it is one thing to study the French spoken in Paris, another to study the French spoken in Louisiana).

- Most everyone else in the world is learning English anyway, and that, together with American military and economic power, makes it unnecessary to worry about knowing the language of a country in which one has business, bases, or hostages.

- Differences in language are essentially of two kinds, right and wrong.

- Verbal fluency and noticeable style are suspicious, except as entertainment (it's what you mean that counts). (Hymes 1996, 84–85)

Each of these assumptions is in fact fundamentally flawed, and the list as a whole is grounded in a lack of understanding of the nature of language, a confusion of historical mythology with historical fact, and is replete with both factual and normative errors. This having been said, Hymes' list nevertheless does, I think, fairly accurately reflect commonly held beliefs about language in the United States.

Although Hymes' analysis may help to contextualize a "social grammar" of the LCTLs, on its own it is obviously far from sufficient for this purpose, as indeed are the related, and conceptually powerful, notions of linguistic imperialism and linguicism (see, e.g., Phillipson 1988, 1992, 50–57; Skutnabb-Kangas 1988; Tollefson 1995). Rather, what is needed is a framework for classifying the LCTLs, coupled with a discussion of the explanatory factors for why particular LCTLs fall where they do within this framework. It is to a discussion of such a framework that we now turn.

It is clear that there is a hierarchy of LCTLs, but it is also clear, as we have seen, that this hierarchy is not one grounded in *linguistic* factors. In order to be useful, the hierarchy of LCTLs is better envisaged as one reflecting the likelihood of a particular LCTL being offered as a foreign language option in a public school. Thus, looking at foreign language education in the United States as a whole, we can talk about a hierarchy of five levels:

Level 1	Commonly Taught Languages
Level 2	Most Commonly Taught LCTLs
Level 3	Rarely Taught LCTLs
Level 4	Never/Virtually Never Taught LCTLs
Level 5	The "Non-Languages"

Level 1 refers not to LCTLs at all, but rather to the languages most commonly associated with foreign language education in the United States: French, German, Spanish, and probably Latin. Although there are significant differences with respect to student enrollment among these languages, all four are widely offered throughout the United States, certified teachers are generally readily available in all four languages (though, to be sure, there are periodic shortages), a variety of textbooks and supplementary pedagogical materials are available for all four languages, curricular guides are widely available and thorough, and all four languages are seen as fully legitimate objects of study. To a very significant extent, when one talks about foreign language education in the United States, it is with these languages that one is concerned.

Level 2 encompasses the LCTLs that fairly routinely appear in public school curricula in most if not all parts of the United States, albeit considerably less frequently than even Latin and serving far fewer students. Included among the Level 2 languages would be Russian, Chinese, Japanese, and Arabic. It is interesting to note that these languages, the most commonly taught of the LCTLs, all involve substantial orthographic challenges for English-speaking students, and all involve considerable interlingual distance from English (though learning Russian is obviously, on both counts, clearly easier for English speakers than learning the other Level 2 languages). Although shortages certainly exist, teacher certification in Level 2 languages is commonly possible and teachers for these languages can be found, textbooks and supportive materials are available (if limited), and curricular guides have been prepared in many states and local school districts.

Level 3 refers to the LCTLs that do, on occasion, make their way into the public school curricula, but do so fairly rarely (even when compared with the Level 2 LCTLs), and often in geographically restricted contexts. Included here would be such heritage languages as Polish, Italian, Portuguese, Modern Greek, Hawai'ian, Norwegian, and so on. The key here is that, for the most part, these languages are offered where they are in fact reflective of some element of the ethnic composition and makeup of the local population. In other words, to some extent Level 3 LCTLs are actually examples of ethnic language maintenance or revival efforts as much as truly foreign language efforts. Teaching certification is uncommon for Level 3 languages, and very often non-foreign language educators who speak the target language (often as native speakers) are employed to teach these languages. Textbooks and supplementary teaching materials are available, but quite limited, and few formal curricular guidelines exist for most Level 3 languages.

Level 4 is by far the largest and most inclusive category, and would include the overwhelming majority of the world's languages. Examples of Level 4 languages would include virtually all African languages,[4] most Asian and Oceanic languages, indigenous Amerind languages, and many smaller European languages, among others. This is, to some extent, a category of exclusion, in that it includes all languages that do not fit anywhere else. What holds this very large and diverse group of languages together (rather as a category of "nonelephants," as Walker [1989] would have it) is that they are virtually never offered as foreign language options in American public schools. As a general rule, teaching certification is not even possible in these languages, textbooks and pedagogical materials are difficult to come by and often of poor quality where they exist at all, curricula for public school classes do not exist, and, perhaps most important, there tends to be virtually no interest among either students or in the community at large for offering these languages. To a considerable extent, Level 4 languages are perceived, in the American context, as simply irrelevant.

The last category, Level 5, differs from the others in that it includes what can be termed "non-legitimate" languages—that is, languages and language varieties that the society appears to view as fundamentally different from "real" or "legitimate" languages. Such a distinction is, of course, linguistically nonsensical—the idea that there can be "legitimate" and "non-legitimate" languages makes no sense at all on any reasonable set of linguistic criteria. The distinction, though, is not a linguistic one but a social and ideological one, and it is one that is all too commonly made in American society to dismiss certain languages as legitimate objects of foreign language study. Two of the better examples of this phenomenon are the cases of American Sign Language and Esperanto (see Reagan 1997b). An especially interesting element of these Level 5 languages is the degree of controversy that often surrounds them. Both American Sign Language and Esperanto are, in fact, offered in American public schools, and yet the resistance to them is surprisingly strong and often highly emotive in nature (see Reagan 1998; Vandenberg 1998).

With respect to providing an explanatory model for why *specific* languages are located in a particular level, I would suggest that there are six fundamental factors which, taken together, determine a language's status. Specifically, these six factors are:

- the size of the language's speaker community;
- the geographic spread of the language (including its use as a second language or *lingua franca*);
- whether the language constitutes a heritage language in the local American setting;
- whether the language is a language of wider communication;
- whether the language has an established and recognized literary/written tradition; and
- whether the language is a "living" or "dead" language.[5]

It is important to note here that it is the *interaction* of these six factors that could be expected to determine the status of any particular language; no single factor could ensure either the presence or absence of a language in the public school curriculum.

EDUCATIONAL IMPLICATIONS

The articulation of a social grammar of the LCTLs has significant and timely educational implications in the U.S. context, in terms of foreign language pedagogy, multicultural and global education efforts, and the politics of education (especially with respect to critical and emancipatory education). Each of these areas will now be briefly explored.

In terms of foreign language pedagogy in the United States, an examination of the extralinguistic factors which determine the relative status of particular languages is an important aspect of language studies with which foreign language educators, and indeed all educators, need to be familiar (see Reagan 1997a). Language is a profoundly social activity, inevitably embedded in a cultural, political, economic, and ideological context, and yet all too often language educators assume a narrow, essentially positivistic view of both language and language teaching. The consideration of the status of the LCTLs can help to ameliorate this situation, just as serious discussion about foreign language teaching methods and strategies can generate important ideas and contribute to a cross-fertilization among foreign language teachers. In the past, this cross-fertilization has tended to move from the traditionally taught languages to the LCTLs; a clear example of movement in this direction is Catherine Ball's interesting effort to incorporate text-based reading strategies in her teaching of Old English (see Ball 1995).[6] Similarly, the development of more student-friendly textbooks in some LCTLs is another obvious example of such bene-fits. The possibilities for cross-fertilization, however, are in fact very much two-way. Indeed, as Allen has argued,

As guidelines for such languages as Hebrew, Thai, Hausa, and Hindi take their place alongside Russian, Chinese, Japanese, and Arabic, we all begin to realise that teachers of languages from the various regions of the world have an enormous amount to contrib-ute to, and learn from, each other about every aspect of their joint enterprise. (1992, 237)

A related area in which there is considerable potential for worthwhile inter-action is between foreign language educators, teachers of English as a Second Language, and teachers working in bilingual education programs—where, in-cidentally, some LCTLs are far more likely to appear than in the traditional for-eign language curriculum.[7]

Multicultural and global education programs, which have become increas-ingly popular in the United States in recent years, are another area where con-cerns with and interest in the LCTLs is relevant. The fundamental challenge in such programs, from a linguistic perspective, is the minimal concern with lan-guage and language diversity that is generally found in multicultural and global curricula. There is, to be sure, a significant difference between the two types of programs in this regard: multicultural education programs do include some concern about language minority students (see Gollnick and Chinn 1994, 219–50; Ovando 1993), though not, for the most part, about other language issues, while global education programs tend at best to give passing mention to language issues. Indeed, in the U.S. context, global education is most commonly completely separate from foreign language education, and tends to be entirely monolingual in nature. As Reagan and Díaz have suggested,

it simply does not make sense to think or talk about global education as a monolingual activity. Further . . . the idea that a global education curriculum could be developed, or that a global education unit could be taught, in a monolingual fashion (as, indeed, the literature seems not merely to accept but to assume) ought to be viewed by reasonable people in roughly the same way that claims about the world being flat are viewed—in short, as utter nonsense. To propose that we can prepare students to deal with issues of internationalization and globalization exclusively through the medium of English, with little or no exposure to other languages, is rather like imagining that we can pre-pare students to be scientifically literate by ensuring that they read their horoscopes each day and are taught to be sure to keep their healing crystals on hand in case of ill-ness. In short, the very message of global education would seem to require that one challenge the dominance of monolingualism in our society (1996, 7–8)

Foreign language programs in elementary school contexts are an increas-ingly popular option in many parts of the United States (see Curtain and Pesola 1994; Lipton 1992). Although FLES (Foreign Language in the Ele-mentary School) programs almost always provide students with an introduction to one of the commonly taught languages (most often French or Spanish), the same is not true for FLEX (Foreign Language Exploration/Experience) programs, where the focus is more on language awareness and exposure and less on acquiring a specific language. It is in FLEX programs that issues related to LCTLs are most likely to be, and most easily addressed in the elementary school context (see Lubiner 1996; Reagan and Case 1996).

Last, we come to the contribution that can be made by consideration of the "social grammar" of the LCTLs to the politics of schooling and to the empowerment and emancipation of both students and teachers. Dell Hymes has argued that "It is probably through education—taken in its broadest sense, as schooling and instruction of all kinds—that the peculiar, latent, tacit American view of language most powerfully exercises cultural hegemony" (1996, 83). It is also, therefore, in educational institutions that we may have the best opportunity to challenge and repudiate this cultural hegemony—to engage, that is, in what Osborn has called curricular nullification (Osborn 2000). This can be done through the inclusion of critical language exploration and awareness programs (see Andrews 1997; Carter 1990; van Lier 1995) in foreign language classes themselves, and in other school contexts in which issues of language, power, and domination can be raised (see Fairclough 1989; Reagan and Osborn 1998), not to mention contexts in which issues of language rights can be discussed (see Benson, Grundy, Itakura, and Skutnabb-Kangas, in press). As Michael Byram et al. have pointed out in their discussion of "language and culture teaching as political education":

By making comparisons, learners are deliberately led into relativisation of their own perspective through prioritisation of the perspective of others. Comparison is not only a technique for highlighting similarities and differences as a means of making them more perceptible. It also serves as a step towards the acceptance of other perspectives, and the valuing of them as equally acceptable within their own terms. (1994, 177; see also Byram 1989)

In short, the consideration of the "social grammar" of the LCTLs provides us with a powerful opportunity to address a broad range of language-related issues in the school context, helping students to become more aware of the nature and role of language in society, language bias and discrimination, and the ways in which language is used and misused with respect to other social, political, and economic issues.

NOTES

1. It is important to note that the focus of this chapter is on foreign language education in the United States, and specifically excludes the use of LCTLs (less commonly taught languages) in bilingual programs. The use of LCTLs in bilingual education in the United States, in essence, is transitional in nature, and the primary articulated objective (especially in programs using LCTLs) is the transition of stu-

dents into English-medium environments. Thus, the fact that the LCTLs may be used in such programs does not in any way detract from the central argument pre sented here.

2. Although "less commonly taught languages" (or LCTLs) is the most common term used to describe the languages under discussion here, other terms are sometimes used as well, especially in other countries. Among the more common alternatives are "lesser-used languages" (Grin 1993) and "minority languages" (Williams 1991).

3. It is interesting to note that of the three commonly taught languages (French, German, and Spanish), two are in Group I (French and Spanish), and one is in Group II (German). The complete list is as follows, with increasing time requirements for each group: GROUP I consists of Afrikaans, Danish, Dutch, French, Haitian Creole, Italian, Norwegian, Portuguese, Romanian, Spanish, Swahili, and Swedish; GROUP II consists of Bulgarian, Dari, Farsi, German, Greek, Hindi, Indonesian, Malay, and Urdu; GROUP III consists of Amharic, Bengali, Burmese, Czech, Finnish, Hebrew, Hungarian, Khmer, Lao, Nepali, Pilipino, Polish, Russian, Serbo-Croation, Sinhala, Thai, Tamil, Turkish, and Vietnamese; and GROUP IV languages are Arabic, Chinese, Japanese, and Korean (see Liskin-Gasparro 1982).

4. The only African language that might, to some extent, count as a Level 3 language in the U.S. context is Swahili.

5. An additional factor which does not appear to be especially relevant in the *contemporary* United States context, but which has been important historically in the United States and continues to be so in many societies, is that of ideology (whether religious or political in nature). It is this factor which provides powerful explanatory and heuristic insight, for instance, into the anti-German language hysteria in the United States during the First World War, the role of the development of critical lan guage training in the United States during the Cold War, and, more recently, some of the concerns among secularists in Turkey to the increased offering of courses in Otto-man Turkish, which is in some instances believed to be symbolically linked to the rise of religious fundamentalism.

6. Along the same lines have been changes in the pedagogy of Latin in recent years. The challenge here has been that the most common approach to the teaching of ancient and classical languages has tended to be, and, with the possible exceptions of Latin and perhaps Classical Greek in some limited instances, continues to be essentially that of grammar-translation.

7. An important point to stress here is the difference in educational aims and objectives between bilingual education programs and foreign language programs. This difference is perhaps best seen in terms of the kind of language proficiency that is our goal. In the literature on contemporary U.S. bilingual education, a common distinction is made between what are called basic interpersonal communicative skills (BICS) and cognitive academic language proficiency (CALP) (see Baker 1993, 11; Spener 1991, 440). The former refers to the language skills needed for casual conversational use of the L2, while the latter refers to the degree and kind of proficiency needed for intellectual and academic purposes. Bilingual educators argue that students achieve BICS far sooner than CALP, and that this distinction makes necessary extended transitional programs for non-English-speaking students in the U.S. context. Although the distinction between BICS and CALP is in fact questionable (see Martin-Jones and Romaine 1986; Spolsky 1989), it is an interesting one for discussion purposes here, since the kinds of language proficiency included in BICS probably more than exceed

typical expectations for student functioning in the target language in foreign language education programs.

BIBLIOGRAPHY

Allen, R. 1992. Teaching Arabic in the United States: Past, present, and future. In *The Arabic language in America*, ed. A. Rouchdy, 222–50. Detroit, MI: Wayne State University Press.

Altmann, G. 1997. *The ascent of Babel: An exploration of language, mind, and understanding.* Oxford: Oxford University Press.

Andrews, L. 1997. *Language exploration and awareness: A resource book for teachers.* Mahwah, NJ: Lawrence Erlbaum Associates.

Appel, R. and P. Muysken. 1987. *Language contact and bilingualism.* London: Edward Arnold.

Audi, R., ed. 1995. *The Cambridge dictionary of philosophy.* Cambridge: Cambridge University Press.

Baker, C. 1993. *Foundations of bilingual education and bilingualism.* Clevedon, UK: Multilingual Matters.

Ball, C. 1995. Providing comprehensible input in a dead foreign language: Two text-based strategies. In *Linguistics and the education of language teachers: Ethnolinguistic, psycholinguistic, and sociolinguistic aspects,* ed. J. Alatis, C. Straehle, B. Gallenberger and M. Ronkin, 498–511. Washington, DC: Georgetown University Press.

Benson, P., P. Grundy, H. Itakura, and T. Skutnabb-Kangas, eds. In press. *Access to language rights.* Amsterdam: John Benjamins.

Brecht, R. and A. Walton. 1994. National strategic planning in the less commonly taught languages. In *Foreign language policy: An agenda for change,* ed. R. Lambert, 190–212. Thousand Oaks, CA: Sage.

Bunge, R. 1992. Language: The psyche of a people. In *Language loyalties,* ed. J. Crawford, 376–80. Chicago: University of Chicago Press.

Byram, M. 1989. *Cultural studies in foreign language education.* Clevedon, UK: Multilingual Matters.

Byram, M., C. Morgan, and colleagues. 1994. *Teaching-and-learning language-and-culture.* Clevedon, UK: Multilingual Matters.

Carter, R., ed. 1990. *Knowledge about language and the curriculum: The LINC reader.* London: Hodder and Stoughton.

Crookes, G., R. Sakka, S. Shiroma, and Ye Lei. 1991. *Towards a generic curriculum for the less commonly taught languages.* (Research Note #1). Honolulu: University of Hawai'i, Second Language Teaching and Curriculum Center.

Crystal, D. 1987. *The Cambridge encyclopedia of language.* Cambridge: Cambridge University Press.

Curtain, H. and C. Pesola. 1994. *Languages and children, making the match: Foreign language instruction for an early start, grades K–8.* 2d ed. White Plains, NY: Longman.

DiPietro, R. 1971. *Language structures in contrast.* Rowley, MA: Newbury House.

Draper, J. and J. Hicks. 1996. Foreign language enrollments in public secondary schools, Fall 1994: Summary report. *Foreign Language Annals* 29 (3): 303–14.

Everson, M. 1993. Research in the less commonly taught languages. In *Research in language learning: Principles, processes, and prospects*, ed. A. Hadley, 198–228. Lincolnwood, IL: National Textbook Company, in conjunction with the American Council on the Teaching of Foreign Languages.

Fairclough, N. 1989. *Language and power*. London: Longman.

Fromkin, V. and R. Rodman. 1978. *An introduction to language*. 2d ed. New York. Holt, Rinehart and Winston.

———. 1993. *An introduction to language*. 5th ed. Fort Worth, TX: Harcourt Brace.

Gollnick, D. and P. Chinn. 1994. *Multicultural education in a pluralistic society*. 4th ed. New York: Merrill.

Grin, F. 1993. European economic integration and the fate of lesser-used languages. *Language Problems and Language Planning* 17 (2): 101–16.

Hadley, A. 1993. *Teaching language in context*. 2d ed. Boston: Heinle and Heinle.

Haugen, E. 1987. *Blessings of Babel: Bilingualism and language planning*. Berlin: Mouton de Gruyter.

Hawkins, E. 1981. *Modern languages in the curriculum*. Cambridge: Cambridge University Press.

Hymes, D. 1996. *Ethnography, linguistics, narrative inequality: Toward an understanding of voice*. London: Taylor and Francis.

Ihde, T. 1997. Teacher certification and less commonly taught languages. *Journal of Celtic Language Learning* 3: 41–50.

Jacobs, R. 1996. Just how hard is it to learn ASL? The case for ASL as a truly foreign language. In *Multicultural aspects of sociolinguistics in deaf communities*, ed. C. Lucas, 183–226. Washington, DC: Gallaudet University Press.

James, C. 1979. Foreign languages in the school curriculum. In *Foreign languages in education*, ed. G. E. Perren, 7–28. London: CILT.

Jordan, E. and A. Walton. 1987. Truly foreign languages: Instructional challenges. *Annals of the American Academy of Social and Political Science* 490: 110–24.

Lipton, G. 1992. *Practical handbook to elementary foreign language programs*. 2d ed. Lincolnwood, IL: National Textbook Company.

Liskin-Gasparro, J. 1982. *ETS oral proficiency testing manual*. Princeton, NJ: Educational Testing Service.

Lubiner, E. 1996. *Learning about languages: A comprehensive FLEX activity book*. Lincolnwood, IL: National Textbook Company.

Martin-Jones, M. and S. Romaine. 1986. Semilingualism: A half-baked theory of communicative competence. *Applied Linguistics* 7: 26–38.

Osborn, T. A. 2000. *Critical reflection and the foreign language classroom*. Critical Studies in Education and Culture Series, ed. Henry A. Giroux. Westport, CT: Bergin and Garvey.

Ovando, C. 1993. Language diversity and education. In *Multicultural education: Issues and perspectives*, ed. J. Banks and C. Banks, 215–35. 2d ed. Boston: Allyn and Bacon.

Pennycook, A. 1994. *The cultural politics of English as an international language*. London: Longman.

Phillipson, R. 1988. Linguicism: Structures and ideologies in linguistic imperialism. In *Minority education: From shame to struggle*, ed. T. Skutnabb-Kangas and J. Cummins, 339–58. Clevedon, UK: Multilingual Matters.

———. 1992. *Linguistic imperialism*. Oxford: Oxford University Press.

Reagan, T. 1997a. The case for applied linguistics in teacher education. *Journal of Teacher Education* 48 (3): 185–96.

———. 1997b. When is a language not a language? Challenges to "linguistic legitimacy" in educational discourse. *Educational Foundations* 11 (3): 5–28.

———. 1998. Rejoinder to Vandenberg. *Educational Foundations* 12 (1): 87–90.

Reagan, T. and K. Case. 1996. Linguistic pluralism for internationalization: The case for non-traditional approaches to language study for U.S. schools. In *Language status in the post-Cold-War era*, ed. K. Müller, 97–107. Lanham, MD: University Press of America and the Center for Research and Documentation on World Language Problems.

Reagan, T. and E. Díaz. 1996. Monolingual global education: The "flat earth" alternative. Presented at the Languages and Global Education Conference sponsored by the Center for Research and Documentation of World Language Problems and the Office of Conference Services at the United Nations, May 3.

Reagan, T. and T. A. Osborn. 1998. Power, authority, and domination in foreign language education: Toward an analysis of educational failure. *Educational Foundations* 12 (2): 45–62.

Ryding, K. C. 1989. Less commonly taught languages: The current situation. In *Language teaching, testing, and technology*, ed. J. Alatis, 114–21. Washington, DC: Georgetown University Press.

Skutnabb-Kangas, T. 1988. Multilingualism and the education of minority children. In *Minority education: From shame to struggle*, ed. T. Skutnabb-Kangas and J. Cummins, 9–44. Clevedon, UK: Multilingual Matters.

Spener, D. 1991. Transitional bilingual education and the socialization of immigrants. In *Language issues in literacy and bilingual/multicultural education*, ed. M. Minami and B. Kennedy, 424–46. Cambridge, MA: Harvard Educational Review.

Spolsky, B. 1989. *Conditions for second language learning.* Oxford: Oxford University Press.

Tollefson, J., ed. 1995. *Power and inequality in language education.* Cambridge: Cambridge University Press.

Vandenberg, D. 1998. Rejoinder to Reagan. *Educational Foundations* 12 (1): 83–85.

van Lier, L. 1995. *Introducing language awareness.* London: Penguin English.

Walker, G. 1989. The less commonly taught languages in the context of American pedagogy. In *Shaping the future: Challenges and opportunities*, ed. H. Lepke, 111–37. Middlebury, VT: Northeast Conference on the Teaching of Foreign Languages.

———. 1991. Gaining place: The less commonly taught languages in American schools. *Foreign Language Annals* 24: 131–50.

Walton, A. 1992. *Expanding the vision of foreign language education: Enter the less commonly taught languages.* National Foreign Language Center Occasional Papers. Washington, DC: National Foreign Language Center.

Wardhaugh, R. 1987. *Languages in competition: Dominance, diversity, and decline.* Oxford: Basil Blackwell, in association with André Deutsch.

Williams, C., ed. 1991. *Linguistic minorities: Society and territory.* Clevedon, UK: Multilingual Matters.

9

Reversing Language Loss in a Multilingual Setting: A Native Language Enhancement Program and Its Impact

Claire Sylvan and Migdalia Romero

> One of our national ironies is that the United States is short on the language expertise needed for national defense, international business, and local government services at the same time that unprecedented numbers of immigrants are arriving in the United States thoroughly fluent in languages other than English.
>
> —Marcos 2000, 6

Linguistic and cultural diversity in U.S. public schools is becoming the norm rather than the exception, not only in large cities that serve as ports of entry into this country but more recently in smaller communities across America. The languages spoken by these new immigrants are as diverse as the cultures they represent, from Albanian to Vietnamese. This diverse population creates new contexts for language educators. It also raises new questions.

While for many educators the linguistic ability of these new immigrants may represent an academic liability and an impediment to the learning of English, language educators inside and outside the United States generally agree that the ability to speak more than one language is an asset and a skill to be nurtured. However, in this country, language educators are often at a loss as to how to work with the student who comes to school speaking a language other than English. As a result, these students are often doomed to forget their native language—at best by benign neglect and at worst by outright condemnation.

Still, there are some educators who believe in nurturing native language skills together with English proficiency in order to make students globally competitive. The question is: How do language educators support the plethora of languages that students bring to the American classroom without the traditional academic and linguistic capacities to do so? Furthermore, is language loss inevitable or can it be reversed? If reversible, how can so many languages be supported outside of traditional language education programs? And what are the benefits of doing so?

The advantages of maintaining students' first languages while they acquire English are manifold. Students who are biliterate enter the job market with enhanced marketability. At this juncture in our history, social and political relationships are important with countries from whence these languages emanate. These students have the potential to construct these relationships.

Without support for maintaining and developing their native language(s), students usually begin to lose the communicative skills they brought from their native countries and homes (Seliger 1991; Silva-Corvalan 1991). As a result, communication breaks down with parents, grandparents, and relatives because, quite literally, the young people speak a different language (Wong-Fillmore 1995). Over time, the language is either forgotten or rejected.

However, if students see that their school values their native language, their own attitudes toward the language and culture are enhanced. These positive attitudes translate into a positive attitude toward themselves and an interest in the maintenance of the first language (Auerbach 1993).

Despite the advantages of supporting students' native languages, educators are often uncertain as to how this can be done outside the parameters of traditional language education programs. Part of the problem is that multilingual student populations frequently have no access to programs that focus on developing their native languages. This may occur because the number of students speaking one language does not reach a threshold level (either because it is a low incidence language; or because there are few speakers of that language in a particular school) and/or because there are no certified language teachers available, especially in the multiplicity of languages spoken by students. Even when there are sufficient numbers of students and teachers, many administrators do not feel the value or need for such an effort. Their contention is that any attempt to support the native language will only interfere with the acquisition of English. As a result, these students are deprived of developing proficiency in their native languages. In essence, the neglect of the skills they bring when they enter school in the United States turns an advantage or asset into a loss. It limits rather than enhances their job marketability in a global economy and quite literally robs the United States of an important linguistic resource in global markets and politics.

This chapter describes a multilingual program in a New York City high school that demonstrates that even in school settings that preclude traditional foreign language education programs, schools can create an environment that supports students in developing proficiency in their native languages as they simultaneously acquire English. Such a program is made possible by the combined use of small group collaborative learning and peer-mediated instruction within multilingual, heterogeneous classrooms. Native language proficiency is promoted in a variety of ways. Students' primary languages are vehicles through which students explore content even when teachers do not speak those languages.

The article focuses on the impact of the program on both teachers and students, particularly the ways in which participants grew and changed as a result of their participation. Personal, professional, linguistic, and academic change was documented through interviews, personal narrative, and logs. A content analysis of the three major sources of data points to a powerful transformation in the way teachers teach and students learn as well as how teachers and students view themselves, each other, and their languages. The implications of these lessons for the discipline of language education are examined.

INSTITUTIONAL CONTEXT

The International High School (IHS) at LaGuardia Community College is a microcosm of the diversity burgeoning all over the United States. It is a multilingual public high school that serves 460 youngsters from sixty countries who enter the school speaking forty-one different languages. A typical class of twenty-four students might have representatives of as many as fifteen different languages. The school admits only students of limited English proficiency who have been in this country under four years at the time of application. Once accepted, students may remain in the school until graduation.

The school's mission is to enable each of its students to develop the linguistic, cognitive, and cultural skills necessary for success in high school, college, and beyond. Until recently, with the exception of Spanish, the native languages of students had not been systematically maintained even though the school's staff recognizes that students' native languages are resources for themselves, the school, and society. Posters and performances in the school, as well as informal use of the language by students and teachers, give testimony to this sentiment. So too does its stated philosophy:

In an increasingly interdependent world, fluency in a language other than English must be viewed as a resource for the students, the school, and the society. (The International High School Partnership 1994)

Students in the school have varying levels of proficiency in English and in their native language. From its inception, the school has capitalized on this diversity by grouping classes heterogeneously, with a strong emphasis on peer-mediated instruction and collaborative learning (Personnel Procedures 1985).

Teachers at this school have long understood the need to teach language through content. However, during the first years of the school's existence, the focus was on the development of English curriculum and the use of ESL techniques by content area teachers. Attention to native language development occurred in native language classes for Spanish-speaking students, in after-school clubs for other language groups, and sporadically in Global Literature courses. In addition, a linguistics class eventually taken by some students provided an opportunity for students to do some comparative analysis of their language and English.

In 1993, the entire school reorganized into six interdisciplinary teams of four teachers, each representing a different discipline. Each team coordinates instruction over a twelve-week period around a theme. Each thematic twelve-week program offers the equivalent of four traditional high school classes (See Figure 9.1). The classes are linked according to the preselected theme. For example, one team developed an interdisciplinary curriculum based on the theme of motion. Students taking this program examined motion from the perspectives of mathematics, science, literature, and physical education. In such a structure, the theme drives the curriculum.

Each of the six teams offers two thematic programs that students take consecutively. In order to graduate, students must complete all twelve interdisciplinary programs. Teams offer only one of their two programs during each twelve-week cycle. During the cycle, the team works with sixty to ninety students, who are organized into three or four "strands." Each "strand" is a group/cohort of students who attend classes together, a form of block-programming.[1]

NATIVE LANGUAGE ENHANCEMENT CLASS

The reorganization of the school gave teachers and administrators the opportunity to refocus attention on how the school promoted students' native languages. This, in turn, led to the creation of an approach that applied the same practices to native language development as the school used in the development of English language skills. The challenge, however, was to develop language skills in a variety of languages simultaneously, languages in which the teacher would have little or no knowledge.

In developing the approach, one of the six teams designed an interdisciplinary program around the theme of change, called "American Reality: Changes." Within this program, the team offered a class in native language enhancement. This course, first taught in the Fall of 1993, was initiated in order to promote, in an organized fashion, the native languages of all students. It is one of two courses in the school that makes active use of the students' native languages. The other course that does this is linguistics, within the "Structures" theme.

Composition of Class

Students at International High School are block programmed. That is, they generally remain with the same group of students (their "strand") for all their

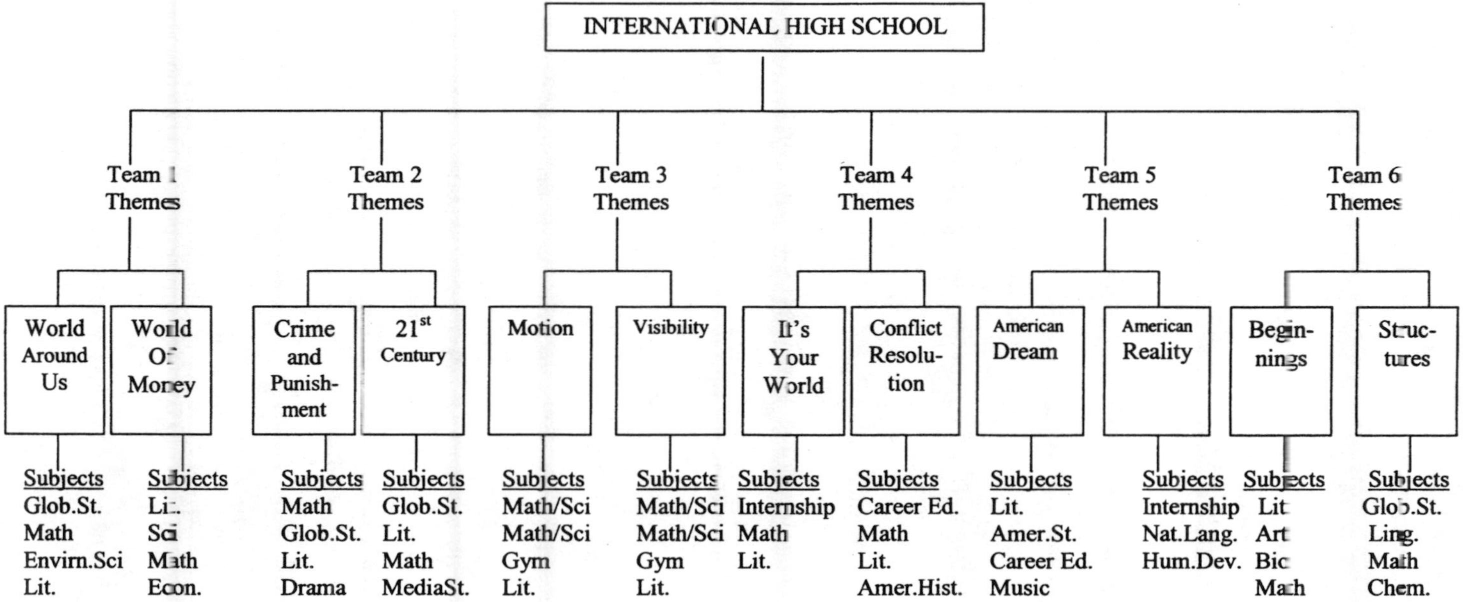

COMMON ELEMENTS

Eventually all students take all 12 themes
12 weeks are spent per theme
4-6 teachers per team
60-90 students per team
70 min. are spent per interdisciplinary subject

Figure 9.1
Curriculum Organization Chart

classes during any given semester. While registering students for strands in the American Reality interdisciplinary program, teachers paid great attention to two key factors—diversity and congruity.

Teachers selected students in order to retain a level of linguistic diversity reflective of the school. Since one-third of the school is Spanish-speaking and about one fifth speaks Polish, care was taken to ensure that the class (strand) was not overwhelmingly representative of just those two linguistic groups. At the same time, teachers wanted to avoid, whenever possible, having only one speaker of any particular language (singletons). While this was not always possible, the targeted diversity was achieved. That first year, one strand included speakers of Spanish, Polish, Korean, Romanian, Chinese, Tagalog, Portuguese, and Armenian. The ensuing diversity mitigated against any one language dominating the class.

For purposes of learning, students were grouped with others who spoke their language, thereby providing linguistic congruity. This congruity allowed students the opportunity to use their native language to interact with and learn from each other. The diverse levels of proficiency that the students brought enabled the less proficient to learn from the more proficient. The approaches relied on were peer-mediated instruction and collaborative learning in students' own languages.

The result was a linguistically heterogeneous class but with enough homogeneity that small groups of each language could be formed. While students used their native language within each language group, they used English across language groups in order to share projects, knowledge, and insights gained.

Description of Program

The instructional program was designed to allow native language enrichment to take place naturally in meaningful and purposeful contexts. To this end, teachers developed collaborative, interdisciplinary activities and projects. These projects provided multiple contacts with the native language. They also provided diverse opportunities for students to interact with ideas, skills, and content inside and outside the classroom. Their native language, was used continually as a medium for communicating, learning, and thinking. English, their second language, was drawn in as a common point of reference, a way of sharing ideas and experiences between language groups and with the teacher.

As an example, students started the cycle in "American Reality: Changes" by examining a poem about change. They proceeded to translate the poem, written in English, into their own native languages in linguistically homogeneous groups. Then, they wrote their own poem about change in their languages, and followed by translation of these poems into English. Throughout this introductory activity, students were asked to reflect on their feelings and thoughts about how they changed, their feelings changed, and the poems changed as they moved back and forth between their first and second languages. Finally, they read their poems aloud in both English and their native languages, compared and contrasted poetic styles and devices used in their different languages, and displayed copies of the poems in the class, placing English and their native language side by side.

Other activities included reading and analyzing newspaper articles and poetry in their native language, conducting surveys of community attitudes, and doing research in and about their communities. Independent reading was always followed up with written reading logs, which were shared among speakers of the same native language. In all cases, students read, wrote, spoke, and listened to their native languages. Frequently, they were expected to share the results of their work in English with others in the class. Chapter Appendices A and B are examples of native language activity guidelines used for two of the written projects students were expected to produce.

Students also worked collaboratively with students who spoke their language to produce a magazine in that language. As they worked on activities exploring their native language literature, culture, community, and career opportunities, as well as the theme of changes in human development, they produced articles, drawings, cartoons, and advice columns for their magazines.

Throughout the twelve-week instructional program, students were prompted to write in journals and reflect on their experience as learners. One aspect of their learning that they examined was their attitude toward and development of their native language. Students were encouraged to think in metalinguistic terms as they were asked to compare working in a native language group with working in a mixed language group. In their journals, responses were written weekly in their native language and English, and then read by teachers who responded in English.

At the end of the program, as a culminating experience, students from the four strands of the American Reality program came together for an end term activity. As part of this activity, students were grouped across strands by native language. This gave students a broader audience for their own native language projects, as well as the opportunity to listen, read, and react to projects done by other students in their own languages.

This instructional program requires teachers to be facilitators of content learning as they promote native language development. Students' primary languages are vehicles through which content is explored even when teachers do not speak those languages. Translation both from the native language to English and vice versa serves multiple purposes in this process: content learning, native language development, and English language acquisition. In addition, by moving from the native language into English, all students are provided access to the work and thoughts of all their peers.

Materials Acquisition

With grant support from 1993 to 1996, the school bought dictionaries, native language books of various genres, newspapers, and magazines. One teacher described the difficulties inherent in buying books in languages not spoken by teachers, as well as the successful, innovative approach she developed to solve this problem:

It was bewildering to order materials I could not read. In addition, book companies that are on approved Board of Education lists are very limited and provide mostly Spanish works or elementary school level books in a few other languages. At this point, I turned to the students for help in locating materials in their languages. What originated out of my feelings of frustration and desperation became an important way of including students in their own learning experience. At first, I went on shopping sprees with groups of students who directed me towards things they were interested in buying. Eventually, I gave students money to go shopping in their own neighborhoods for magazines and newspapers since there was no one location that could provide everything we needed. Parents also became involved in shopping for books, together with other staff members throughout the school.

Clearly, what evolved was student involvement in the learning process. To a large degree, students were given control over what and how they learned. Their judgment was sought out and this meant that they were trusted and by extension empowered. The involvement of parents also let students know that their parents' opinions were respected and that they had something important to offer the educational system.

Assessment

Visitors to the International High School often asked what teachers do when a student's project or portfolio was written in a language other than English. Who did the assessment and how was it assessed?

There were five sources of information on student proficiency and growth: peers, teachers, other staff, community members, and the students themselves. Peers and others competent in the language of a written assignment read it and provided feedback to the student in open forums. In addition, student writing was read by or discussed with the teacher. The writers used teacher response to revise their written work. If the teacher did not speak the student's language, he or she approached the work using a writing process approach. One teacher, a monolingual English speaker, and a licensed high school English teacher with over fifteen years of experience described how she did this:

I sit down with students and ask them to talk to me about their native language articles. I point to a paragraph and ask them to tell me about it. I continue to ask questions about the content as well as the structure.

This teacher, who has worked as a teacher trainer with the New York City Writing Project and is an expert in writing process, pointed out that:

146

My background as an English teacher made it very easy to suggest structural changes in their writing. What makes a powerful story stays the same in any language. If you push the student to write in his/her own voice and include personal narratives, then you are helping the writing become stronger.

The two languages worked together in this consultative process. Interspersed in a student's written narrative in the native language, teachers commented and made suggestions written in English. This teacher's comments were the result of a writing conference with the student about his/her paper. In this way, the two languages worked together to support each other.

In addition to peers and teachers, other staff and community members were involved in reading and responding to student's work:

If the teacher does not speak the student's language, the teacher may call on other staff members, who collectively are proficient in 22 languages, to help in assessing the content of the portfolio. When the language of the student is not found among the languages spoken by the staff, then a parent, student, or community member may be called upon for help. The translator assists the teacher and student in discussions, in writing comments, asking questions, or giving suggestions. These kinds of assessments and interchanges focus on the content of the piece and its general structure and organization. (Sylvan 1994)

Summary

Having described the native language enhancement project, we will turn to a discussion of the impact of this initiative on teachers and students alike. Our discussion will focus on describing how the project changed teachers and students in very fundamental and lasting ways, including their attitudes, their actions, and their degree of personal and professional awareness.

IMPACT OF PROGRAM

What happens when teachers are put into the position of having to teach or helping to facilitate the learning of a language over which they have little or no knowledge? How do they respond? What do they gain in the process and what do their students gain, if anything? What happens when students are made responsible for their own learning? In order to shed light on these questions and to better understand the impact of this native language enhancement (NLE) initiative on students and teachers alike, oral and written forms of data were collected. We were particularly interested in examining unplanned change that resulted from participation in the program, that is, change that went beyond growth in language. We wanted to understand it qualitatively from the perspective of the teachers and students who participated.

To these ends, teachers and students who participated in the project were interviewed as two separate cohorts. Group interviews afforded interviewees the opportunity to build on the responses and experiences of each other in discussing personal change that resulted from their participation in this venture.

In addition to the interviews, three sources of written data were examined from students: questionnaires, journals, and essays. At the beginning of the course students were asked to complete a questionnaire about their attitudes toward their native language, English, and the class they were about to take. The questionnaire (Chapter Appendix C) served as a catalyst to get students to think about language use, loss, and growth. On a weekly basis students were expected to make entries into a journal. The journal was both personal and reflective of their experience with the American Reality theme. However, it was understood that teachers would read and respond to journal entries. At the end of the cycle students prepared a portfolio that included two essays. The first was a personal statement reflecting on their growth throughout the cycle. The second was a mastery statement about what was learned in the three areas in which the student had participated: human development, native language, and internship work experience.

Data on teacher change came from both the group interviews and from teachers' self-evaluations written at the end of the year. In these written reflections, teachers commented on their personal growth as well as that of their colleagues.

In analyzing the data, each oral and written comment related to the personal impact of this program was listed as a separate entry. Entries were coded according to the type of transformation each suggested. Coding by one reader was either confirmed or altered in consultation with the second reader. Once coded, entries were then grouped by category in order to facilitate their inclusion in the narrative on change that follows. Coding was not intended to be used to quantify change or impact, but rather to qualify it.

DIMENSIONS OF TEACHER CHANGE

The Native Language Enhancement program was less about teaching a language than it was about learning a language, specifically helping students become independent learners, responsible for both what they learned and how much was learned. In the absence of knowing the multiplicity of languages that their students spoke and were there to learn, teachers, by necessity, focused on how their students learned. More specifically, they wanted to know how they as teachers could facilitate the learning process.

Three distinct categories of change emerged from teachers' commentaries. The first was change in attitudes both toward the students' native languages and toward the native language initiative in which teachers were participating. The second was change in action specifically in the way teachers approached the teaching-learning process. A third area of change was in the teacher's level of awareness about their students, the learning process, and language development.

Changes in Attitudes

From conversations with teachers it was obvious that a positive attitude prevailed regarding the use and maintenance of the native language at The International High School. In part this was a reflection of the philosophy of the school. Teachers have intellectualized the advantages of maintenance. They speak favorably and even passionately about the value of the students' native languages. One wrote of her "profound love" for Spanish, a language she acquired as a second language. She expressed "deep-rooted concern for those who are wrenched from their countries and languages," comparing that separation to the one she experienced as a child when Yiddish was "stolen" from her, first by parents who used it to keep things from her, second, "by Hitler who virtually wiped out an entire people, their culture, and their language in Europe, as well as much of my family; and third, by an assimilationist attitude prevalent in the United States in the early 1900's." Other teachers also spoke about their commitment to native language maintenance in interviews and in their written self-evaluations. This commitment was also evidenced throughout the school in posters and school assemblies.

Teachers also understood the positive correlation between high proficiency levels in the native language and the acquisition of a second language (Cummins 1989). They were also aware of the fact that gains in one language help promote gains in the other. This understanding was even passed on to their students. In interviews teachers commented: "We tell them being fluent in L1 helps them later on," and "that skills are transferable."

Teachers nevertheless realized that in spite of their good intentions, students were losing their native language proficiency. They had observed that "students do little native language reading and less writing." It was this realization that helped teachers buy into the project.

However, operationalizing a program of native language maintenance in a multilingual classroom challenged teachers' convictions at multiple levels. It challenged their convictions about maintenance. It also made them reevaluate their role as teacher as well as the role of their students in the teaching-learning process. Finally, it made them appreciate their students in new and profound ways.

By and large, teachers did not buy into this project without reservation. On the one hand, there was a great deal of surface appreciation for the multiplicity of languages spoken by their students and for the maintenance of that proficiency. However, this surface appreciation did not parallel how teachers initially felt about the native language enhancement initiative and about teaching out of license. They spoke and wrote about their initial resistance and fear—feeling a loss about what to do, feeling "left out," even "terrified originally." They felt like "outsiders." Early on they realized that they knew less than their students, did not understand everything, and were not in control of what was being said or written. Teachers commented:

How can I read this? How do I know it's not nonsense?

What are they talking about?

How can I respond to the native language if I don't know it?

I wasn't used to it (teaching multiple languages). I didn't know what to do.

One teacher was so immobilized that she put off starting the project for six weeks. She said that she "didn't know what to do."

Teachers' feelings of being an outsider and out of control augmented their resistance. It also challenged the way they thought about teaching and learning. If this project were to succeed, the teachers would have to find new ways of approaching their subject matter—languages they could neither speak nor understand. Over time some of their fears, resistance, and discomfort dissipated. They actually started feeling comfortable with not understanding everything said in class.

I became comfortable with eight languages spoken that I didn't understand.

So what if I don't understand what kids were saying and why they were laughing.

Students were maybe having too much fun. That's when I would ask what they were discussing and draw them back to the assignment.

Teachers moved from feeling left out of the learning process to feeling a part of it. Eventually they learned to become comfortable facilitating the process. They also realized that the use of the native language both engaged students and expedited learning. The attitude became contagious. Teachers had bought into and now owned a new vision of the role of the native language in learning. In sharing their vision and enthusiasm, they enlisted the support of their colleagues.

In terms of attitudes, what started as surface appreciation, for language maintenance as an ideology but with resistance to an institutional maintenance effort, ended up as a new and deeper understanding of the impact of native language mastery. Teachers saw that unforeseen benefits accrued. Students were "writing extended discourse in languages that could be lost." They were also "reading more" and enjoying it more, and "If they love to read they will read more." As another teacher put it: "learning is learning. By becoming more literate in the native language, students become more literate in general."

Changes in Action

Teachers' insights into the learning process evolved both out of necessity and frustration. As questions about the process surfaced so too did the search for solutions. In the absence of a curriculum, teachers had to become innovative. Once they realized that their role was truly one of facilitation, as one teacher put it, "the philosophy was liberating," allowing him to act in new ways. Another teacher noted that she felt she was a "more creative and more interesting teacher" when she "went out of license."

The philosophy of facilitation that emerged allowed teachers to relinquish control, share power, and enlist the assistance of others. They consulted with colleagues, parents, and students about issues of content, form, feedback, assessment, and materials acquisition. Teachers were "eager to adapt and learn new things." In the absence of a model for this approach or any curriculum guides, new approaches to learning had to evolve and greater collaboration ensued. "We talked and came up with ways of active listening, making connections."

New problems also had to be faced. The most obvious one was how to help students learn a language the teacher doesn't know. Strategies evolved in the form of native language activity guides, which were discussed earlier, two of which appear as Appendices A and B. Other activity guides were developed to guide students through the use of native language newspapers, responding to literature, and investigating their communities and cultures.

Another problem was how to promote language development for students without a linguistic partner and therefore without an audience. One teacher noted: "Some kids were alone. We had to look for outsiders to enable them to practice. I thought of bringing in an adult." Other teachers had students seek out native language informants in and out of school.

Yet another problem was how to be sure students were talking and writing about the subject at hand. It was decided that students would respond to each other in their native language and then report back in English to the teacher.

The instructional repertoire of teachers was extended in a number of other ways. What evolved was the promotion of "real interaction among students" both within language groups and across them. The heterogeneity of the linguistic groups in terms of their literacy skills enabled the more proficient to serve as models, leaders, and tutors for the less proficient. This resulted in a great deal of consultation among peers, as well as a great deal of purposeful talk and sharing. "Kids shared the native language readings they had done in their own countries." By extension, greater sharing led to greater listening among students—a truly active learning environment, facilitated by the teacher's openness and trust of students. Teachers' concepts of student-centered learning were pushed to a new level. The result was true empowerment of students. In the face of not knowing students' languages, there was no alternative.

Teachers relied heavily on translation and questioning as their way of knowing what was being discussed in small native language discussion groups. A five- to ten-minute conversation among students would yield a thirty-second translation. This would be followed up by questions from the teacher seeking clarification and/or the extension of ideas by students.

In addition to extending their teaching repertoire and engaging students in greater dialogue, teachers became more astute observers of their students. They realized early on the extent of students' language loss as they read students' commentaries and listened to them talk. Students talked and wrote about "Americanisms slipping into their native language writing," that they were reading less in the native language, if at all, and that they were now having to look up more words than before. "One Polish boy had no trouble when he was 13. He was appalled he had lost vocabulary." Another student "was embarrassed by reading his native language out loud. While he never got over it, he was pleased with his final project." All were observations made by teachers.

Teachers newly sensitized observation skills allowed them to notice that language loss being reversed. They noted that "students were writing extended discourse in languages that could be lost" and that students were "excited about what was read." They "started reading novels in Spanish and Polish." Students "became interested in native language literacy and in sharing it." They "were excited about seeing books in the native language which they had read as young teens." They also "gobbled up magazines and newspapers," and "started keeping up with current events." A Christmas card sent to one teacher said that the teacher had made the student "love literature." Another teacher noted that the NLE class "reawakened in students a love of their native language and country and of not wanting to lose either." One teacher synthesized the process and impact on students quite succinctly:

Students read a lot in their native language. For many, it was the first time in a very long time. They were startled to find out that they had forgotten so many words, and suddenly it hit home that if they didn't actively read and write in their native language, they would lose it. It wasn't enough just to speak the language.

Teachers garnered from students' comments that the study of the native language was having its impact at home on intergenerational communication as well as in the community. A student shared with the teacher the fact that she had read with her grandmother at home. Another had showed his older sister his work. And yet another had translated in a hospital for an elderly Russian, feeling "good she was able to help."

As a result of reflective observations, teachers gained a new appreciation for their students. Students' writing and their presentations provided everyone with insight on their plight as immigrants and their migration experience, as well as their cultures. Teachers also had greater insight into their students as language learners and of the language and cultural losses their students were experiencing. The teachers' feelings, of being an "outsider" and of their discomfort with languages they didn't understand, helped them appreciate their students feeling left out and not understanding English.

Teachers found students' writing to be "thoughtful and powerful." One teacher commented on the power of kids sharing their reading logs and commenting on each other's entries. Another remembered vividly Ali, a shy student, who "did a marvelous dance for us." She noted that it was powerful for him as well as his classmates. The feeling was that the program had an "emotional impact on kids." It enabled them to "bond with their country, their culture, and themselves." Sharing their experiences "brought tears to the eyes of students," made them "miss their country," and in some cases "brought out the pain associated with the American dream and reality." A composition written by one of the students best exemplifies these feelings.

My country, Vietnam, has passed 4,000 years of history. More than 99% of this time, my country had struggled under the aggression from the Eastern imperialists to the Western imperialists. Thus, my people and I were born with a strong nationalist spirit in our soul. No piece of literature I've read can fully describe how I love my country. No piece of music I've heard can meaningfully express how I feel about my country. No piece of painting I've seen can exactly picture how my country is to me. Only deep, deep inside my heart actually knows how I miss those coconut trees running along the riverside, the tender sweet taste of the mango, the intensely warm flavor of the durian. I don't want to recall any further of my country because this just makes me sad.

I left my country when I was just thirteen and now I have been in America for more than three years. The only thing that keeps me in touch with my country is my native language. I read newspapers, magazines, books in my language almost everyday. I also spend time talking with my people to keep my memories of my country alive. That is why I really appreciate that I can work and do a book in Vietnamese in our class.

In terms of action, teachers had moved from being in control of their subject matter to being real facilitators of students learning languages that teachers did not know. Further, in light of not knowing the language, teachers became more astute observers of their students in general as well as of the impact of the NLE initiative on their students. Their involvement in this initiative enhanced their understanding of student-centered learning while also extending their teaching repertoire. It forced them to seek solutions to learning problems that they never would have faced otherwise. In the process, they were able to see and appreciate yet another dimension of their students.

Metacognitive Awareness

The approach that evolved in the absence of models or guides was one of experimentation and role redefinition. As teachers redefined their role within the NLE initiative, they also redefined it more globally. They thought critically about learning and what fosters it.

You know what you say and what you've taught when it's in a language you know. But that doesn't mean you know what kids have learned. Therefore, what is taught is not always what is learned. When teaching in another language (one you do not know) that realization is made obvious.

The issue of control generated much reflection and commentary. One teacher commented that "control is an illusion," and that "when you can't have control you must face some issues," such as the relative importance of knowing what everyone is doing. Teachers agreed that "not having control leads to more trust of students." Another observed: "Relinquishing authority and control is difficult to unlearn. I am uncomfortable at times with not being the center of learning in the classroom." Yet this same teacher noted a year later in her annual self-evaluation:

In the past, I was always uncomfortable when groups would speak in their native language, feeling they were excluding everyone else at the table, including me. Now that they were purposely being grouped by their native language, this was no longer a concern, but mainly the change was in me. I felt comfortable.

Since they were "teaching" a language they did not know, teachers had to develop strategies that would enable students to use their native language, push it to new limits, and assess their own progress. This put teachers in the role of learners. Being learners helped them understand the learning process in a very personal way. Learning became the primary and only focus in their classrooms since teachers could not really teach what they did not know. They had no alternative but to become facilitators of learning.

Eventually the program led to changes in the way all content was taught by the participating teachers. The most obvious change is that the native language became infused throughout the curriculum. The more profound change was in the subordination of teaching to learning.

Beyond participating teachers, others bought into the power and potential of developing the native language as a catalyst for learning, a source of involvement, as well as a means of improving the English language proficiency of their students. As mentioned earlier in this chapter, three of the six interdisciplinary teams submitted proposals for the funding of small native language initiatives within their teams.

Teachers involved in this initiative gained confidence in working with students who spoke very little English. As one teacher noted, what was challenged was "the old traditional mold that I am supposed to be everything for students, provide all the answers, all the direction."

DIMENSIONS OF STUDENT CHANGE

Through participation in this class, student attitudes toward language and learning went through major transformation. In addition, student behavior was affected and students began to develop a more global understanding of themselves as bilingual learners and people. All student excerpts in this section are included as they were written, without changes to grammar, punctuation, or spelling.

Students' Attitude Changes

Students entered the native language class with certain attitudes about language and language learning. These attitudes influenced their attitudes toward the NLE class. For example, students entering the class often expressed

154

their initial resistance to working in their native language because they wanted to learn English and because they believed they already knew their native language. In reflecting on this, some students noted:

I tried very hard to learn the English language . . . it was like that was the only thing I was interested in and I did not even bother to read or write in my native language. . . . Before this course I wasn't reading too much in my native language because I was thinking that the most important thing for now is to learn more and more English. . . . But I didn't realize that slowly I started to forget my native language.

Many students assumed that since they spoke their native language, and often had studied it before coming to the United States, they had complete command of it. Once students were again placed in a position where they had to use their native language for academic purposes, often for the first time in many years, they became poignantly aware of their own language loss.

When I started writing articles for the [native language] magazine, I forgot a lot of words and it seem hard for me to write. I was a little upset about it, because I'm Chinese. I'm supposed to know my language as good as I speak.

I realized how much of my language I have forgotten. I wrote articles for the magazine in both English and Croatian.

I feel upset when I do not understand or cannot concentrate in reading the newspapers in my native language. . . . I remember I used to read very fast in Chinese, but because I didn't work on Chinese for two years, I have forgotten some words. Now there are many words I did not understand and it takes long time to go to the dictionary.

The more English I learned, the more Portuguese went away. . . . When my teacher said that we have to write in our own native language, I said to myself, it's going to be terrible. I will be ashamed writing in Portuguese because I think my Portuguese is first grade level.

In at least some cases, part of the initial resistance by some students was due to embarrassment at their proficiency level in their own language. Still, participation in the native language class made them more aware of their own language loss. This, in turn, led them to change their attitudes. From their initial resistance to working in their native language, they moved toward embracing their language more deeply. Students came to value their knowledge and acquisition of their native language for both instrumental and affective reasons.

I don't want to forget my Polish because I know that in my future I will need it a lot. For example, if I want to be a lawyer I can help people from my own country and Americans.

It is important for me not to forget my native language (Tagalog) because it's where I come from and it's good to be able to speak, write, and read in two different languages.

Native language . . . is a way of looking back to my roots. To me [if] I don't understand in Bengali, I am not going to get clear thought in English.

Living far away from native lands, people forget their culture and social activities. The native language class helped me to retain my culture and heritage. . . . After doing their course, I come to an opinion that native language is sweeter to everybody than English. We can express our feelings easily in native language.

The projects we did in native language have made me remember all of the words that I had forgotten. In a way, I rediscovered myself.

Students' Behavioral Changes

The changes in student attitudes about the importance and benefits of enhancing native language proficiency were accompanied by changes in behavior. Students acted differently toward their native language. Their relationship with their community and their family also saw a change.

Students learned to appreciate the literature of their countries and to pursue it.

I have read a lot in my native language. I read "Painted Bird" and Polish magazines. Before I didn't like to read or write in Polish and now . . . I love to read in my native language.

I have some Polish books at home and I think that I will start reading them to improve my native language.

They also realized that they needed to be proactive if they wanted to stem the language loss that was occurring. They talked and wrote about what they needed to do.

I could see that I need to practice my language or otherwise I may forget how to read and write in Spanish.

As my English is improving, I didn't really care about my Chinese. Since I took native language, I realize that just reading newspapers and writing letters and talking to my family is not enough to improve my Chinese.

While we were working on one of the articles and we started reading and writing, after a while I was improving and remembering. . . . Now I am going to read and write in my native language at home so I don't forget.

Students often expressed their desire to take action to stem language loss in terms that indicated their reconnection with their roots.

I learned that it is really important to practice writing and reading in my native language more because . . . my roots are . . . important because it's my origin and I should not leave it aside. From now on, I would read and write more often in my language.

I feel comfortable working with a group of people who speak the same language as me. I feel I'm in China and it reminds me of my school life in China. My feelings of missing China are getting stronger and stronger. . . . I would feel close to my country and hear the laughing sound come from my childhood. I miss China so much.

Students also noted how studying their native language had improved relationships at home. A young Haitian student explained how he "Got to know what [his] mother went through when she was a young lady." Another noted:

The last and most important thing I had got from my native language activities was that it got me closer to my parents. Since I had to ask them for help and to answer my questions, I communicated with them frequently and it became OUR homework not just mine. When I translated that poem from English to Indonesian, my mom and dad were actually fighting on getting the words that resemble the real meaning. It was a lot of fun. It got my family closer together. Thank you.

Students' Metacognitive/Metalinguistic Awareness

Students began to see how improving their skills in their native language aided them in increasing their proficiency in English.

In my mind, I was thinking that the improvement in Vietnamese helps me improve in English. . . . [If] the writing in Vietnamese are well, then my writing and understanding in English are well too.

When you are learning your own language, for example, you learned a new word and right away you want to know how to say it in English.

Others developed more advanced understanding of language learning. One student's insights paralleled those of one of the foremost theorists on language learning, particularly the notions of a "common underlying proficiency" and of "transfer" (Cummins 1989).

The similarities in writing in Chinese and writing in English are the ideas, the way to organize, and how to learn the way of expression. . . . If you know how to organize an article well in your native language, you will also do a great job in your English writing because the idea of how to organize the article is the same, no matter what language you use. So it seems to me that if I improve my Chinese writing skills, I will also improve my English writing skills. The reason is the whole idea about how to write is almost the same.

Students also gained a broader metacognitive awareness of how they learned, who was responsible for their learning, and who should, could, and did control the learning process.

We weren't doing all this stuff just because the teachers wanted us to, we were doing it for ourselves. We don't want to forget our own language, at least I don't. . . . I thought that when we did the native language project the teachers will give it to somebody who is from the same country to check it, but then D— told me that he didn't give it to anybody, he didn't even grade it. I think that was good. He may think that we would be cheating because he doesn't understand Polish, but the truth is that we weren't because we did it for ourselves.

How could I forget the one activity where we had to read a rather thick novel in my language and respond to it in Indonesian? That was a little weird in the beginning. I mean, who would understand anything I wrote? I was going to write nonsense, but you know something—it was even harder. I ended up writing a brief summary regarding the plot and put down my feelings about it.

Teachers also noticed that students were clearly taking over their learning. They were initiating projects both within the class and outside of it. They carried over the use of the native language to other subjects. Some students did a project on birth control in Spanish for human development, their sex education class. The teacher went on to explain that the project was done by students who decided that incoming freshman needed immediate information about birth control. The students took it upon themselves to organize a workshop in Spanish for them.

As they became more involved in the assessment of their own work and that of their peers, they resisted interference from the outside. Some students were described as "hostile to outsiders." One teacher analyzed it in this manner:

The idea of having outside help, of having staff members read their work had mixed results. . . . The reactions from the students were surprising. They felt it was not their teacher giving them the criticism and they really balked. Partly it was the timing. It was nearing the end of the cycle and time was very short. Their magazines were already in their final state and at this point, they were not eager to receive constructive criticism or do lengthy revisions.

The behavioral changes and broader awareness that students gained led them to further change their attitudes toward the native language initiative. Excerpts from one student's weekly journal showed a transformation typical of many other students.

[Week 1] Probably I will be very rude saying that taking the native language class is a waste of time for some of the students. Many students, including me, don't know English perfectly and we need more time and practice to learn this language. Moreover, we deal with our native language every day, at school and at home. I don't think we need special classes where we can learn the native language.

[Week 2] I know I said that by taking native language class is a waste of time for some of us, but right now I have to say the class will be very helpful with finding out how much we understand the importance of practicing and knowing our language. Right now, I understand why we took this class, to not stay at the same level in our native languages as when we left our countries.

[Week 5] Honestly, at the beginning of this cycle, I thought that I will not [be] learning anything. . . . I wasn't so happy by taking the American Reality program, but right now I feel great that it turned to be interesting and knowledgeable. I really learned a lot from these classes, for example that it's very important for me to still learn in my native language, to increase my growth from the level that I left when I came here and improve my writing and reading skills in native language.

SUMMARY

The Native Language Enhancement (NLE) initiative affected both teachers and students. What evolved was a transformation in the way teachers teach and students learn as well as how teachers and students viewed themselves, each other, and their language. The class promoted changes in the attitudes, behavior, and awareness of participants.

Teachers and students went through a parallel transformation. They both started out with a positive attitude toward the multiple languages spoken by the students in the school. However, there was some resistance or skepticism on the part of both to the NLE initiative. They differed in that teachers believed that without native language support, students would inevitably lose whatever language ability they brought from their native countries. Students, on the other hand, did not acknowledge the encroaching loss of native language ability or the need for enrichment, until they were well into the class. Once realized, students applied themselves and took charge of their own linguistic growth. They embraced their language and saw unanticipated benefits in its development. There was a reconnection to and deeper understanding of their families, an appreciation of their literature, and an active pursuit of maintenance.

Teachers moved in their teaching toward greater facilitation of learning, something that had already permeated the school, but not to the extent that this project necessitated and engendered. In the absence of knowing the students' native languages, teachers both consciously and openly transferred control of the learning process to the students. In addition, teachers found new ways to facilitate this process.

Both teachers and students gained greater awareness of the process of learning and of the power of trust in that process. Students also gained insight into the paths and ways of linguistic transfer and how knowledge of their native language enhanced learning of their second language, English. The awareness and insight they gained further empowered students to become better learners and more integrated people with the linguistic, cognitive, and cultural skills necessary for success.

Part of the success of this project was predicated on its underlying philosophy. There was a fundamental belief at the International High School that the enhancement of one's native language impacts positively on the development of a second language, especially when both languages are used to facilitate learning and good writing. Said another way, gains made in one language promote gains in the other. A second belief was that good writing is good writing is good writing. In her annual self-evaluation, coauthor Claire Sylvan, the catalyst for this initiative and a teacher in the project, encapsulated the context and rationale behind the NLE initiative.

Adolescents are going through major changes in general. Throw in moving to a new country, and a new trauma is added. Next, remove their language, which allows them to express their being, which is in turmoil, and you have the potential for real difficulties. No wonder some kids resist learning English. Even for those who do well in English, what is the psychological cost if their own language is neglected, discarded, while learning English? Why should bilingualism be subtractive (lose your language while learning another)? Why can't it be additive (keep and develop your language while learning another)? What message do we send if, as a school, we don't, in practice, transmit the message of additive bilingualism to our students? Cumulatively, the psychological cost of depriving students of their native language must translate into sociological costs. Obviously, there is a linguistic cost as well, to the society.

CONCLUSIONS AND IMPLICATIONS

The NLE initiative evolved as a learner-centered instructional program that provided a language-rich environment that made language maintenance possible. It built upon the philosophy that students learn best when teachers use their professional expertise, not principally as providers of knowledge, but as facilitators of a process that enables students and faculty to learn while making language choices to accomplish meaningful activities.

However, what started out as a project to initiate a native language enrichment program in a multilingual environment, ended up as a project that created fundamental and pervasive change in attitudes and practice of participants. Beyond its impact on participants, the initiative left its mark on curriculum and practice across the entire school community. The NLE initiative had a catalytic effect on the school community, affecting other teachers and their perceptions of students and the languages they bring to school. This translated into school-wide support for institutionalizing the maintenance of the linguistic resources that students bring to school and to the United States. This support was concomitant with continued pursuit of the mission of the school to prepare students for higher education within an English speaking country. Further, this support resulted in an infusion of native languages across many strands and disciplines at the school and the requirement that the graduation portfolio include documentation of students' growth in their native language. One teacher noted that "the critical mass in favor of using native language has grown." What seems to have evolved is an understanding of how two languages can work together to complement each other in the learning process and in the acquisition of a second language. In addition, there was the realization that gains made in the latter do not have to be at the expense or result in the loss of the native language.

The educational innovation begun in one class by one team clearly spread throughout the school. The small group of teachers who started out in the project became catalysts for change and created the critical mass needed for bottom-up reform. They bought into and shared a vision of how the native language could be used to enhance all learning. Teachers sharing their transformation and success, and students sharing their enthusiasm and commitment have moved nonparticipating teachers throughout the school to action. Indeed, when so many people are struggling to promote educational reform, it would be useful to investigate further ways in which the educational innovation was diffused throughout the entire organization.

In addition to issues of reform which need exploration and on which this initiative has helped to shed light, there is still the issue of language education and its relative importance in a society which values monolingualism so highly. The value of native language maintenance for all students is illuminated very ably by a student who wrote:

I feel sorry for people who disregard the importance and value of maintaining their language. I just want to say to all immigrants that America may be your home for the rest of your life, but don't forget where you came from. It's like you're in the present and heading to the future, but don't forget your past no matter how good or bad it was. You can't go forward unless you know what steps you have passed. Everyone has a country.

A recent *New York Times* article highlights the importance of supporting the maintenance and development of the native languages of increasingly diverse student populations throughout the United States for the country.

While the cold war's end has brought waves of immigrants with knowledge of obscure languages to the United States . . . linguistic shortfalls [have] gone from an episodic to a chronic problem. "It's now affecting the ability of federal agencies to address their missions." (Schemo 2001)

The issue originally posed is: Can language educators support the plethora of languages that students bring to the American classroom without traditional academic and linguistic capacities? These traditional capacities include classrooms aimed at encouraging development in one language, and a teacher who is an expert in that language. This program indicates that even in the absence of these conditions, students can enhance their native language skills provided that the approach to teaching and learning is changed.

The language educators in this initiative moved from being the source of language knowledge to being the facilitators of language development. The students in this initiative could not be perceived as vessels into which language is poured. Rather, of necessity, teachers came to view students (and their communities) as the experts whose knowledge needed to be reawakened, built upon, and expanded. Materials for this program were collaboratively acquired and definitions of assessment were expanded to encompass growth on performance-based tasks.

These changes are fundamentally changes in how teachers view themselves and their students, how they understand their role as language teachers, how they understand the nature of teaching and learning, and how willing they are to share power in the language learning community. Despite the plethora of languages that might seem to preclude traditional language education, in fact this language diversity has the seeds within it that enable all schools and all language educators to support the development of the many languages that populate and enrich our schools and our society.

There are no preconditions in terms of language expertise of teachers. Nor do small numbers of speakers of a single language limit the capacity of a school or teacher to develop such a program. Rather, what is required is the courage to change fundamental assumptions about who is the expert, and how teachers and students interact in a language class when students come from diverse corners of the world. The courage to make these changes opens wide the door of possibilities to enrich our schools and our society with the language wealth that our students bring.

APPENDIX A: SAMPLE NATIVE LANGUAGE ACTIVITY GUIDE

American Reality: TRANSITIONS

Teenage Pregnancy: Native Language Activity

Today you will watch a video about four pregnant teenage girls. After the movie, you will have a discussion and do some activities with your internship peer groups.

We would also like you to investigate the attitudes toward teenage pregnancy among people of your native culture.

Instructions:

1. With other students from your native language, prepare a list of questions which can be used to interview teenagers, adults, and elderly people of your culture about their views and attitudes toward teen pregnancy.
2. Put the questions in a logical order. Check the questions to make sure that both you and the person you are interviewing will be comfortable with the way you've asked the questions.
3. Go over the questions with a teacher. Then make copies of the questions for each member of your group.
4. Each group member will use the questions to conduct interviews. Decide in your group:

   How many interviews will each group member do?
5. When your native language group meets next week, you will go over the interviews that each person did and decide how to combine the information. Here are some possibilities to think about:
   a. An article for your native language magazine
   b. An article in your English magazine that compares the attitudes of different cultures toward this issue
   c. A written report describing your findings in your native language, with a summary in English

    d. A poster and oral report, with written interview questions and answers turned in to the teachers

    e. Any other suggestion which you may have

APPENDIX B: SAMPLE NATIVE LANGUAGE ACTIVITY GUIDE

American Reality: CHANGES

Poetry Project

1. Form a small poetry group of speakers of your native language. Each of you will find two poems in your native language that you like. If you can, try to find poems from your own country.
2. Make a copy of the poems. Make sure the title and author and source are on them. Put these in the class poetry file.
3. Bring in your poems to share with your group on _____.
   a. Read each poem aloud.
   b. Select the poem(s) that your group wants to study.
4. Examine your poem together.
   a. Reread the poem at least three times.
   b. Practice reading it aloud in different ways.
   c. Discuss what each line means.
      Are there parts of the poem you still do not understand? Write about these parts.
   d. Pick out interesting images and talk about what they mean.
   e. Find out what makes it look and sound like a poem.
   f. Discuss if and how the poem feels like it comes from your country and culture.
5. Write your personal reactions/responses to the poems. Include:
   a. What you think the poem says. Write about specific lines and words and ideas in the poem that explain why you interpret the poem this way.
   b. What the poem makes you think about. Copy the lines from the poem that help explain your ideas.
      Complete this at home.
6. Choose at least two (2) of the following to work on *together*.
   a. The language of the poem. What makes it sound like a poem? Explain about
      * The sounds of words. What does the poet do to make words sound beautiful or interesting? For example, does the poet use rhyme or alliteration? Give examples.
      * The rhythm of the poem. Does the rhythm repeat or are the lines different? Why did the poet do that? Give examples.
      * Other poetic devices

   b. An important image from one of the poems and illustrate it.

- Draw or paint it in a colorful way to be hung in our class.

- Write a paragraph saying why you chose this image and what you think it means.

- Copy the line or lines from the poem that contain this image.

- Translate the line(s) into English. Put these lines on the picture.

   c. Translation of the poem into English. Include the titles of the poems and the names of the persons who wrote them. Include other information you know about the poems or the poets such as when they were written, why they were written, under what circumstances, etc.

Teach the poem to the class.

- Give each member of the class a copy of the poem in both your language and English.

- Read it aloud in your language and English.

- Select your favorite lines/images and explain them.

- Describe what makes it sound like a poem in your native language.

- Explain what changes occur when you translate the poem.

   d. Compare the poem with a poem on the same topic in English. Example: love, friendship, honor, death. Make a copy of the poem in English. For each poem, write about:

- How the poet feels about the topic.

- How poetic language is used.

- What your favorite lines and images are and explain them.

For both poems, summarize their similarities and/or differences:

- How the topic is treated.

- How poetic language is used.

- How culture may influence the poet's view of the topic.

Journal question: How do you feel when you read a poem in your native language? Compare this with your feelings about reading poetry in English. The poems can be obtained from

- A book you have at home

- A book a friend or relative has at home

- The International High School Library

- The Donnell Library in Manhattan on 53rd Street between 5th and 6th Avenues

- Your neighborhood public library

- The LaGuardia Library

APPENDIX C: STUDENT QUESTIONNAIRE

1. How do you feel when you use your native language?
2. How do you feel about reading and writing in your native language?
3. In what circumstances and with whom do you usually use your native language?
4. How do you feel when you use English?
5. In what circumstances and with whom do you usually use English?
6. What changes have you made in your use of English since you came to this country?
7. What changes have you made in your use of your native language since you came to this country?
8. How has your knowledge of English changed your use of your native language?
9. How do you feel about the changes in your use of language?
10. How do you feel about using your native language in this course?

NOTE

1. Since the research was completed, the school has undergone further restructuring, modifying in part the organizational structure described in this article.

BIBLIOGRAPHY

Auerbach, E. R. 1993. Reexamining English only in the ESL classroom. *TESOL Quarterly* 27 (1): 9–32.

Brown, H. D. 1993. *Principles of language learning and teaching.* Englewood Cliffs, NJ: Prentice Hall Regents.

Cummins, J. 1989. *Empowering minority students.* Sacramento: California Association of Bilingual Education.

The International High School partnership assessment guidelines and graduation requirements. 1994. New York: The International High School.

Lucas, T. and A. Katz. 1994. Reframing the debate: The roles of native language in English-only programs for language minority students. *TESOL Quarterly* 28 (3): 537–61.

Marcos, K. 2000. Are we wasting our nation's language resources? Heritage languages in America. In *Biliteracy for a global society: An idea book on dual language education,* ed. K. Lindholm-Leary, 6. Washington, DC: National Clearinghouse for Bilingual Education.

Oller, J. W., L. L. Baca, and A. Vigil. 1978. Attitudes and attained proficiency in ESL: A sociolinguistic study of Mexican-Americans in the Southwest. *TESOL Quarterly* 11, 173–83.

Pease-Alvarez, L. and A. Winsler. 1994. Cuando el maestro no habla Espanol. *TESOL Quarterly* 28 (3): 503–35.

Personnel procedures: Peer selection, support and evaluation at the International High School. 1985. New York: The International High School.

Project Propel handbook: Resources for adopting sites: Program Reorganization Promoting Excellence through Language. 1993. New York: The International High School.

Schemo, D. J. 2001. Use of English as world tongue is booming, and so is concern: In Washington, a lack of linguists to take key security jobs. *New York Times*, April 16: 1, 10.

Seliger, H. W. 1991. Language attrition, reduced redundancy, and creativity. In *First language* attrition, ed. H. W. Seliger and R. M. Vago, 227–40. New York: Cambridge University Press.

Silva-Corvalan, C. 1991. Spanish language attrition in a contact situation with English. In *First language attrition*, ed. H. W. Seliger and R. M. Vago, 151–71. New York: Cambridge University Press.

Sylvan, C. 1994. Native language development in a multilingual setting. *NABE News*, August 1: 35–36.

———. 1994. Assessment in a multilingual school: The International High School. *Educational Forum* 59 (1): 74–80.

Wong-Fillmore, L. 1955. When learning a second language means losing the first. In *Compendium of research on bilingual education*, ed. G. Gonzalez and L. Maez, 19–36. Washington DC: National Clearinghouse for Bilingual Education, George Washington University.

———. 1991. Language and cultural issues in early education. In *The care and education of America's young children: Obstacles and opportunities. The 90th yearbook of the National Society for the Study of Education*, ed. S. L. Kagan. Chicago: University of Chicago Press.

10

Authentic "Migratory" Experiences for Language Learners: Macrocontextualization as Critical Pedagogy

Xaé Alicia Reyes

A recent visit to a local high school on the night of student inductions into the variety of language clubs housed under the umbrella of World Languages confirmed my suspicions about the state of affairs in the teaching of Spanish. Each group of students to be inducted was introduced by the chair of the corresponding department. In the case of the Spanish department, the chair was a pleasant young New England native with a distinct peninsular Spanish accent. I shifted my weight in my chair as I heard the thick "zetas" (z's) and aspirated "jotas" (j's) as she addressed the students. Our pleasant introduction to each other was a little unsettling as I spoke in my most neutrally enunciated Spanish, which the majority of native speakers of Spanish fail to trace to any ethnic group, but that is decidedly not peninsular Spanish. Most Spanish speakers welcome the opportunity to practice the language; however, the level of enthusiasm is dictated by the perceived hierarchy of superiority of spoken peninsular Spanish over other varieties. After a polite exchange of introductions and some small talk, the Spanish teacher moved on to other guests and left me with the French teacher who had invited me.

As someone who taught Spanish language and culture for many years, I am able to move in and out of different varieties of Spanish depending on the setting. My spoken Spanish varies according to my interlocutor and my context. It ranges from a formal, neutral intonation that resembles the Spanish spoken in countries such as Colombia and Venezuela, to a more relaxed and elliptical Spanish spoken in my country of origin, Puerto Rico. Even within the locations mentioned, one finds variations that relate to levels of formal education of the speakers. The devaluing of Spanish varieties spoken outside of Spain, has been a constant in Spanish departments across the country. In this chapter I will discuss the impact of this hegemonic view of Spanish and the missed opportunities to enhance language fluency through what I call "authentic" migratory experiences. Critical pedagogy in the foreign language classroom is proposed as a framework to embrace a foreign language learning stance that considers power relationships among speakers of a language.

WHO GETS TO TEACH LANGUAGES?

My first foreign language experiences came about as a military dependent in Munich, Germany, where as a fourth grader I was introduced to German and went from beginning to advanced German as I completed sixth grade. The teacher was Frau Schatz and our classes consisted mainly of grammar lessons and some practice in reading and singing songs in German. Although I did not live in a fenced army post, our interactions with the local community would have been minimal to none had it not been for my parents. They made friends with locals and struggled with the language as we shopped in neighborhood stores and socialized with folks in the area. We visited and had friends over but none of them had children my age. This limited my potential to practice the language but it provided the realistic contexts to learn about the culture at deeper levels than most of our peers were able to experience. Hence, I identified foreign language teaching with native speaking ability and perhaps even with "foreign" born individuals.

Back in Puerto Rico, from seventh grade through my Master's degree, my teachers of English were nuns, from the United States. Later in public high schools and at the University of Puerto Rico, they were either Puerto Ricans educated in the continental United States or continentals living on the island. Many of my Spanish teachers at the college level were educated in Spain, and in courses such as Spanish grammar and syntax, my professors were from Galicia and the Canary Islands. I began to identify the higher variety of English with U.S. continentals and the higher variety of Spanish with Spaniards. While in graduate school I took German with a professor from Heidelberg, Germany. These experiences decidedly marked my understandings of who was allowed to teach a language. Furthermore, although practicing the language was encouraged, there were never discussions about language varieties and their relationship to world politics and power. Instead, the discussion was centered on the power struggles between those who supported Spanish as the official language on the island and those who felt that English should have equal status in order to further the cause of U.S. statehood for the Island (see Negrón de Montilla 1977). Language teachers would look to Spain for reinforcement and authority in the case of Spanish and to the United States (rather than Great Britain) in the case of English. Immersion in U.S. settings was constantly encouraged as the way to enhance native-like speaking ability. Some families would send their offspring to visit relatives in the United States to perfect their English. The goals or purposes of these exchanges were not met in cases where the students would wind up in a setting where all communication could take place in their native language.

Teaching Spanish at the college level in the United States gave me my first glimpse into the hierarchic relationships in Foreign/Modern Language departments. I taught Spanish in a number of colleges in the Northeast and in two different locations in the Southwest. As I assessed my environments, I soon discovered that, with few exceptions, the elite faculty in most departments were Spaniards, some Cuban-Spaniards, Argentineans, and Colombians, in this order. Seldom was there a "Puerto Rican" faculty member unless he/she was a graduate teaching assistant. There were always a large number of Spaniards, usually teaching the higher-level literature courses. These were often followed by a number of South Americans, usually from Argentina or Chile. As the "literary boom" of the seventies brought writers such as Borges, Cortázar, Vargas Lllosa, Allende, and García Márquez to the forefront, hiring of South American faculty became a little more attractive because students had to learn a repertoire of regional terms and modalities of language use in order to relate to the most prolific literary production in the last century. This legitimation of writings has not been as prevalent with regard to locations closer to the equator. Thus Puerto Rican, Cuban, and Dominican writers have commanded less attention in Spanish departments. A good number of graduate teaching assistants were Spaniards, Argentineans, and Colombians. Again, these students were usually assigned the higher-level courses as well.

In my view, content knowledge has been taken for granted in the hiring of language teachers in K–12 settings because candidates are usually referrals from colleges and universities. There is usually a pipeline through which language departments continue to relate to schools through their alumni. Pronunciation and native-speaking ability have been weighed more heavily. The major influence in deciding who would teach what, appeared to be the pronunciation patterns of the individuals vis a vis the status assigned to the different varieties of spoken Spanish. The closer it resembled peninsular Spanish, the higher the likelihood of the assignment of upper-level courses. In my case, my teaching assignments were usually at the beginner and intermediate levels. I didn't expect higher-level courses to be assigned to me as a graduate teaching assistant from outside of the language department. However, in many cases I was more qualified to teach the courses because I had completed a Master's degree in translation which included thirty credits in each language. My course work included grammar, syntax, contrastive analysis, and writing courses in both Spanish and English.

In my work with high schools, I have seldom encountered native speakers of Spanish from non-European backgrounds teaching language courses. This phenomenon is probably linked to certification requirements for teachers. A good number of immigrants with literacy and educational backgrounds that would make them an asset for Spanish language instruction in our K–12 class-rooms, are unable to teach because they are not certified by the state. Certification requirements include a number of college courses offered in English and for which you have to be a full-time student in a teacher education program. Hence, these individuals would have to apply for admission to a program. The process involves recommendation letters, interviews, and evidence of experiences with children and young people. It is unlikely that a recent immigrant would obtain these documents quickly. Some states and school district offices have created alternative routes to place some of these teachers in emergency appointments or as paraprofessionals in areas of need. Some have provided alternative routes for meeting the certification requirements.

Many of the undergraduates who seek teaching credentials in the education programs I have worked in, are students who have experienced a year abroad within the context of an exchange program at an affluent public or private high school. Students who are native speakers of Spanish from the Caribbean, Puerto Ricans and Dominicans, have often faced difficulty in college language departments. I have often heard colleagues refer to these students' language usage as problematic and many of them struggle with the discourses of exclusion and devaluation related to their language usage.

Judith, a bright Puerto Rican student in one of my graduate education courses, sat in my office one afternoon and asked if she could take one of her courses elsewhere and still get certified to teach Spanish in the state. She was, in my experience a "true" bilingual. Both her Spanish and English were native-like and her writing in both languages was proficient. Her Spanish methods professor wanted her to pronounce her words as a Spaniard would and she constantly criticized her by making disparaging remarks about Puerto Rican Spanish. I consulted with the chair of the department and she sympathized with Judith, admitting to me that this was not the first time she had this kind of feedback about this professor. She shared that she felt sorry for the U.S. Latino students because this professor had very low opinions of their language abilities. Unfortunately, there was no one else to teach this course and our only hope was to await her retirement. Judith persevered and completed the course and eventually became a much sought after Spanish high school teacher. (Journal entry 1996)

If students like Judith do beat the odds to complete a program, they are seldom recommended for jobs in affluent school districts. Most eventually find themselves in urban settings and are assigned the lower level and even "remedial" levels of Spanish. These dynamics maintain the hegemonic status of peninsular Spanish. In Judith's case she earned a strong teaching reputation in less than two years and eventually was recruited by an affluent district.

"YEAR ABROAD" PROGRAMS

Many foreign language departments recommend and encourage students to spend a year abroad in a country where the language is spoken. In most cases, Spanish departments have arranged for these opportunities in Spain. Many universities practically have a satellite language department established in Spanish cities. A few have made arrangements with Mexico and in recent years a few Latin American countries such as Costa Rica, have begun to partner with U.S. universities to offer immersion opportunities for students. Other venues are not considered unless a faculty member takes an interest. In my years of working in these settings, I never saw partnerships with Puerto Rico until a former colleague of mine, herself a Puerto Rican, set up an exchange between her U.S.-based college program and a small college campus on the island. This type of experience is often logistically and financially impossible for many of our students of education. Program sequence, work situations that fund their schooling, and other commitments are obstacles to this enrichment. For this reason I would propose that students engage in what I describe as "authentic migratory" experiences and that the teaching of languages be approached from a constructivist perspective. Authentic migratory experiences are basically interactions with and in immigrant communities. The interactions may include volunteering as translators/interpreters for different situations that arise in these communities. For example, it is imperative that schools communicate with parents regarding requirements that need to be met by parents and students. Some families need orientation in their languages regarding social benefits and housing. Individuals need interpreters for medical and immigration information. Perhaps language teachers can organize teams to volunteer in different communities thus providing service and constructing knowledge that is purposeful within a real context. The activities and participation may be monitored by teachers from other content areas as well, if we can develop interdisciplinary links that could include sociology, history, political science, ecology, and many other disciplines.

Following the Freirian model of dialogical learning and acknowledging prior experiences, our language programs could also benefit from the richness in language and culture of the diverse students in our classrooms. Students could be involved in tutoring and mentoring in ethnic communities, and through service learning (Coles 1993) they could acquire language in a contextualized manner. Tanno (1998) stresses that "one of the most important components of graduate education in the twenty-first century should be community service" (372). Although Tanno's text is within the context of intercultural communication theory, it can be closely linked to any discipline if we use the term education in the broadest sense. I would suggest that community service become a part of education at every level and that language teaching can be enhanced by activities that involve practice in the language as well as sociocultural awareness.

The immigration patterns in the United States and the impact of Latin American music on the U.S. landscape, have created interest in the broader conceptualization of Spanish language and culture. This conceptualization is more inclusive of the Spanish varieties found in the American continent and even among the U.S. ethnic communities such as Puerto Ricans and Chicanos. This latter group's presence preceded that of Anglos in the United States and many history and research opportunities could be developed around this fact. Hence, many of the conditions described by linguists as necessary for successful language acquisition are present in our environments. "Language needs to be firmly context embedded. Story lines, familiar situations and characters, real-life conversations, meaningful purposes in using language—these will establish a context within which language can be received and sent and thereby improve attention and retention. Context reduced language in abstract, isolated, unconnected sentences will be much less readily tolerated by children's minds" (Brown 1994, 93).

POPULAR CULTURE COUNTS

Students are motivated to learn Spanish to relate to its music, literature, or cultural features and ultimately to make themselves more marketable in different work settings. Media reports of demographic patterns reflecting an increase in the Latino population, much earlier than expected, and economic trade agreements such as NAFTA, create a need for a workforce with Spanish-speaking skills. Technology needs, and an entertainment industry with a notable Latino presence demand, new approaches to marketing that consider the interests and trends among Latino and Spanish-speaking consumers in the United States and around the world.

A recent perusal of a cable audio channel devoted to international love songs yielded more than 90 percetage of songs in Spanish in a whole afternoon tuned in to the station; surprisingly, only one French song and another in Italian added to the repertoire along with a few songs in Portuguese. The variety of songs in Spanish included numbers from every Spanish-speaking location known to me, evenly represented. Ballads from every Caribbean, Central American, and South American country were played with a Spanish ballad included at least every hour. In the audio channel labeled "Tropical," a predominance of Puerto Rican and Dominican music was dotted with Colombian and Panamanian "cumbias" and "bachatas," but salsa and merengue were the predominant genres.

The proliferation of dance clubs in major cities, where salsa and merengue are the mainstay, have created a demand for salsa lessons in colleges, community centers, and exercise programs. Ethnic foods are available in most mainstream supermarkets where ten years ago one had to go to an ethnic community to find these staples. Plantains and Goya products are everywhere and those of us who consume these products couldn't be happier. A delightful experience I often encounter during grocery shopping is when another customer asks me about a product and how to prepare it. This interest shows a willingness to explore other cultures at those levels. When I teach courses that touch on issues of diversity, students are always interested in experiencing the foods and music and understanding cultural behaviors related to social events such as weddings, "quinceañeros" (equivalent of the sweet sixteen party but more extravagant), or behaviors and expectations at christening celebrations, wakes, and other rituals that are often not touched upon, but which nonetheless may be important rituals to relate to in their future interactions with co-workers. This type of cultural knowledge is only accessed through authentic migratory experiences acquired by interacting in and with communities.

Language teachers can inform of these practices, but only experiencing them will create the awareness of their meaning. Language teaching embedded in critical pedagogy would contribute enormously to the design and implementation of foreign language experiences that are meaningful and realistic. This approach is an example of what Osborn (2000) describes as *macrocontextualization*. It is "the process of planning and implementing language instruction by incorporating the local political, economic, and cultural factors related to linguistic diversity with the intent of developing students' skills in understanding the role that language plays in society" (114). Macrocontextualization will further enlighten our students by having them consider the sociopolitical and historical factors that contribute to the changes in the practices in our communities. "Quinceañeros," for example, are a cultural manifestation that has the purpose of celebrating a girl's entrance to womanhood, but the celebration is a prelude to the wedding ceremony. As such, the white dress is a symbol of purity and the expectation that virginity is honored and protected between the "coming of age" and matrimony. Many of our Latino immigrants cling to these traditions in the face of the social pressures of sexual liberation they perceive as a lure to their daughters in U.S. society. The complexity of the dual standards that young people from different cultures, not just Latinos, confront in this society has been documented in Gibson's (1987, 1988) work with Punjabi youngsters. In her studies, Gibson describes dynamics where students acted more like their U.S. peers and then came home and followed the norms of their culture.

Another important context for authentic migratory experiences could be the religious institutions where ethnic communities congregate. My personal experiences with Catholic churches have been very enlightening. I have chosen deliberately to attend a parish outside of my community because I can hear and participate in mass in Spanish. An added bonus that I have gained from attending mass here is the opportunity to extend my circle of friends and to strengthen bonds with people from Puerto Rico who live in the area. Although the parish has grown to serve an almost equal number of Mexican immigrants and a smaller group of citizens from other Latino countries, several non-Latinos attend the parish because the sense of community that is more familial is very welcoming. Macrocontextualization applied to language education would find multiple issues with which to create dialogues. The church serves as a location for information on school programs, immigration orientation, jobs, and housing issues. Forums on situations such as the bombing on the Puerto

Rican island of Vieques, and ways to aid victims of earthquakes are also held in the church's community room. The church hosts a small number of social events which provide recreational opportunities to families with limited resources. Many opportunities to practice Spanish are available through the church and the local schools. We need not travel abroad to practice the language; we have many opportunities at our fingertips and in our own back yards. Even becoming a mentor to younger children or keeping company with an elderly immigrant will engage us in the culture, history, and language in ways we never imagined. And as we learn about those histories and cultures, we may reflect critically on how schooling has not included the voices of those who have lived experiences of labor exploitation, and political oppression and struggle. Thus we are simultaneously practicing language in a relevant setting and developing new and important understandings about the world around us. The outcome may be, for example, increased communicative proficiency in Spanish and a critical stance that will generate a commitment to social justice on the part of our students.

"REAL" PRACTICE MAKES PERFECT

The most frequent complaint one hears from foreign language learners, as an explanation for their lack of fluency in foreign languages they have studied for years, is that they did not practice speaking the language. Some claim they can understand it if it is spoken slowly but that, for the most part, instruction focused on memorization of grammar, or of scripted dialogues that attempted the re-creation of social contexts for meaningful communication. The problem seemed to be that the contexts provided by many of the foreign language texts lacked the relevance needed to make the connections "real" for the students. Why not provide or suggest opportunities for authentic exchanges with native speakers of the target languages? An approximation to this approach, and a worthy one, if I may add, is the opportunity to participate in international exchanges through visits to other countries and/or through hosting visiting students from foreign countries during their stays in the United States. These exchanges provide realistic experiences for students but are often out of reach for those outside of the upper socioeconomic brackets.

Teachers who embrace social reconstruction and encourage opportunities to examine issues of equity are exemplifying critical pedagogy in their decision making and in their teaching practices. This is done every time they consider these issues with their students in their own environments. When this approach becomes part of their teaching, the context of language instruction becomes meaningful and relevant. Not only does it open possibilities for critical analysis of issues related to immigration, the job market, and education, but it also validates the possibility of macrocontextualizing language experiences right in our backyards. Students could find opportunities to interact and communicate in linguistic and cultural settings of our many ethnic communities.

174

The hierarchies assigned to language varieties have affected the perceptions of many of our language teachers. Consequently, teachers may have transmitted their value systems to their pupils. This is why many students may be convinced that they have nothing to gain by interacting and communicating in ethnic communities. It is likely that they have accepted the views held by those who are convinced that no language variety spoken in these communities is "worthy." Studies by Valdés et al. in the Southwest have found that a surprising number of Spanish-speaking students were still being placed in beginning Spanish classes with the goal of helping them "unlearn their bad habits" (1981, 7). The belief is more along the lines of denying the value of these language varieties and even of considering them "adulterated" versions of the "real thing," thus not recommendable as a learning tool (see Reagan and Osborn in press). These arguments are reminiscent of the hegemony assigned to British English among English teachers in the old days. The same hegemony is apparent in the relationship between peninsular Spanish and the Spanish spoken everywhere else.

Many of our language teachers are not ready to capitalize on the potential richness of resources represented by native speakers of Spanish in local ethnic communities. For one, teachers tend to teach as they were taught, even when exposed to current learning theories and research on teaching and learning. The power of their own learning experiences and the observation of teachers that continue to emphasize traditional audio-lingual methods over the natural approach, influence their choices in the classroom. Furthermore, this traditional approach is embedded in a detachment from the social context in which teaching and learning take place. Rather than integrating and engaging in discourses about the issues that affect our society, there is an avoidance of such topics and an understanding that they should not be a concern in our classrooms. Teachers then resort to artificial scripts about students' experiences in foreign countries, usually countries where the target language is spoken. The approach used by many of these texts is "tourist-like." They usually include vocabulary related to family members, landmarks, and traditions of the target cultures.

A more relevant curriculum would address realities of communities where target languages are spoken. These communities could be in or outside of the United States and the awareness gained with regard to their social realities will contribute to students' development of values and commitment to justice and the overall improvement of society. Some teachers resist the characterization of teaching as a role where issues of values and morals are addressed. Instead they argue that parents are solely responsible for the development of character and values. It is imperative that we revisit this understanding with teachers in our preservice programs so that prospective teachers realize that their involvement in this aspect of students' lives is inevitable because of the amount of time the students spend with their teachers vis a vis the time spent with parents.

The increase of two-working-parent families, single parent families, and mobility, reduces access to extended families and support systems. Continued exposure through media images of behaviors and practices that are often controversial and unfamiliar to students, transforms teachers into interpreters of these realities for their students. Teachers will often be called upon by their students to mediate and interpret for and with them to understand and adopt views as their own. Thus the teacher's responsibility includes the empowerment of students to participate in the construction of their world through the development and validation of their voices. Voice is the central ingredient of critical pedagogy (Ruiz 1997, 321). In language learning, all of these contextual elements could enhance and make learning relevant and meaningful.

PRACTICES THAT TRANSFORM

Two-way bilingual or dual language programs are probably the most desirable school environments for language learning because they are based on a premise that assigns equal value to both languages in the setting. If more schools were to adopt this model for language instruction, student language learning would probably contribute to better social interactions with ethnic populations from the languages represented in the schools. This may translate into better attitudes toward those who appear to be or sound different from us, in general. It is only through these positive experiences with language and linguistic contexts that language learners will find meaning and purpose in acquiring fluency in other languages. The implications of assigning languages equal value in classrooms and schools will help bolster the image of those who speak the languages both in the eyes of others and in regards to themselves.

The language programs in most schools exclude speakers from classes in their own native languages rather than encouraging their involvement in higher levels, whenever possible. In many cases, native speakers' proficiency in pronunciation and oral communication could allow for their validation and participation as conversation partners. This validation will carry over into other social interactions. Eventually, students feel respected by their peers and their teachers and this will enhance their self-esteem. Current practice discourages "native" speakers of a language to study that language, with the notable, but largely isolated exception of advances being made in "heritage language learning" pedagogy. In some cases, students whose speaking ability is native may pose a threat to a teacher who speaks the language with an accent. But more often the devaluing of students' skills correlates to the teachers' perceptions about the language groups in question. If our teacher education programs emphasize the critical issues of hegemony related to language and culture (Darder 1991), foreign language teachers will develop a more reflective constructivist stance toward their students and the communities they serve. An approach that visualizes students' roles as bridge builders in society and contributors to positive cross-cultural communication will include all students and value all language varieties.

An atmosphere that fosters positive attitudes toward diverse languages creates the necessary comfort levels for language appreciation and language learning. Rather than hearing an angry "don't these people know they are in 'America,'" or "speak English" that I often overhear when I am in public settings where people are speaking languages other than English, one would like people to react indifferently or interested. Recently I observed a father and his toddler in a parking lot as a couple walked by them speaking another language. The father promptly started making faces ridiculing the couple to make his child laugh. Eventually he started making silly noises as if imitating their talk and the child laughed in delight. This behavior modeled by the adult will undoubtedly shape the child's reactions to languages and cultures and the people who are different. A very different situation occurred when I walked into an auto shop and another customer immediately asked me, in perfect Spanish, if I spoke Spanish. I was surprised to find that he was not a native speaker although the quality of his pronunciation was native-like. He was happy to have someone to practice with and no one around seemed to be phased by our ongoing conversation in Spanish. I was delighted to hear that he became proficient in the language by interacting in the local ethnic community. His interest in the language and his sense of comfort and confidence allowed him to enjoy the opportunity and not feel that it would pose a threat to non-Spanish-speaking patrons.

As cross-culturalism and multilingualism become more of the norm and less the exception, our need to understand other languages and experience other cultures increases. Language teaching has to reinvent itself and respond to the demands of specific contexts. More and more language programs that address specific needs, called language for specific purposes, such as health, business, education, law, and social services, to name a few, change the nature of language instruction from an abstract concept to a relevant and more concrete one. Students are more involved with the classes that provide the skills that they need to participate more fully in diverse settings. Teaching strategies that involve role-playing and fieldwork in the form of service learning will provide opportunities to practice languages and will certainly contribute to developing the skills and vocabulary needed to succeed in a variety of work settings and locations. Macrocontextualization within foreign language classrooms is a valuable strategy to prepare our students to access the curriculum and to develop critical awareness of the myriad of social issues that impact on language teaching and learning.

BIBLIOGRAPHY

Brown, D. H. 1994. *Teaching principles: An interactive approach to language pedagogy.* Upper Saddle River, NJ: Prentice Hall Regents.

Coles, R. 1993. *The call of service: A witness to idealism.* Boston: Houghton Mifflin.

Darder, A. 1991. *Culture and power in the classroom*. Westport, CT: Bergin and Garvey.

Darder, A., C. Torres, and H. Gutiérrez. 1997. *Latinos and education*. New York: Routledge.

Gibson, M. 1987. Punjabi immigrants in an American high school. In *Interpretive educational ethnography at home and abroad*, ed. G. Spindler and L. Spindler, 281–310. Hillsdale, NJ: Lawrence Erlbaum.

———. 1988. *Accomodation without assimilation*. Ithaca, NY: Cornell University Press.

Giroux, H. 1986. Radical pedagogy and the politics of student voice. *Interchange 17*, 48–69.

Negrón de Montilla, A. 1977. *La americanización en Puerto Rico y el sistema de instrucción pública*. 1900–1930. Rio Piedras, PR: Editorial Universitaria.

Osborn, T. A. 2000. *Critical reflection and the foreign language classroom*. Westport, CT: Bergin and Garvey.

Reagan, T. G. and T. A. Osborn. In press. *The foreign language educator in society: Toward a critical pedagogy*. Mahwah, NJ: Lawrence Erlbaum.

Ruiz, R. 1997. The empowerment of language minority students. In *Latinos and education*, ed. A. Darder, R. Torres, and H. Gutiérrez, 319–28. New York: Routledge.

Tanno, D. 1998 "At the helm" in graduate education: Service as preparation for intercultural communication theory. In *Communication: Views from the helm for the 21st century*, ed. J. Trent, 370–74. Boston: Allyn and Bacon.

Valdés, G., A. Lozano, and R. García-Moya, eds. 1981. *Teaching Spanish to the Hispanic bilingual: Issues, aims, and methods*. New York: Teachers College Press.

Index

Index

Venezuela, 167
Vieques, 174
Vietnam, 83–87
Vietnam War, 84–87
Vietnamese, 126, 135
Visual, 35
Vocabulary, in language education, 71
Vogely, Anita, xv
Voice, 176
Von Glasersfeld, E., 46–48
Vygotsky, L., 41, 49, 72

Washington Post, 87
Watzke, J., 3, 12, 17, 23
Weiner, L., 109, 120
Weinland, T. P., 77
Weltansichten, 5

White, 2
White-collar, 3
Whitman, C. T., 19
Whorf, B. L., 5
Widdowson, H. G., 54
Wieczorek, J. A., 83
Wiley, T., 10, 121
Williams, T., xvi, 72
Wink, J., 112
Wong-Fillmore, L., 140
World languages, 18, 167
World War I, 6, 121

Zeichner, K., 56
Zevin, J., 78, 88
Zone of proximal development, 72

About the Contributors

Philip M. Anderson is Acting Dean of the Division of Education, Queens College of the City University of New York. He is coauthor of *Enhancing Aesthetic Reading and Response* (1991).

S. Alenka Brown-VanHoozer is Director for the Center for Cognitive Processing Technology at Oak Ridge Y12, and President of Human Dynamics, LLC. She is a former research scientist for Argonne National Laboratory, instrumentation and control engineer for Rockwell International/Babcock and Wilcox, research engineer for Rockwell International/EG&G, and Micro-Research, Inc. Her research involves modeling subjective experience, cognitive coding of representation systems, behavior profiling, learning behavior, decision making modeling, states of awareness, and adaptive systems. She is the author of *Say It Right (NLP Focused)* (2nd ed., 1997).

Jacqueline Davis is an Assistant Professor of Language Education at Queens College, CUNY. Her research interests include teacher educator practice, preparation, and development; teacher education and socialization; sociocultural dimensions of language and teacher education; teacher knowledge; language learning; and applied linguistics. Her work has appeared in *ESPecialist, Studies in English Education, Voices in the Field,* and *Foreign Language Annals.*

David Gerwin is Assistant Professor of Secondary Education and Youth Services and cocoordinator of the Program in Social Studies at Queens College, CUNY. His research interests include the lifetime career development of social studies teachers, the creation and development of professional practice networks, and the ways faculty and students experience the "methods" course. He is also interested in the use of oral history in the classroom and in historical research. As a historian he has written about community organizing during the 1960s in Newark, New Jersey.

Deborah M. Herman is an interdisciplinary doctoral candidate in Foreign Language Education, Border Studies, and Educational Sociology at the University of Iowa. She has presented at local and international conferences on stereotypes among foreign language students and in foreign language textbooks, attitudes toward "official English" legislation in Iowa, popular perceptions of language acquisition, and immigrant labor issues. She was the founding editor in 1996 of "Intercambios," the statewide newsletter of the Iowa chapter of the American Association of Teachers of Spanish and Portuguese. Her research interests include regional perspectives on the "official English" movement, border issues in the Midwest, the impact of nationalism on foreign language education, and the history of foreign language education in the United States.

Stephen W. Kercel has been a researcher in the Advanced Methods Group on the Instrumentation and Controls Division of Oak Ridge National Laboratory for the past ten years . His research interest is on-line intelligent sensors; he has won two R&D 100 Awards for real-time implementations of wavelet-based sensors. He has published approximately eighty technical papers. He is an Adjunct in Electrical Engineering at the University of Tennessee and teaches a graduate course in Engineering Applications of Wavelets. He is a Registered Professional Engineer in Tennessee, a Certified Computer Professional, and a Senior Member of the Institute of Electrical and Electronic Engineers (IEEE). He is Conference cochair of Artificial Neural Networks in Engineering (ANNIE) 2000 and has chaired a Special Invited Track on Bizarre Systems at ANNIE 99 and a Special Invited Track in Semiotics at IEEE-Systems, Man, and Cybernetics 97. He has been an Invited Plenary Speaker on wavelets and bizarre systems at various international conferences and an invited guest lecturer at many universities.

Terry A. Osborn is Assistant Professor of Educational Linguistics and Second Language Education in the Department of Curriculum and Instruction, Neag School of Education, University of Connecticut. He is author of *Critical Reflection and the Foreign Language Classroom* (Bergin & Garvey, 2000). His areas of research interest include critical pedagogy and literature in the language classroom and his work has appeared in *Educational Studies, Educational Foundations, Multicultural Education,* and *Foreign Language Annals.*

Timothy Reagan is Associate Dean and Professor of Educational Studies and Foreign Language Education in the Neag School of Education at the University of Connecticut. He has written extensively in the areas of educational linguistics, foreign language education, and language policy in education.

Xaé Alicia Reyes is currently an Associate Professor at the University of Connecticut-Storrs, with a joint appointment in Curriculum and Instruction in the Neag School of Education and the Puerto Rican and Latino/a Studies Institute. Her interests include educational ethnography, critical pedagogy, and teacher education as affected by language, culture, and migration. Recent publications include "Puerto Rican Return Migrants" in Nieto's *Puerto Rican Students in U.S. Schools* (2000).

Migdalia Romero is Professor in the Department of Curriculum and Teaching at Hunter College, City University of New York. Her research has focused on effective programs for ESL students and heritage language learners and her publications have addressed programmatic and instructional issues impacting on bilingual and ESL teachers.

Claire Sylvan is a substitute Assistant Professor at City College of New York, CUNY. She has worked for the past ten years at the International High School developing programs of native language instruction and has taught a wide range of courses to heritage language learners. Her research interests include the relationship between native language and English language proficiency, first and second language literacy development, authentic assessment and the impact of high stakes testing on progressive education in general and for English language learners in particular as well as best practices in preparing English language learners for college and beyond. Her work has appeared in *ACTFL Foreign Language Education Series, The Educational Forum, NABE News,* and *Options.*

W. R. VanHoozer is CEO of Human Dynamics, LLC, founder and managing editor of McClure-Brown Press, and founder of TranceFormations, Unlimited, a private practice. He is a former behavior counselor for private counseling centers in Colorado and was a psychotherapist in the military. His research addresses the nature of hypnosis and applications of hypnosis in clinical and nonclinical environments, including altered states of awareness/consciousness. Additional areas of research interest are NeuroLinguistic Programming (NLP) approaches to individual and group therapy, NLP and normalcy, modeling subjective experience, success modeling, representation systems and submodalities, and representation systems and learning behavior. He is the author of *It's All in Your Head: Trance Scriptions for a Healthy You* (1994).

A. J. Vogely, ENFP, has spent the last ten years at Binghamton University in New York. During that time, many "radical" teachers have graduated from her Masters of Arts in Teaching Foreign Languages Program and most are still teaching today. Her research on listening comprehension strategies and listening comprehension anxiety has been published in *Modern Language Journal* and *Foreign Language Annals*. She received the Stephen A. Freeman Award for best published article on language teaching techniques presented by the Northeast Conference of the Teaching of Foreign Language (NECTFL) in March 2001. Other publications include a guidebook for students and teachers of introductory Spanish literature that is driven by the latest reading comprehension research and several invited chapters. Her interest in psychological type theory began in 1993 and she has regularly presented sessions on using type in education at the Association for Psychological Type (APT) conferences. She is dedicated to making a difference in education.